3 0050 01440 7349

D1739232

CAL STATE UNIVERSITY, HAYWARD LIBRARY

ROBERT WORTH BINGHAM AND THE SOUTHERN MYSTIQUE

Robert Worth Bingham around the mid-nineteen twenties. From the Barry Bingham, Sr., Collection. Reprinted with permission of The Filson Club Historical Society, Louisville, Kentucky.

Robert Worth Bingham and the Southern Mystique

From the Old South to the New South and Beyond

William E. Ellis

THE KENT STATE UNIVERSITY PRESS
Kent, Ohio, and London, England

CAL STATE UNIVERSITY, HAYWARD LIBRARY

CT
275
B5737
E45
1997

© 1997 by The Kent State University Press, Kent, Ohio 44242
All rights reserved
Library of Congress Catalog Card Number 97-6779
ISBN 0-87338-578-0
Manufactured in the United States of America

04   03   02   01   00   99   98   97   5   4   3   2   1

Library of Congress Cataloging-in-Publication Data

Ellis, William E. (William Elliott), 1940–
    Robert Worth Bingham and the Southern mystique : from the Old
South to the New South and beyond / William Ellis.
        p.   cm.
        Includes bibliographical references (p.   ) and index.
    ISBN 0-87338-578-0 (cloth : alk. paper) ⊗
    1. Bingham, Robert Worth, 1871–1937. 2. Bingham family. 3. Publishers and
publishing—Kentucky—Biography. 4. Newspaper publishing—Kentucky—History.
5. Louisville (Ky.)—Biography. 6. Southern States—Social life and customs—1865–
I. Title
CT275.B5737E45   1997
976.9'041'092–dc 21   97-6779
[B]   CIP

British Library Cataloging-in-Publication Data are available.

CAL STATE UNIVERSITY, HAYWARD LIBRARY

Contents

Preface

FOR OVER THREE-QUARTERS of a century the history of the Bingham family of Louisville, Kentucky, has been one of tragedy and controversy as well as wealth, power, and prestige. Robert Worth Bingham (1871–1937), the subject of this biography, lived a significant life as a lawyer, progressive mayor, newspaper publisher, and ambassador. A native of North Carolina, the young lawyer voiced opposition to several cherished Kentucky political traditions from the beginning of his career in the mid-1890s. During the Progressive Era at the beginning of this century he opposed the powerful liquor and racing interests in the Commonwealth of Kentucky. His service in the summer of 1907 as interim mayor of Louisville illustrated several salient features of southern progressivism in that decade.

A few years after the accidental death of his first wife, he married one of the richest women in America, Mary Lily Kenan Flagler, who herself soon died in the summer of 1917. Charges that Bingham in some way directly contributed to the death of the wealthy heiress followed him to his grave. With a large bequest from Mary Lily's estate, Bingham purchased control of the *Courier-Journal* and the *Louisville Times* and became a regional power broker in the twenties and thirties. As an early supporter of Franklin Delano Roosevelt for president, Bingham received the reward of being named ambassador to the United Kingdom.

Little was written about Bingham until 1980 when *The Filson Club History Quarterly* published my piece on his career as a progressive in the Louisville political arena during the first decade of this century. Research for that article came from secondary sources and the Robert Worth Bingham Papers at The Filson Club in Louisville. I began researching in the summer of 1977—long before the row among the contemporary Binghams that preceded the sale of the newspapers and the spate of books published between 1987 and 1991. The Filson Club collection spans the years of Bingham's life up to the early twenties. Barry Bingham, Sr., donated another set of papers to the Library of Congress covering the remaining years of his father's life. As time permitted, I made trips to Washington, D.C., supported by travel grants from Eastern Kentucky University, to delve into these extensive Bingham manuscripts.[1]

In the next few years I produced two more articles, one about Bingham's efforts in behalf of the cooperative marketing movement in the twenties and another about the southern moorings of the Bingham family. In the background was the idea of working toward a full biography of Bingham.[2]

In 1983 a series of events began to unravel the Binghams' control over their media empire in Louisville. Sarah Montague Bingham, or Sallie, as she is known, the granddaughter of Robert Worth Bingham, precipitated a disintegration of the Bingham holdings. She claimed that her brother Barry, Jr., as publisher of the papers, kept her and her sister, Eleanor, from achieving full equity of leadership in the family enterprises. The disintegration of the Bingham dynasty included a family schism vividly chronicled in the press and on CBS television's *60 Minutes*.[3]

This publicity also revived the old rumors and innuendos about Mary Lily Bingham's death. Writing about the Binghams created a small cottage industry among journalists and writers of the popular press. David Leon Chandler, the author of a biography of Henry Flagler, and Mary Voelz Chandler, his wife, added fuel to the fire by producing a muckraking manuscript biography of Robert Worth Bingham in 1986 under a contract with Macmillan. Barry Bingham, Sr., hired the largest law firm in Kentucky to study the manuscript. After reading Barry Bingham's response, Macmillan refused to publish the manuscript. However, another press published the book in late 1987. The Chandlers' *The Binghams of Louisville: The Dark History Behind One of*

America's Great Fortunes turns out to be little more than one "heavy on speculation and short on direct proof," according to historian Robert M. Ireland. More to the point, the book is a malicious mishmash of unsubstantiated constructed melodrama.[4]

In 1988 Random House published Marie Brenner's *House of Dreams: The Bingham Family of Louisville,* a volume that concentrates on other themes. Her book deals mostly with the latter-day Binghams and their travails, particularly concentrating on the marriage of Barry and Mary Bingham and how that union led to trouble among their squabbling children. Brenner declares Louisville to be "a Jell-O and Velveeta town." Though the book is more objective in content, it still has a journalistic flair rather than a true historical approach to the subject.[5]

Passion and Prejudice: A Family Memoir by Sallie Bingham reels back to the Chandler side of the ledger. Bingham goes even further than the Chandlers in not only attacking Judge Bingham and his life and times but also sparing no one else in the family, particularly if they are of the male gender. As a matter of fact, a *Time* magazine reviewer declared Bingham's perspective to be that of a "millionaire Marxist-feminist," a seemingly contradictory position until one reads the book.[6]

Susan E. Tifft and Alex S. Jones, a husband-and-wife team, produced *The Patriarch: The Rise and Fall of the Bingham Dynasty* in 1991. One has only to look at the chapter titles, such as chapter 2: "Beautiful Bob Bingham," chapter 3, "The Mad Woman in the Attic," or "Mr. Clean's Newspapers," chapter 14, to get the general drift of the semisensationalist nature of the book. Where appropriate, all of these works will be responded to in this book either in the text or in explanatory endnotes.[7]

I make no proprietary claim to writing about Robert Worth Bingham. Particularly missing in the previously named books is historical context. For example, Chandler and Bingham display little knowledge of the Progressive Era, other than a misplaced belief that everything that occurred then was mistakenly called "progressive." The reading public in the final analysis will decide if I have been successful in producing a credible biography of a fascinating and important, though neglected, figure in twentieth-century American history.

It is time, then, to find out about the real Robert Worth Bingham, founder of a short-lived dynasty. Who was this man? How was he influenced by his southern background? What really happened to Mary

Lily Bingham? What was the impact of Bingham on his city, state, and nation? What was his role in international affairs? What were his strengths and weaknesses? What were the legacies that he bequeathed to his family, state, region, and nation? The answers are not always clear-cut, and the story includes the ironical and paradoxical twists that often times occur in American history. His roles as a southerner, lawyer, reformer, businessman, publisher, political figure, and diplomat demand to be viewed from the perspective of a working historian.

I wish to acknowledge several individuals and institutions for their support in producing this book. Eastern Kentucky University generously contributed research funds for the book. Archivists at The Filson Club, the Manuscript Division of the Library of Congress, the National Archives, the Franklin D. Roosevelt Library, and the North Carolina and Southern collections at the University of North Carolina at Chapel Hill were helpful on every occasion. Nelson L. Dawson and James J. Holmberg of The Filson Club in Louisville encouraged the research and writing of this biography. James C. Klotter of the Kentucky Historical Society, Richard Lowitt of Iowa State University, George Brown Tindall of the University of North Carolina at Chapel Hill, and Nancy K. Forderhase and George Robinson of Eastern Kentucky University have read all or parts of the present manuscript. Their critiques are appreciated, and I, of course, take full responsibility for this book. Former Eastern Kentucky University graduate assistants John Ernst, Harold Jones, William Sariego, and Janet White also deserve special thanks for their assistance.

Interviews proved critical in producing this book. Barry Bingham, Sr., consented to several oral-history taping sessions that provided valuable insights of a devoted son about his father. John Herchenroeder, a retired editor of the *Courier-Journal*, gave much-needed anecdotal information about the inner workings of the staff of the Bingham papers.

I dedicate this book to my grandchildren: Andrew, Elise, Jordan, Caitlin, and Meredith, and to the memory of John Herchenroeder.

chapter one

From the Old
South to the New

AFTER READING Margaret Mitchell's *Gone with the Wind* in early 1937, Robert Worth Bingham, ambassador to the Court of St. James's and the son of a Confederate veteran, lauded the novel's evocation of the Old South. He exclaimed, "I do not thank you for "Gone with the Wind"—I bless you. . . . I know every phase of it all; the poverty and the pride, the gentility, the gracious manners, the romance, the preservation of dignity and high and generous humanity in rags and semi-starvation."[1]

Though born in 1871 during the era known as Reconstruction, the Old South governed the life of Robert Worth Bingham as it did most other southerners of his generation. Antebellum mansions, the old plantation ways, ex-slaves, and Confederate veterans were constant reminders of the old days. In the stories of Confederate glory, heroism, and tragedy he heard from his father and others, his youthful imagination soared. The New South, the new order of things into which he came of age, also became a tangible part of his life. Hopes of economic development for his region and personal success filled his early dreams.

As a child and as a young man, Bingham internalized the myths and legends of the Old South, Civil War, Reconstruction, and New South eras. The forces of family and culture, time and place, profoundly influenced the reactions of all the North Carolina Binghams to their environment. They reflected and amplified the most salient

features of southern life and history for a century and a half. For bet-
ter or worse, Robert Worth Bingham would always be a southerner.
The Bingham School tied together all these elements of Robert Worth
Bingham's acceptance of the southern mystique.

"Mens Sana in Corpore Sano" (A healthy mind in a healthy body),
the motto of the Bingham School of North Carolina, a prototypical
nineteenth-century southern boarding school for males, echoed the
ethos that ruled the lives of many educated Americans in the nineteenth century. In the South that belief system took on special features because of the development of the institution of slavery. It envel-
oped the lives of all the Binghams.[2]

Three generations of Binghams controlled the school from its
founding in the 1790s to the closing of the institution in the late 1920s.
William Bingham, a Scots-Irish Presbyterian minister from Northern
Ireland and graduate of the University of Glasgow in 1774, arrived at
Wilmington, North Carolina, in 1789. Within a few months he opened
a school. Over the years the Bingham School moved several times,
from the Wilmington area to Hillsborough and other locations in
Orange County, then to Mebane, and finally to Asheville on a site
later called Bingham Heights near the French Broad River.[3]

William James Bingham, born in 1802 in Chapel Hill during a brief
time when his father William taught Greek and Latin at the University
of North Carolina, took over direction of the school in 1826, continuing in that role until his death in 1866. The Bingham School prospered in the years before the Civil War, moving to Oaks, a rural village
on the western fringe of Orange County in 1845. Before the onslaught
of the Civil War in 1861, enrollment often exceeded one hundred
students. The school maintained a rigorous classical curriculum, emphasizing the study of Greek, Latin, mathematics, and history. From
the beginning the Binghams stressed quality education, discipline,
character, and hard work.[4]

Living in a southern state, the Binghams settled into the institutional pattern of slaveholding. Although the family never became part
of the elite planter aristocracy, it did occupy upper-middle-class status
among slave owners in the mid–nineteenth-century North Carolina
Piedmont. From 1840 to 1860 the number of slaves owned by William James Bingham increased from ten to fourteen, a substantial number for that area of North Carolina. The slaves served as a vital source
of labor around the school by tending the crops and livestock that

provided much of the food set before the students. Typical of many southern families, a slave "mammy" looked after the needs of the youngest children of the Bingham family. Owing to the "flush times" of the fifties, the wealth of the family substantially increased from $3,556 in real estate in 1850 to $9,000 in 1860. The combining of slavery and agriculture with their school enterprise proved to be profitable for the Binghams. They represented the traits of a typical middle-class family in pre–Civil War North Carolina. Because of their school they took on a special role of leadership that extended beyond their economic station.[5]

Like many southern families in the antebellum period, the Binghams never completely reconciled themselves to the institution of slavery. William James, the patriarch of the family, expressed interest in the organization of the early antislavery societies. After that avenue of opposition to slavery closed in the South, he joined the colonization movement. For two decades he supported the Whig party in an era when Orange County became a stronghold of that party. Presbyterian industriousness, self-assurance, and morality ruled the behavior of the Binghams. The schoolmaster's two sons, William (1835–73) and Robert (1838–1927), who matured in the immediate antebellum period, also conformed to basic southern cultural mores of race, class, and society, and followed their father's whiggism.[6]

Another instititution, the University of North Carolina at nearby Chapel Hill, played an important role in the lives of the Bingham family. After the first William Bingham taught at the fledgling university from 1801 to 1804 (earning the nickname Old Slick because of his baldness), three successive generations of Bingham men attended the school. They all joined the Dialectic Literary Society, one of two such groups on the campus. William James graduated with honors in 1825. Sons William and Robert followed in his footsteps in 1856 and 1857 and joined their father as teachers at the Bingham School.[7]

With the first rumblings of secession in 1860, the Binghams, like a majority of their fellow North Carolinians who had supported the Whig party, favored the cause of the Union. Although Orange County contained a substantial number of slaveholders in 1860, that year it gave a clear majority (52 percent) of its votes to John Bell, the Constitutional Union party candidate. However, John C. Breckinridge, the southern Democratic party standard-bearer, carried North Carolina by a slight margin. Governor John W. Ellis, an advocate of secession, did not push firmly for joining the new Confederate States of America until after southern armies had fired on Fort Sumter and President Abraham Lincoln had called for seventy-five thousand men from the states remaining in the Union. Momentum for secession built slowly in North Carolina. After Virginia left the Union, it was only a matter of time until the Tarheel State did the same. The North Carolina legislature voted for a secession convention to convene on 1 May 1861, not long after which Governor Ellis ordered seizure of all federal property in the state. By the middle of the month the convention voted to sever ties with the United States, repealing an ordinance that made North Carolina part of the Union in 1789.[8]

The Binghams agonized over the secession crisis. For old Whig William James, nearing sixty years of age and in declining health, the choice came particularly hard. Once the decision had been made, however, the Binghams gave everything to the fate of the Confederacy. They kept the school open through most of the war, accepting Confederate money even after that currency lost most of its value. The school also took produce in lieu of money to make ends meet. Financial sacrifice increased as the war continued.[9]

All members of the family made their contributions to the war effort. Robert organized a company of men and mustered into the 44th North Carolina Regiment. When he marched off to war, he left behind a young wife, Delphine (Dell) Louise Worth, the daughter of Dr. John M. Worth, a pre–Civil War North Carolina state treasurer, and a descendant of William Worth, a native of Barnstaple, England, who settled in Massachusetts in the seventeenth century.[10]

Owing to ill health, William Bingham did not join the army but accepted more responsibilities for operating the school. Commissioned a colonel in a North Carolina army unit, he turned the Bingham School into a military training facility. Young cadets received their first military training as officers at the school before entering the service of the South upon graduation. Although the school took on the appearance of a military encampment, with older students patrolling the countryside around Oaks, Colonel William did not alter the classical curriculum. He not only stressed Latin and Greek studies but also continued work on classical textbooks, and published one volume during the war.[11]

While William James and his eldest son struggled to keep the Bingham School functioning, Robert, from nearly the time he enlisted, found himself in harm's way. With only minimal training, the 44th Regiment moved toward the North Carolina coast. After minor engagements there, the regiment moved on into Virginia to support General Lee's invasion of Pennsylvania in June 1863. In an attempt to hold two bridges, a Union force captured Robert's company and dispatched him to a prison at Fort Norfolk, Virginia. The harsh conditions there and later at Johnson's Island in Lake Erie embittered the young North Carolinian against the "yankee" and reinforced his faith in the southern cause.[12]

After being exchanged in early March 1864, Robert came home to heartrending tragedy. He returned to find that his first son, James Worth Bingham, born shortly after his last trip to Oaks, had died. His wife also had been seriously ill and would suffer poor health for the remainder of her life. Deteriorating conditions around Oaks after mid-1863 contributed to these tragedies. Medical aid and food supplies ran short as the war moved ever closer. Union sympathizers, known as Red Strings, roamed the countryside and sometimes harassed the school's cadets. Therefore, on Christmas 1864 the Bingham School closed forever at the Oaks location.[13]

At home the Binghams became so destitute that Robert borrowed money from Jonathan Worth, postwar governor of North Carolina and uncle of his wife, to outfit himself with clothing and firearms for his return to the battlefield. Worth admitted that "the military sky does not look bright," but still held out hope that Lee had a chance of stopping Union general U. S. Grant. With the remnants of the 44th Regiment, Bingham joined Major General William MacRae's Brigade of North Carolinians who linked up with the Army of Northern Virginia in the defense of Richmond. General Lee and his forces survived to fight another day, but retreated from their elaborately built redoubts toward the eventual surrender point, Appomattox Courthouse. Along the way Bingham successfully moved 250 men across a stream to the final bivouac of the Army of Northern Virginia. Bingham, overcome with the emotion of the surrender and Lee's farewell to his troops, set off for North Carolina. Finally, "lousy, ragged, hungry and barefooted," the North Carolinian returned home to the uncertain future of the South that became Reconstruction.[14]

The Bingham School also entered a new era by moving to a site one mile east of Mebaneville, now Mebane, in Alamance County, just a few miles north of the old Oaks location. After closing for several months during construction of a few buildings, the school reopened in late fall 1866. William James, in declining health for years, died just before the opening of the new facilities. Generally credited as one of North Carolina's educational pioneers, he developed the Bingham School into one of the premier private schools in the antebellum era. Though the tragedy of the Civil War left a bitter legacy to be faced by his sons, he bequeathed to them a tradition of educational merit.[15]

Building a new school would have been difficult under any circumstances but proved particularly trying in the immediate postwar era. During that time the Binghams continued to play a prominent role in the education of young men in their native North Carolina. Moreover, Robert Bingham's influence in development of the New South milieu melded with his Old South heritage.

At the same time Robert and Dell put their lives back together. Over the next eight years four children would be born to the Binghams during Reconstruction: daughters Mary Kerr (1865–1932) and Sadie Alves (1867–1955), and sons Robert Worth (1871–1937) and William (1873–1891). While the girls attended private schools, the boys took their early training at the Bingham School. Sister Sadie, in particular, became a close companion and confidante of Robert Worth.[16]

The wartime experiences of the Bingham family profoundly influenced the remainder of their lives. Indeed, Robert harbored some bitterness. The prison experience, a dead first son, a wife with delicate health for the remainder of her life, harassment of the school by the Red Strings, and the death of the elder Bingham so soon after the war could not have but conditioned Robert for strong opposition to Republican-led Reconstruction in North Carolina.[17]

During the early Reconstruction era in North Carolina, radical Republicans, led by Governor William Woods Holden, a native "scalawag," and North Carolina Supreme Court justice Albion Winegar Tourgée, a "carpetbagger," clashed with a group generally known as Conservatives. The latter were a synthesis of prewar Whigs and Democrats and others wishing defeat of the radical Republican government. The Binghams and other Whigs meshed nicely with the dictates of the Conservative party. Eight years after the war and the completion of their control of North Carolina state politics, Conservatives finally changed their name to the Democratic party. The activities of men like the Bingham brothers spelled the difference between success and failure for the designs of the Republican state government in the late sixties and early seventies.[18]

The adjoining Piedmont counties of Orange, Alamance, and Caswell proved to be the pivotal areas in deciding the fate of Republican control of Reconstruction throughout the state. Conservatives in these counties, aided by the violent specter of the various groups associated with the Ku Klux Klan, presented a united front against Republican political control and its quest for racial justice. The Bingham brothers took part in this movement by joining one or more of the local Klan-like associations. While the extent of their participation is not known, William was one of over sixty Alamance Countians indicted in 1870 in the effort of Governor Holden to crack down on Klan activities. In the end a judge friendly to the Conservative "redeemers" dismissed the indictments. Even less is known about the Klan connections of Robert, but his son, Robert Worth, recalled late in his own life the family's role in the Klan. "My earliest memory is of clutching my mother's skirts in terror at a hooded apparition," he remembered, "and having my father raise his mask to relieve me."[19]

Sustained Klan violence centering in Alamance County directly contributed to the end of Republican control in North Carolina. With the election of 1870 the Conservatives swept into a majority of county and state offices. The combined efforts of Governor Holden and Judge Tourgée could not bring about successful prosecutions of Klan members. Their crusade not only failed, it soon led to the impeachment of Holden. Conservatives, with the Klan always lurking ominously just beneath the surface of public life, resumed control of the state and decided the place of Negroes in the new regime long before the alleged Compromise of 1877 more or less officially ended Reconstruction in the South.[20]

Historian Allen W. Trelease claimed that during Reconstruction "the local establishment" led the Ku Klux Klan. But why did these "best men" of southern white society participate in atrocities and mayhem under the hood of the Klan? Why did the Binghams become part of such activities? After all, here were men who held positions of leadership in southern Presbyterianism. They presumed to lead in the education of the region's young men. How could they condone or participate in such violent acts and, apparently, never question for the remainder of their lives the means used?[21]

The Binghams did not react out of blind instinct, as southern journalist W. J. Cash, author of *The Mind of the South*, once suggested about his fellow southerners, but rationally participated in organizations and activities outside the law because they believed that they followed higher laws: those of racial supremacy and the preservation of southern cultural mores and political autonomy. Accepting defeat on the battlefield, they determined not to lose their status as pre–Civil War overseers of southern life. They swept aside any suggestion of compromise. Losing to the force of arms made them even more determined to regain control of local and state government. In the end, perhaps even murder of innocent victims became pardonable if the South retained self-rule.[22]

As the Conservatives and their Klan adjunct inexorably worked their way toward a return to power in North Carolina, the Binghams, now settled near Mebane, reopened their school. William took over as chief officer of the school when his father died, and Robert settled into academic life once again. Having taught only briefly at the school before the war, Robert deferred to his older brother's judgment on most school matters. William provided strong executive leadership as well as being a widely known classical scholar.[23]

Family life for the Binghams stabilized in the late seventies and early eighties. Robert Worth, or Rob, as he was known to family, became a considerable source of pride for his father. Students in the seventies later remembered seeing the elder Bingham with Little Bob, as they called the youngster, seated before his father on a white horse riding about the school grounds. As the younger Bingham grew older, the students gave him another nickname, Hard Money, because he demanded the same for the sale of firewood, apples, and sundry items at the barracks. From an early age Rob developed a fondness for the out-of-doors and hunted in the fields around the school. He developed into a crack shot and often contributed to the family larder with his hunting skills. More important, he absorbed the cultural, religious, and political views of his father and the surrounding region.[24]

With the death of brother William in 1873, Robert, now using his military title of major, assumed full charge of the school. Although financial problems nearly brought ruin in the early seventies, by the mid-eighties the Bingham School could boast of extended facilities. About this time Bingham again became a military school, with Robert taking the rank of colonel in the North Carolina state militia. Enrollment expanded, usually exceeding 150 students. The Bingham School made a few concessions to modernity by fielding highly competititve athletic teams and building one of the first gymnasiums in the South, but continued to stress classical education.[25]

The school reflected the general cultural milieu of educated middle-class southerners of the era. For example, a listing of declamations for the 23 April 1880 exercises included topics dear to the hearts of most southerners: "Let Us End Sectional Strife," "Southern Chivalry," and "Adieu to the Confederacy." A debate on the topic "Would a Large Army and Navy Be Beneficial to the United States?" identified another bent of the southern mind of this era. Bingham boys and Rob learned that their nationalism could and should subsume their old southern cultural traditions. But the latter always lingered just below the surface.[26]

Bingham students came from mostly North Carolina middle-class families with occasional students from as far away as Texas attending the sessions. They descended from solid Scots-Irish stock who, although often lacking wealth, represented the business, agricultural, and political establishment of the postwar years. Their families opposed the radicalism of the farm movements of the Alliance and Populist parties. Owing to their property ownership, they disliked tampering with the monetary system. They tended to be hard-money, low-tariff Grover Cleveland Democrats. One observer of this self-contained world, Woodrow Wilson, described a visit to the school in 1884. His future father-in-law Edward Axon attended school there in the prewar years. In a letter to Ellen Louise Axon, his fiancée, Wilson described a typical southern boy's boarding school, praising the hospitality of the Bingham family. He also admitted, jokingly, that he flirted with the two Bingham girls.[27]

In the years from the end of the Civil War to just after the turn of the century, Colonel Robert played a prominent role in the New South era while Rob grew to manhood and absorbed the values of the South, both old and new. The colonel personified this synthesis to his son, and, as a southern educational leader, played a prominent role in the development of these ideals. Both were part of a larger movement of ideas and culture, and each embodied characteristic reactions of two generations of southerners to the ideas and ideals of the New South.

The New South, according to historian Paul M. Gaston, began as a creed, or reaffirmation of southern potentiality, but ended as a myth, in which southerners rationalized success for their dreams of material advance. As part of this mental construct, southerners developed their own peculiar ideas about the history of their region and the nation. This consensus reinforced southern provincialism, contributed to the institutionalization of racism, and strengthened the hold of the Lost Cause on the southern mind.[28]

Colonel Robert's contributions to the New South as creed and myth came primarily through his intense activity in the educational affairs of North Carolina and the region. However, his views of race and history predetermined almost any response to practical matters, whether in education, politics, or economic affairs. For example, although he urged the education of all children and even asked for large expenditures of local, state, and federal governments for such purposes, he stressed that the races must "BE DEALT WITH SEPARATELY." The colonel defended secession, but not slavery, finding the South's "peculiar institution" to have been even more disastrous for the white than the black race. He endorsed segregation as "race instinct" and gave no quarter to any suggestion of immediate suffrage rights for Negroes, proposing that blacks should be enfranchised only after they had been schooled in democratic institutions.[29]

Yet in nearly the same breath the colonel could claim that "I have always loved the negro [sic] and I shall never cease to love him. My father and mother reared seven children in a slave woman's lap. She loved us better than her life. We loved her next to our parents." Although this statement appears typically apologetic of a white southerner justifying the development of post–Civil War segregation, Bingham was being consistent, given his background. Undoubtedly he loved the slave woman. Wars, lost and won, are given meaning by those who fight or live through them. If Bingham mythicized the Old South, secession, and the Civil War, he could do no other and continue to live with the memories of the pain and suffering of the war. Adoption of the Lost Cause mental construct became consistent with the struggle of Reconstruction and return of native white rule in the South. All became part of the colonel's historical view of himself, his race, his section, and, ultimately, his nation. Several generations of southern young men came under this influence at the Bingham School, where they absorbed the value system of their schoolmaster, which they, in turn, carried into adulthood. Young Rob would be as profoundly swayed as any other.[30]

After a fire destroyed several buildings at the Mebane location in 1890, Bingham decided to move to a location that could provide better fire protection and a somewhat better environment for the young men in his charge. He chose Asheville and moved there the next year. On a hill near the French Broad River, later named Bingham Heights, the colonel built in the early nineties what would become the last Bingham School.[31]

At least two prominent literary figures took notice of the life of Bingham and his school in its Asheville setting. If the colonel exemplified the chivalry, sense of honor, and devotion to the Lost Cause of many of his generation to his son and other southerners, to another North Carolinian, novelist Thomas Wolfe of Asheville, he epitomized something much different. Wolfe never attended the Bingham School but could have taken a teaching position there after graduation from the university at Chapel Hill. His refusal indicated a desire to break with what he considered the stifling past of his native southland. In *The Hills Beyond* he immortalized his impressions of Colonel Robert Bingham, apparently using the headmaster as the prototype for the character Theodore Joyner. To Wolfe, Joyner represented the pretentiousness and shallowness of the professional Confederate veteran. Joyner, like Bingham, headed a neo-Confederate military academy on Hogwart Heights and gave speeches expounding on the glory of the antebellum South and the heroism of the Civil War. One of Joyner's sons, Gustavus Adolphus "Silk" Joyner, bears a striking resemblance as an adult to Robert Worth Bingham. Both leave the school environment, take law degrees, and become successful apart from the Old South dependence on their fathers.[32]

Walter Hines Page, ambassador to Great Britain during World War I and an alumnus of the Bingham School, demonstrated a more ambivalent attitude toward his alma mater and its headmaster than did Wolfe. A critic of the New South mentality, Page blamed the Lost Cause encumbrances of southerners like Bingham for the lack of general progress in the South in the late nineteenth century. However, in one of his famous "Mummy" letters written in 1886, he cited Bingham as one of the more enlightened citizens in a culturally moribund state. Twenty years later, after forsaking the South and winning success in the publishing world, Page only thinly disguised the Bingham character in his autobiographical novel, *The Southerner*. Much like Wolfe's Colonel Joyner, Page's Colonel Graham typified nearly all that a progressively minded southerner should abhor. But in the end Page found something positive about the influence of his old teacher. In summing up his experience at the Graham School, the fictitious Nicholas Worth declared, "My hearty Colonel, it was a narrow segment of life that you moved in and marched us over in those years of guns and drums and paradigms and Presbyterianism. I recall with a smile and yet with affection your amusing pomp and your martial precision. But you stood erect; and that is a pleasant memory in a world where I have seen men cringe."[33]

The real Colonel Bingham (and his literary counterparts) can be faulted for their obeisance to the absolutist mentality that existed within the Old South–New South ruling elite. This slavish behavior blinded him to the exigencies of the postwar southern environment of the late nineteenth century. Yet his efforts in behalf of education should receive credit. As the South struggled with important social, economic, and political questions, progressive individuals like Bingham meliorated conditions, particularly in education, that could have been much worse. He represented the best the New South era had to offer and helped educate hundreds of young southerners, who later provided more enlightened leadership than their mentor.

As the Civil War generation of the elder Bingham gave way to its postwar descendants, the legacy of the Old South remained strong, yet not immutable. In the case of Robert Bingham and his son, the father bequeathed to his offspring a legacy of undying loyalty to the South and its traditions. The environment that Thomas Wolfe and Walter Hines Page so vividly described, including the continual Presbyterian affirmation and military school discipline, profoundly influenced Rob.

In his formative childhood years young Rob also came under the care of a loving, self-sacrificing mother. Although unhealthy from the time of the Civil War, Dell Bingham had a profound influence on her family and the students at the school. A convert to Presbyterianism, she instructed her children in religion at an early age and generally supervised the spiritual life of the young cadets at the Bingham school. Some of the younger cadets, who missed their own mothers, looked to her for a softening of the military discipline represented by the colonel. Her impact on the life of Rob was more subtle than that of her husband, but nonetheless crucial in his childhood years. Late in his life Rob compared his mother to Melanie in *Gone with the Wind*. By that time his mother had been dead for half a century. He remembered her as the epitome of the southern gentlewoman who persevered through the Civil War and Reconstruction years. Dell died on 24 February 1886, at forty-four years of age, when Rob was only fifteen. Five years later his younger brother William died at the age of eighteen.[34]

Issues other than race racked the North Carolina in which Rob came of age. Economic and political turmoil of the eighties and nineties severely tested the Bingham's adherence to the Democratic party. The Panic of 1893 frightened property owners like the Binghams into reordering their national political priorities. When William Jennings Bryan challenged the political status quo and fused the Democratic and Populist parties in 1896, the Binghams supported the candidacy of William McKinley, but not loudly. The colonel's advocacy of the Cleveland gold variety of the Democracy would not allow him to support the Nebraskan. The Binghams continued their "Whiggery" throughout the nineties while stoutly opposing the radicalism of southern Populists.[35]

Just before reaching his seventeenth birthday and after graduating from the Bingham School in 1888, Rob followed the family tradition by entering the University of North Carolina. Like his father and grandfather before him, he joined the Dialectic Literary Society, took part in debates, and developed an interest in history. Before the turn of the century, debating societies ruled life at Chapel Hill, and most students belonged to one of two such groups. Rob enjoyed sports and, although weighing only about 150 pounds and standing five feet eight inches in height, he participated in the university's first organized football game with Wake Forest College in October 1888. He served as captain of the sophomore football team and played a little baseball as well.[36]

While in Chapel Hill and later at the University of Virginia, Bingham established a network of friends that remained an important part of his life in the years ahead. He joined the Alpha Tau Omega social fraternity soon after coming to Chapel Hill. Fraternity brothers Shepard Bryan, William Watkins Davies, and Harrison Randolph became his closest friends. Bingham later served as provincial chief of Ohio and Tennessee ATO fraternities for a while just after coming to Louisville. Rob and a few friends organized another social group at North Carolina in the autumn of 1899 with the intriguing name

Order of Gimghouls, a fraternity for juniors and seniors. Davies, Bryan, and Wray Martin wrote up an appropriate medieval ritual complete with a hierarchical order in which "Sir Knight R. W. Bingham" played a role. Through the years Bingham continued to contribute money to the Gimghouls, including funds for the building of Hippol Castle, which still stands near the Chapel Hill campus. More important, however, were the friendships made in the ATO fraternity and the Gimghouls that became part of a lifetime of legal, political, and business networking.[37]

Rob also paid close attention to his studies. Besides history, he enjoyed languages and took several Latin, Greek, and German courses. Even later in life he kept up his German, taking private language lessons, reading the *Louisville Anzeiger,* and corresponding in German with a Louisville lawyer. Displaying a restlessness to get on with the study of a profession, Bingham did not graduate with his class at Chapel Hill. Nevertheless, he took part in the ceremonies and festivities attending the commencement of 1890. At one of these exercises he spoke on the topic "Manifest Destiny and Manifest Duty," winning the Representative Medal for Oratory, the highest award given for student presentations. In his speech he stressed: "The Teuton is the noblest race that has existed and the most progressive," echoing his father's racism. The growing spirit of expansionism found especially fertile ground in the South. Not coincidentally, another student who preceded Rob to the podium spoke on "The Color Line," advocating that "the danger from the growth of members of the negro [*sic*] can only be met by the restriction of suffrage on an educational basis." For these young southerners expansion complemented their native racism. Bingham's schooling either at the family school or at Chapel Hill received no reformist stimulus in the eighties or nineties.[38]

After leaving Chapel Hill in 1890, Bingham attended the University of Virginia for two years, where he first studied medicine and then turned to law. Again he played some football. There he met Hugh H. Young, a young medical student who later became director of the Brady Urological Institute at The Johns Hopkins University Hospital and one of the most prominent surgeons in the United States. Bingham and Young developed a close, enduring friendship.[39]

Unsure about his future, Rob returned to the Bingham School as a Latin and Greek instructor in 1892. However, in 1896 he severed his relationship with the old school, breaking a three-generation tradition. He took up again the study of law, a field that his old North Carolina friend W. W. Davies also entered. Moreover, about this time Bingham's personal life also took a different turn.[40]

In the summer of 1894 the twenty-three-year-old North Carolinian met the slightly older Eleanor E. Miller, a resident of Louisville, at the luxurious Grove Park Inn outside Asheville. Eleanor came to Asheville with her family because of the ill health of her father, Samuel A. Miller. Miller, afflicted with what was described in the press as a lung disorder, made periodic trips to such mountainous areas as Colorado and North Carolina. He also suffered from mental depression. Rob and Eleanor courted for several weeks that summer.[41]

Eleanor came from an old Kentucky family, socially prominent and financially well-off. Her maternal grandfather, Dennis Long, started a company that built steam engines and manufactured iron pipe in Louisville. The owners of Bashford Manor Farm, the Longs bred three Kentucky Derby winners and other bloodstock. Samuel A. Miller entered into various business ventures with the Longs and soon became involved with such firms as B. F. Avery, a Louisville farm machinery manufacturer, and several private waterworks owned by the family. Mary Henrietta Long Miller and Samuel had two other children: Katherine Anna, who married Americus Franklin Callahan, and Dennis Long Miller.[42]

In early 1895 Samuel Miller, under a doctor's care for a serious lung infection, moved back to Asheville. A physician also noted that the Louisvillian suffered from "melancholia." On February 2 he and his son Dennis traveled to the railway station to meet Eleanor, who came not only to visit her father but also to spend time with Robert. Just as the train pulled into the station, Miller leaped into its path. Dennis tried to save his father and only narrowly missed being struck and falling under the wheels of the locomotive. Samuel Miller died instantly.[43]

Over the next few months the romance between Rob and Eleanor became more serious, and eventually he asked Mrs. Miller's permission for an engagement. "I am not asking you to let her marry me yet—only to agree to her engaging herself to me," the young teacher requested. Bingham made a point in his letter to assure his future mother-in-law that his intentions were honorable and that he was a young man of the highest ambitions and work habits. By that time he decided to continue his pursuit of a law career.[44]

After finishing what he considered a final obligation to his father by finishing out the 1895–96 school year at the Bingham School, Rob moved to Louisville. With a little money saved from his meager salary and a loan of twenty-five hundred dollars from grandfather John Milton Worth, he immediately entered the University of Louisville law school.[45]

On 20 May 1896 Rob and Eleanor married in Louisville at the Calvary Episcopal Church. A large reception complete with orchestra followed the ceremony at the Miller home. Bingham soon switched his religious affiliation to that of his wife: the Episcopalian Church. He and Eleanor moved in with Mrs. Miller in her spacious home on Fourth Street.[46]

A year after his marriage Bingham received his only academic degree, the L.L.B. W. W. Davies, his old friend from Chapel Hill days, also moved to Louisville after practicing law briefly with Shepard Bryan in Atlanta. The two transplanted North Carolinians formed a law partnership. With a wife from a prominent Louisville family, and the beginning of his law practice, Robert Worth Bingham could not but have been optimistic about his future in the Falls City.[47]

As Bingham began his new life in a border-state city, one influenced by the Midwest as well as the South, he brought with him the intellectual, moral, and spiritual heritage of his North Carolina upbringing. Colonel Robert made the pilgrimage from the Old South to the New South. Rob moved beyond even these confines into vibrant turn-of-the-century America.

chapter two

From the New South to Progressivism

THE KENTUCKY WHERE BINGHAM settled in the mid-nineties differed little from his native North Carolina. His accent would not have been out of place in this border-state city of the upper South, sometimes called the "great city of compromise" between North and South. One student of the history of the Commonwealth of Kentucky in the late nineteenth century has asserted that the state "waited until the war was over to secede from the Union." This belated "secession" had several manifestations. Ironically, Louisville, the stronghold of Unionism and the Union army in Kentucky during the Civil War, became a most "southern" city after the war. The growing power of the L. and N. Railroad in the postwar southern economy welded the thriving manufacturing and commercial interests of Louisville to the South more so than to the adjacent Midwest. Louisville built monuments to the Confederacy as it tied itself more closely with the fate of the South. Many Kentuckians treasured their horse racing, mint juleps, Stephen Collins Foster's *My Old Kentucky Home* (based on an old slave lament), and the Lost Cause of the Civil War South. Kentuckians in the early twentieth century spearheaded the construction of a Todd County concrete obelisk to mark the birthplace of Confederate President Jefferson Davis. The state's regionalism allowed northern Kentuckians to present more midwestern than southern characteristics, but even there the appeal of the myths and legends of the Old South, the southern mystique, had its followers.[1]

Neo-Confederatism appeared everywhere in Kentucky. Confederate veteran Henry Watterson at the *Courier-Journal* became a prominent spokesman for the New South creed and the Old South myth. At the level of state government, Confederate veterans dominated the legislature, the courts, and the statehouse in Frankfort into the nineties. About the time Bingham migrated to the Commonwealth, the Republican party reasserted itself first in state and then national races in Kentucky. However, even the inroads of that party belied the hold of southern culture, literature, agriculture, religion, politics, and mores on Kentuckians. Bingham and Davies, his law partner, would have recognized few discernible differences from their native North Carolina. They willingly participated in the southern contexts of Louisville and Kentucky. However, they also became part of the vanguard of progressivism that brought about significant change in the nation and region in the period from the nineties through World War I.[2]

In 1900, second only to New Orleans in population in the South, Louisville combined the charm of a "big country town," according to Barry Bingham, Sr., with that of a bustling industrial and commercial city. The conquering of the treacherous "Falls of the Ohio" with the Portland Canal, and the spanning of the Ohio River with bridges, gave Louisville vital contact with all regions of the country. Louisville's bourbon distilleries and tobacco-processing plants became known all over the world. Large corporations such as the L. and N. Railroad and the B. F. Avery and Son Company, the largest producer of plows in the world, drew more headlines, but a host of smaller industries specializing in paint, hardware, and provisioning of the southern trade made the Falls City an important trade and commercial center. Dennis Long and Company became the "nation's largest producer of cast-iron pipe." Other industries in cement, meat processing, woodworking, and textiles added to the prosperity of the city. Louisville entrepreneurs pioneered such diverse products as chewing gum with the Kis-Me Gum Company becoming a leading manufacturer. River traffic continued to prosper even as the railroad increased its hold as the more important regional transportation linkage.[3]

Louisville demonstrated other outward signs of urban vibrancy in the late nineteenth century. The Southern Exposition of 1883, just south of Central Park in old Louisville, succeeded so well, it continued through 1887. Streetcar suburbs developed on the outskirts of the city proper as the middle class moved to such areas as Crescent

Hill just east of Louisville. Louisville and Kentucky closely followed the economic trends that emanated from the East Coast and Middle West. The general prosperity of the McKinley era encouraged business development and a revived stock market all over the country in the mid-nineties. Even farm prices stabilized and took much of the starch out of the old demands of the Farmers Alliances and the Populist party for special aid for America's agriculturalists. Most people, however, still had vivid memories of the terrible Panic of 1893.[4]

I

Bingham was in his twenty-sixth year as he settled into a law career in the River City on the Ohio. His strong attachment to his father, Colonel Robert, and the ideals of the Bingham School held dominant sway on the young lawyer. The ambitious Rob soon rose to the upper echelons among the city's lawyers, using his own talents and his wife's family connections. Early success propelled him into the political arena in an exciting era of local, state, and national politics during the Progressive Era. Even as he developed his law practice and other business interests and made his entry into politics, Bingham never lost contact with his North Carolina roots while taking a serious interest in his own developing family ties in Kentucky.

Marriage to Eleanor E. Miller brought Bingham into contact with the business interests of the well-to-do Miller and Long families. Eleanor's sister Katie married Americus F. Callahan, who worked for Long and Company and later became a first vice-president of the United States Cast Iron Pipe and Foundry Company in Chicago. Callahan went on to found the Outlook Envelope Company, where he developed the "window" envelope specifically designed for business correspondence. The Millers, Callahans, and Bingham built not only family ties, but productive investment and business associations around the turn of the century.[5]

Eleanor, known as Babe or Babes to family and friends, and Rob became the parents of three children in the early years of their marriage. First Robert was born in 1897, named for his father and paternal grandfather; then Henrietta, named for her maternal grandmother, came in 1901; and finally, George Barry, named for the founder of an Anglo-Irish titled family to which Robert Worth claimed kinship, was born in 1906. The children received the benefits of an upper-middle-class upbringing and the indulgence of their parents. Young Robert attended private schools like the University–Flexner School connected with the University of Louisville. The children were a bit spoiled by their parents. Sometimes they displayed a bit of temper, as when their mother's "nervous indigestion" spoiled a trip to visit the Callahans in Chicago. "Poor little Henrietta went under the bed and stayed for an hour when she found that we were not going tomorrow morning," the father explained, "and we all were greatly disappointed."[6]

Barry, the youngest child, remembered his parents as loving and generous. Eleanor enjoyed music and took time to teach Barry new songs and singing duets with her son. She loved to work in the garden. The children saw less of their busy father, but, according to his youngest son, when Robert Worth Bingham came home from the office, he usually allowed some time to talk and play with them.[7]

By 1900 Bingham had prospered enough to rent a summer cottage near Asheville, North Carolina, for his family, where they stayed to avoid the oppressive summer heat and humidity of Louisville while enjoying contact with his own family nearby. At least one servant always accompanied the family on these occasions. Rob often traveled on business but attempted to spend as much time as possible with his family on weekends.[8]

After living with Mrs. Miller for several years at 1326 Fourth Street, the Binghams, now a family of five, moved into a newly constructed home in the exclusive Cherokee Park area of suburban Louisville. At one time the estate encompassed ten acres of land deeded to Eleanor by Mrs. Miller. Bingham also bought his first automobile, a Cadillac "machine" with acetylene headlamps. Barry Bingham, Sr., remembered growing up in a community atmosphere that allowed children to mix with all types of people, including the servants and tradesmen who plied the area. Roller-skating on residential streets near his grandmother's house did not present this youngster with problems. He was free to roam at will with little concern for his safety.[9]

Bingham's concern for the health of his family and himself extended to securing a cow to ensure wholesome milk for his children, as well as purchasing large quantities of Anita Spring Water for his family's use. For years he suffered from the effects of a form of eczema, a malady that appeared to run in the family, afflicting his sister Sadie. Dr. Michael Ravitch, a Louisville dermatologist, periodically treated the Binghams for their skin disorders. Other recurring health problems added to Bingham's discomfort by the turn of the century, including stomach maladies, problems with sleeping, and headaches. An old college mate diagnosed his friend's problems as the result of working too hard and smoking too much tobacco, the latter, he argued, being a "poison to you." To guarantee security for his family, Bingham took out several life insurance policies on himself with Eleanor as the beneficiary.[10]

Notwithstanding Bingham's apparent health problems, he demonstrated a zest for life and, on occasion, displayed a sense of humor. Law partner Davies was more of an old-fashioned raconteur. Both enjoyed playing on each other's humor. For example, when Bingham complained of a kidney problem, Davies could not forgo describing in a comical way how his life had been saved by patent medicines. When notified by local authorities that a dog license was due for payment, Bingham replied: "Yours is received in regard to the expiration of my dog license. As the dog has expired too I presume I will incur no cost by not renewing his license."[11]

Rob's relationship with Colonel Robert during these early years in Louisville changed as the son accepted more and more responsibility for his father's welfare. Moreover, the son took over much of the financial direction of the Bingham School. He offered legal advice, made loans to his father for major school-construction projects, and gave substantial grants for such projects as building a school clubhouse. In connection with the latter project, the younger Bingham promised to fund the construction if the patrons followed certain rules. Although the smoking of pipes and cigars would be allowed, no cigarettes or gambling would be permitted. Rob handled some investments for his father in the Pipe Trust, where the Longs and A. F. Callahan, Mrs. Long's son-in-law, had some influence after the sale of their company to J. P. Morgan. When Rob feared for his father's safety during a period of lawlessness around Asheville, he mailed a modern rifle along with a hundred shells "of the dum-dum variety" to the Bingham School. Major R. T. Grinnan, the husband of sister Sadie, steadily assumed more day-to-day direction of the school as Colonel Robert aged, a circumstance that created tension as neither the colonel nor Rob held the talents of the major in high regard. From Louisville Rob kept close watch over the school and the welfare of his father.[12]

True to southern mystique and respect for his father's Civil War record, Bingham joined the United Sons of Confederate Veterans soon after arriving in Louisville. He briefly considered running for commander in chief of that organization in 1900, but declined because the responsibilities would take too much time away from his work. However, when the United Confederate Veterans met in Louisville in mid-June 1905, young Bingham worked on the local arrangements committee.[13]

Bingham's career prospered from the day he opened his practice in Louisville. In the early days of their partnership, Bingham and "Will," or "Dave" Davies as he was called, worked together in their cases and invested in many of the same business enterprises. They moved several times in the first decade of the century, but always to more spacious offices. Their firm handled only a few criminal cases, preferring instead to represent major corporations and investors and argue some tort cases involving injuries to clients. Bingham and Davies sometimes sent out-of-state clients "a good representative of the liquid refreshment (bourbon from the Pendennis Club stocks) which made this commonwealth famous" as a gift.[14]

Some of their major corporate clients included B. F. Avery and Sons, United States Cast Iron Pipe and Foundry Company, National Biscuit Company, American Chicle Company, and Coca-Cola in Louisville. For example, such cases included working for incorporation of Swift and Company and National Biscuit in Kentucky and negotiating their tax cases. Bingham and Davies also handled numerous injury cases for B. F. Avery and U.S. Cast Iron Pipe. When three Louisville businesses began "making spurious and imitative articles" in competition with Coca-Cola, Bingham also represented Judge J. H. Candler of Atlanta in pressuring those firms to change their products. Too, Bingham handled land acquisitions in the South for several wealthy Louisville investors.[15]

Bingham and Davies also pleaded tort (personal-injury claim) cases and provided a variety of other services as they built their law practice. Their fees included the usual one-third of recovery plus expenses. Several injury suits against such railroads as the Illinois Central, Southern, Louisville and Nashville, and the Louisville Railway proved to be successful for the plaintiffs. Acting as trustees for estate settlements and bankruptcies and working for the pardon of a few incarcerated Kentuckians added to the firm's workload. On one occasion when glue factories' offensive odors wafted toward the nearby elite Louisville Country Club, the firm of Bingham and

Davies negotiated with the animal rendering plant owners for a relocation.[16]

The close Bingham-Davies partnership in legal and business matters lasted for ten years. They dissolved their partnership, but not their friendship, at the end of the first decade of this century. By 1910 a partnership of John McChord, Bingham, and Robert L. Page took place. Two years later Kohn, Bingham, Sloss, and Spindle formed a new firm.[17]

Bingham's business interests directly related to his legal practice during Theodore Roosevelt's years in the White House (1901–9). Nominally a Democrat and registered throughout his lifetime to that party because of his North Carolina upbringing, Bingham had business contacts that included devout Republicans like the Longs and Millers. But he apparently also had contacts with other supporters of the GOP. For example, a Montana national Republican committeeman gave him tips about mining companies in the West. His network of college friends in North Carolina, Georgia, and other states became business associates for various enterprises. More important, the young Louisvillian's marriage to Eleanor Miller brought an opportunity to participate in the Miller-Long investments and to join the board of B. F. Avery and Sons.[18]

Robert's personal investments grew substantially in the first decade of this century. He invested heavily in Wall Street, and his correspondence indicated that on occasion he played the market with some abandon. His portfolio included railroads, commodity futures, and other securities. Like a number of Americans he got caught short during a severe market fluctuation in 1905, and one of his brokers called for more margin more than once. "Everybody is panicy [sic] and throwing their securities on the market," the broker explained. Sometimes investments almost failed, as when the Western Bank on Market Street in Louisville nearly went under during the Panic of 1905. Bingham worked hard and succeeded in getting support from other Louisville financial institutions to keep the bank afloat and his investment secure.[19]

Part of the Miller-Long business interests included control of water companies in Owensboro, Kentucky; Danville, Illinois; and Defiance, Ohio. Bingham and Davies invested in and handled the legal affairs of the companies, taking one successful case all the way to the United States Supreme Court. George J. Long, the brother of Mrs. Miller, and her son Dennis Long Miller, served as the chief executives of the companies. A. F. Callahan, Bingham's brother-in-law, also participated in the various companies, but principally worked with Dennis Long and Company at the task of making cast-iron gas and water pipe until 1903 when the Louisville-based company merged with J. P. Morgan's United States Cast Iron Pipe and Foundry Company of Chicago. In the Windy City, Callahan cut his connection with the old Miller businesses and eventually left Morgan's firm, becoming an entrepreneur in his own right. "I am damned glad of it," Callahan told his brother-in-law as he severed his connection with the turbulent iron-pipe business.[20]

Apparently Mrs. Miller sometimes proved difficult to deal with on occasion. For example, she differed over the amount of stock used for collateral for cosigning a loan for Callahan, believing that her stock portfolio suffered a loss. "Beyond a doubt she has acquired a deep-seated uncompromising hatred for me and I fear equally strong for you," Callahan told Bingham, and "I honestly think that the greatest worry to me is the greatest joy to her." Once Callahan settled into his own companies in Chicago, including serving as president of the Universal Electric Storage Battery Company, he became fully independent of his mother-in-law's business interests. Bingham, however, continued to serve Mrs. Miller as her chief legal and business adviser.[21]

Bingham also struck out in business ventures independent of the Millers and Longs. He became interested in patents and represented the Howe Manufacturing Company of Louisville in its quest for new patents for high-pressure valves. An avid sportsman, he pushed a patent application for a new type of fishing reel for a client. Moreover, he became involved in organizing various coal, lead, and fluorspar mining companies located in western Kentucky. On one occasion Bingham used his influence at B. F. Avery and Sons to persuade that manufacturer to use the fluorspar of Western Kentucky Mining Company in their smelting process. These mining ventures in Kentucky failed to produce much profit. Other attempts to form mining companies along with Davies in the western United States also proved unsuccessful. Bingham's partner good-naturedly declared to a friend, "Dame nature holds somewhere in her archives and storehouses, something for us and we will find it yet—by gum!" The general prosperity of the Teddy Roosevelt years did not bring automatic success to the Bingham-Davies enterprises, but they prospered like many other young entrepreneurs of the period.[22]

A young Bingham strikes a serious pose around 1902. From the Barry Bingham, Sr., Collection. Reprinted with permission of The Filson Club Historical Society, Louisville, Kentucky.

If the United States is often described as a nation of "joiners," then Bingham would be a prime example. His memberships exemplified not only his business interests, but his predilection toward progressivism as well. It seemed that nearly every organization in Louisville at the turn of the century opened itself to Bingham. His memberships fell into several categories, including fraternal organizations, business

CAL STATE UNIVERSITY, HAYWARD LIBRARY

associations, social groups, and philanthropic affiliations. Like his father before him, he became an active member of several Masonic organizations, which have been described by one student of the South
as bearing "quasi-religious features" well-accepted by southerners.
Some critics of such organizations have assigned special purposes, almost conspiratorial features, to the Masonic brotherhood. Whether
coincidentally or not, a good number of Bingham's associates were
Masons, often beginning their correspondence with "Brother" and
ending with the closing "Fraternally yours."[23]

Bingham also joined several Louisville business and social organizations, including the prestigious Pendennis Club. He belonged to
philanthropic organizations and took a special interest in the Kentucky Children's Home, assuming a role of leadership that lasted for
over three decades. In 1902 he became president of the Kentucky
Children's Home Society, working to meliorate the fate of the state's
orphans. On the other hand, he made a bow to the dominant racing
industry of his adopted city, joining the ranks of the New Louisville
Jockey Club in 1903. Membership in so many organizations extended
Bingham's influence throughout the city of Louisville and the immediate vicinity. These contacts expanded Bingham's network of friends
and business colleagues.[24]

When the opportunity arose, Bingham also began accepting speaking engagements in Louisville and out in the state, traveling to such
central Kentucky towns as Cynthiana, Richmond, and Georgetown
when time allowed. Conscious of the usefulness of speaking well, he
worked on his voice and presentation and even tried his hand at acting in amateur plays, playing a role in *School for Scandal,* a light English comedy in 1899.[25]

Business success also gave Bingham other opportunities. By 1906
he could afford to make annual summer excursions abroad, usually
to Great Britain. In both places Bingham could indulge a passion for
hunting that became almost an obsession. Familiar with all firearms,
he often carried a revolver with him. On one occasion he left a revolver behind at the Callahan's in Chicago and asked for its return.
Bingham's list of memberships included those in various gun, revolver,
hunting, fishing, and field-trial clubs such as the Juniper Club of Louisville. He had a southern sportsman's love of watching a well-bred
bird dog work in the field and, belonging to the Kentucky Field Trials
Club, soon had his own string of award-winning hunting dogs. His

spirit of competitiveness always revealed itself when he hunted with others. He prized his ability to outshoot his hunting companions. Bagging the most birds on a hunt with other men appeared to be just as important as winning an important lawsuit or making a wise business decision. Bingham's success in his law practice and other business ventures coupled with an engaging personality allowed him to join in lockstep an elite group, the rising young professional men in Louisville society.[26]

I I

Just prior to Bingham's political debut in Louisville, he demonstrated several traits that George Brown Tindall in *The Ethnic Southerners* found to be dominant among early-twentieth-century southern "business progressives." These southerners devoted themselves to the spread of majoritarian reform, regulation of business, promotion of both business and government efficiency, and advancement of "the public service concept of government." Moreover, this type and form of progressivism continued to influence the South and the nation long after the demise of progressivism in the 1920s. In his magisterial study, *Southern Progressivism*, Dewey W. Grantham found that southern progressives for the most part reconciled "progress and tradition." The former meant the acceptance of the "Yankee" business ethic, whereas the latter, with a few exceptions, kept to the old racial mores of the New South.[27]

Bingham's career during the Progressive Era typified middle-class business progressivism. He did not attack capitalism, proposing instead that government must regulate business to make it more responsive to the public welfare. Correspondingly, he represented large corporations such as Swift and Company, American Chicle Company, and B. F. Avery and Sons. He lobbied for pure food legislation in Kentucky, Mississippi, Virginia, and South Carolina as a well-paid representative of the National Biscuit Company. Middle-class progressives like Bingham viewed such legislation as a mechanism to assure wholesome food for their families while promoting commerce and business efficiency. Louisville progressives supported their city as a trade center for the upper South. Bingham and other Kentucky progressives, however, did not close their minds entirely to the more radical ideas of the day. For example, the Louisville Conversation Club, a group of professionals, ministers, and businessmen, to which several progressives such as Bingham belonged, provided a venue for discussing the most current and controversial topics of the day.[28]

Neither did Bingham oppose labor organizations as long as they went about their business in a peaceful manner. For example, he helped settle a strike against the Louisville Railway Company, a street-car corporation, during his brief tenure as mayor in mid-1907. The business community supported a quick settlement of that strike in order to keep downtown business active. Bingham skillfully kept the opposing sides from resorting to the use of force. Fearing that the strikers would overreact, he immediately crushed the efforts of the railway company to hire private police to protect their rolling stock. Just as important, he kept the Louisville Police Department under a tight rein.[29]

At best, Kentucky progressives demonstrated paternalistic attitudes toward blacks. Governments in Kentucky and surrounding states, as ably demonstrated in George C. Wright's *Racial Violence in Kentucky, 1865–1940,* did little to control lynching as a form of intimidation of Negroes during the Progressive Era. The Day Law, a statute aimed at separating the races in such private schools as Berea College, completed the process of legal segregation of the races in Kentucky in 1904. However, Kentucky Negroes were never disfranchised by law as they were in the Deep South by various legal devices such as the "grandfather" clause or poll taxes. They usually supported Republican candidates, particularly in Louisville. The Democratic press, led by the *Courier-Journal* of "Marse" Henry Watterson, often used the race issue to attack the Republican party as being boss ridden and anti-Southern in character. No doubt white Republicans often manipulated their black brethren for political gain. Although Kentucky sent two-thirds of her sons to fight for the Union during the Civil War, pro-Southern politics and sympathy for the Lost Cause of the Confederacy, the southern mystique, dominated the Commonwealth after the Civil War. At times Kentucky blacks faced the threat of disfranchisement in addition to the segregationist policies of the white majority. However, progressives did not cut themselves off entirely from Negroes, meliorating racial conditions that could have been much worse. For his part Bingham often addressed meetings of blacks and supported Negro education, but he did not move to overturn the racial mores of the community. He was very much his father's son on the matter of race.[30]

Kentucky progressives did not ignore the problems of the developing urban environment. Bingham and other progressives tried to improve the lives of the less fortunate, and he supported such benevolent organizations as the Kentucky Anti-Tuberculosis Association, Associated Charities, Neighborhood House, Salvation Army, YMCA, and the Newsboys' Home. These associations demonstrated the progressives' desire for efficiency and control over charitable institutions, and as well as a sincere concern for the plight of the poor. The middle-class progressive ethos, which included the Protestant Ethic, placed the highest value on work. Bingham concluded that there should be no "imposition by the unworthy" and that the poor should be provided with jobs.[31]

These represent only a few examples where Bingham's political ideas coincided with that of mainline southern progressivism. On the subject of alcohol, the issue that would eventually destroy progressivism nationally, Bingham supported the enforcement of such laws of control as the state Sunday closing law for saloons. He enjoyed wine with his meals, but apparently never overindulged in the distilled ardent spirits (bourbon) so well-known in the Bluegrass state.[32]

Borrowing from the progressive lexicon, such phrases as "good government," "honest government," "a clean city," "higher service," "progressive element," and other high-sounding phraseology resonated in the Bingham correspondence during this era. In the Kentucky context of progressivism, a strong religious element composed of mainline Protestant ministers and laymen dominated the leadership of that movement. This group formed the nucleus of Bingham's support as he entered political life. In what is seen by historian Ferenc M. Szasz as the last opportunity by the declining Protestant "hegemony" to control and dominate American culture, political reformers of a religious bent gave strong public leadership to the progressive movement.[33]

Robert Worth Bingham played a role in the history of progressivism. Ostensibly a Democrat because of his North Carolina upbringing and the influence of Colonel Robert, he became an active member of the Democratic party soon after settling in Louisville. Like his father, he had no use for William Jennings Bryan, owing to a belief in the sanctity of the gold standard. The younger Bingham did not follow a slavish connection to the Democratic party as he entered an active political life, but did serve as a Democratic committeeman for the forty-third precinct of the city of Louisville in 1898.[34]

However, the following year, during the tumultuous gubernatorial election between Democrat William Goebel and Republican William S. Taylor, Bingham volunteered as a poll inspector for either the Republican party or the "Honest Election League" because "I consider it the duty of every decent citizen to protect the ballot on that day as far as he can." Moreover, Bingham contributed to the defense fund for Republican Caleb Powers, the secretary of state accused in the death of the ill-starred Governor Goebel, because he believed that Powers had been falsely accused. At the same time the young Louisville lawyer supported Charles F. Grainger, the machine candidate for mayor of Louisville, and addressed such local clubs as the Bandana Democratic Club in support of the party. After the election of Grainger in 1901, Bingham thought nothing of asking that the new mayor give a place in the fire department to Pete Edwards, owing to the fact that "he has been a faithful worker for the Democratic party." In his earliest foray into party politics in Louisville Bingham paid his political dues to the Democratic party, while establishing a pattern of independence.[35]

Bingham's political ambitions surfaced in 1902 when he talked to several local political leaders about the prospects of running for the U.S. House of Representatives. Although he did not receive the nod from the Democratic machine, he did make himself known as someone who desired public office. Consequently, after the 1903 general election, County Judge James P. Gregory appointed Bingham to replace Sam B. Kirby as county attorney when the latter moved up to a bench in the Chancery Court. The *Louisville Times*, the afternoon companion of the pro-Democratic party *Courier-Journal*, praised the appointment as a "plum" for the up-and-coming lawyer. To his father Bingham analyzed the opportunity as one too good to pass up. First, the new job would help his law practice with "a large amount of valuable advertising." Although he would have to run in another year and then a year hence for a full four-year term, the salary would more than meet his needs. "It certainly was a great stroke of good fortune," he explained. In the bid for election in his own right in 1904, he ran ahead of the Democratic ticket led by Judge Alton B. Parker, who carried Kentucky for the first time since the 1892 presidential election. Bingham defeated Republican Lafon Allen by about twelve hundred votes.[36]

As chief legal counsel of the most populous and richest county in Kentucky, Binham set out to prove himself a capable administrator of the law. He devoted some time to coordinating construction of a new Jefferson County armory. Opposing the will of the local Democratic machine and its saloon-keeping allies, Bingham moved to enforce state laws regulating the sale of liquor on Sunday. With the apparent approval of Governor J. C. W. Beckham, he set out to close down saloons on the Sabbath, but not without local opposition.[37]

The executive committee of the Jefferson County liquor interests, the Mutual Protective Association, protested vehemently and bluntly told Bingham he could never again expect their support in an election. Bingham countered by also ordering the closing of saloons at midnight, another statutory restriction often ignored in Jefferson County. He allowed no exceptions, denying the right of such elite groups as the Pendennis Club and the Tavern Club to serve liquor on Sunday. Although the local religious establishment fully supported Bingham's efforts, Governor Beckham pardoned most of those convicted of violation of the law because of his desire to be elected to the U.S. Senate in the next election. In the end Bingham's efforts as county attorney to dry up Jefferson County on Sunday did not prevail.[38]

The political climate of Louisville and Jefferson County mirrored that of many other American metropolitan areas in the Gilded Age as machine politics of one variety or another dominated. For a substantial period of that time the political machine of "Colonel" John Whallen, a stereotypical Irish-American saloon-owning politico, who operated out of the Buckingham Theatre, dominated the local Democratic party organization. The Buckingham advertised "The Burlesque Show That Pleases," touting the talents of "The Cozy Corner Girls." Dispensing beer and political favors from his burlesque house-saloon, Whallen manipulated city politics through his control of the labor and immigrant votes. Charles P. Weaver and Charles F. Grainger competed with Whallen for control of the party and the over one thousand patronage jobs on the city payroll. Whallen usually kept the upper hand through the nineties by using Louisville policemen under his control to intimidate voters. During one such episode in 1894, Richard Knott's *Louisville Evening Post* courageously exposed these corrupt tactics. But the "Boss" of the "Buck" received only a temporary setback to his domination of local politics and the Democratic party.[39]

After years of suffering under Democratic party bossism, a number of Republican leaders and independent Democrats joined forces behind a Fusion ticket in 1905 and nominated J. T. O'Neal for mayor. Other reform-minded groups such as the City Club, the Committee of One Hundred, and the Louisville Ministerial Association joined the fusionist cause. Basil Duke, William Belknap, Thomas W. Bullitt, and other prominent citizens supported the reform ticket. Knott, editor of the *Louisville Evening Post* backed the fusionists, as did the *Louisville Herald,* the local Republican organ. The *Courier-Journal,* edited by Watterson, and Colonel William B. Haldeman's *Louisville Times,* steadfastly upheld the Democratic ticket and its mayoral candidate, Paul C. Barth.[40]

This turn of events forced Bingham into a conflict of conscience against the practicality of staying with his party. As a Democratic party officeholder, Bingham was expected to pay a tenth of his salary into the party coffers. The Louisvillian balked at this order from the machine, deducting from that donation several hundred dollars that he considered out-of-pocket office expenses. Both Bingham and his partner Davies understood the complexities of the campaign, which was something other than simply a battle between good and evil. However, to these young law partners the Democratic machine stood out as anathema to their ideals of good government. Bingham determined to rise above partisan politics, and he attempted to use his office to assure a fair election. Although he personally visited several registration stations in the hope of enforcing a fair registration process, in the end he could not be everywhere at once, and the Democratic machine inflated their canvass during the two-day preelection registration period.[41]

On election day both sides prepared for a conflict other than with the ballot. In a flurry of charges and countercharges, Democrats claimed that fusionists appeared at the polls armed with "Ax Handles and Hickory Canes," as the *Courier* headlined, while fusionists charged that policemen and other Democratic henchmen attacked them at the polls. Several fusionists were physically assaulted, at least one ballot box was stolen and its contents burned, and fusion ballots were not counted at all in some precincts. On the first Tuesday in November 1905, reform parties won races for control of Cincinnati, Philadelphia, and a few other metropolitan areas, but in Louisville, Paul

Barth, the personal choice of boss Grainger, defeated O'Neal by over three thousand votes. Bingham, as a candidate in his own right, swept into office along with the other Democratic nominees. Fusionists immediately declared their intention to challenge the results in the courts.[42]

A few days after the election nearly one hundred fusionists convened and subscribed over ten thousand dollars to contest the election. Helm Bruce and William Marshall Bullitt took depositions and prepared the legal briefs for the plaintiffs. They entered forty-five cases of election irregularities in Jefferson Circuit Court, only to have Judge Shackelford Miller return an unfavorable verdict in late December 1905. After raising another ten thousand dollars for appeal expenses, the fusionists went to the Kentucky Court of Appeals, the state's highest court. Both sides marshaled the forces of men and money when the cases finally came before the court in Frankfort in April 1907.[43]

The course of these cases through the Kentucky legal system placed a severe strain on both Bingham's political life and his professional ethics. As county attorney, Bingham was in actuality both a defendant, owing to his election as a Democrat in the November 1905 general election, and a participant in the litigation. On the one hand, he and Davies supported the party in its defense of policemen and firemen who were charged with personal irregularities in the election-fraud cases. For example, they appealed to General Percy Haly, the chief political adviser of Governor Beckham, for information about potential jurors in the upcoming trials in early 1906. As county attorney, Bingham arranged for the collection of a 3 percent assessment from all Democratic candidates, who won their races in 1905, in order to pay for the litigation. However, although part of the group elected, Bingham none too secretly showed his dislike of the tactics used by his fellow Democrats. Davies became a counsel for the Louisville Democratic officials and argued the cases before both circuit and state courts in defense of the party. He took the case "individually" and was paid for his services as such and not through the law firm of Bingham and Davies. Bingham tried to distance himself from the litigation.[44]

Before the court of appeals, the fusionists presented a powerful case. They asserted that city voter registration had been subverted, "repeaters" had been allowed to inflate the Democratic party vote, ballots had been stolen, the police force had participated in violent acts against the fusionists, election officials had acted improperly in some precincts, and armed men had brazenly stolen ballot boxes. By a four-to-two vote the Kentucky Court of Appeals reversed the Jefferson Circuit Court decree, thereby removing from office all elected officials in Louisville and Jefferson County, including County Attorney Robert Worth Bingham.[45]

The former county attorney affirmed the court's decision. "I not only do not regret the decision of the Court of Appeals," he explained to a friend, "but believe it was exactly right, and that it will be a blessing in disguise to the Democratic Party in this community, which has recently fallen under bad leadership, and needs a complete change in order to bring back to it the respect and allegiance of the best elements of the community." Bingham, of course, considered himself and other progressives to be the "best elements of the community"; he declared his intention to be deeply involved in reforming the Democratic party in the coming years.[46]

chapter three

"... And Politics—
The Damnedest in
Kentucky"

WITH THE HANDING DOWN of the court of appeals
decision the task immediately fell on Governor Beckham to appoint
interim administrations for Louisville and Jefferson County. Becoming governor after the assassination of William Goebel, Beckham won
a special election in 1900 and the regular gubernatorial election in
1903. He hoped to be chosen U.S. senator after a Democratic sweep
of the general assembly in the general election in 1907. The interim
government in the state's most populous area would hold office for
only four months until new officials could be elected in November.
Beckham wanted to ensure the continued strength of the Democratic
party in Jefferson County, without whose aid he could not be elected
to the Senate. Yet he also wanted to fulfill the spirit of the court of
appeals decision. Helm Bruce encouraged Beckham to appoint
Bingham as mayor. The governor, who characteristically delayed the
decision while figuring all the political angles, named Bingham to
that post in late June 1907.[1]

Reactions to the appointment were for the most part positive. Colonel Robert declared that his son would have "to be like Sir Galahad"
in order to withstand the pressures of the coming crisis. The *Courier*
reported that the news "came like a peal of thunder from a cloudless
sky." Former Mayor Barth asked that Bingham give Louisville a "business-like administration." Editor Knott of the *Evening Post* applauded
Beckham's choice, finding the new mayor "animated by a zeal for the

righteous conduct of public office." The Republican *Herald* declared the appointment to be a "vindication of the majesty of law and invincibility of justice." Crusty old Watterson proclaimed Bingham to be acceptable though "not a very orthodox Democrat." After Beckham completed appointments of other city and county officials, the venerable editor of the *Courier* found them to be "exceptionable," but he doubted that much could be done in a short span of time to reform the city because the new administration would be "handicapped by immemorial abuses." With the announcement of his appointment, Bingham issued only a brief obligatory statement to the press. He promised to "concentrate every faculty that I have upon the effort to give the people of Louisville an honest and efficient city government and an absolutely fair election in the autumn."[2]

Prohibitionists, representing a growing movement at the turn of the century, served as a vital element in Bingham's coalition. In the late nineteenth century the image of the saloon sharply contrasted with the ideal of the "bourgeois interior" of the family. Many people, ranging from alcoholic novelist Jack London to pietist evangelical ministers, hoped to close the saloon forever, believing that it threatened the emerging middle-class nuclear family structure in America.[3]

Louisville and Jefferson County saloons wantonly disregarded state law and remained open on Sunday, offering a convenient target for temperance advocates of many persuasions. Louisvillians who did not support complete prohibition of the liquor trade found it increasingly difficult to ignore this lawlessness. As county attorney, Bingham had tried to enforce the Sunday closing law. Beckham probably appointed Bingham to the mayor's office without consulting him about the Louisvillian's intentions concerning the saloon problem, but he must have known that Bingham would very possibly repeat his history.[4]

The religious community associated enforcement of law with temperance regulation. Attempting to force their civil religious ideals on the community, the mainline Protestant churches and their allies backed Bingham's stand against opening saloons on Sunday. The Kentucky Anti-Saloon League responded with total support for the reform mayor. Local option successes in the state encouraged antisaloon advocates to anticipate the eventual prohibition of all alcoholic beverages. For a period of four months Bingham and prohibitionists became nearly inseparable in thought and action.[5]

Bingham took the oath of office on Saturday, 29 June 1907, and immediately ordered Police Chief Sebastian Gunther to enforce the Sunday Closing Law. The mayor warned that saloon keepers serving alcohol the next day would have their licenses summarily revoked. The *Courier* reported a "Louisville Dryer Than Ever Before in History" with the "Lid" on and "screwed down" tight by the mayor and the police department.[6]

In July 1907 (a month of record-setting temperatures in the state), the Sunday saloon disappeared in Louisville as police-court judge Randolph H. Blain, appointed by Beckham, enforced the law. County Attorney Robert Lee Page, Bingham's successor and later his law partner, also took an active interest in this law and closed the Sunday saloons in the county. Popular summer retreats at Fontaine Ferry Park and the Whallens' White City Park complied with the law. Success in closing down saloons on Sunday indicated that Bingham would not be a caretaker administrator. Throughout Bingham's brief tenure as mayor, the police and courts enforced the Sunday Closing Law.[7]

The mayor and governor faced other problems in cleansing the political atmosphere of Louisville and Jefferson County. Beckham's appointments reflected his desire to fill city and county offices with men untainted by the machine or connected with an opposing faction. The governor appointed Walter Lincoln as county judge and A. Scott Bullitt as sheriff. Bingham and Beckham met on several occasions during the late summer, considering appointments and strategies. After nearly a month of indecision, Beckham finally appointed aldermen and councilmen to the Louisville General Council. The board of public works, a board of public safety, a building inspector, and many lesser positions also had to be filled by Bingham.[8]

When Bingham took over as mayor, Louisville had no civil-service program. Similar to other cities at the turn of the century, over one thousand jobs were part of a nearly universal patronage system. The new mayor did not lack for advice from his constituents about appointments. Ministers, labor leaders, politicians, and friends of the mayor sought to have their favorites appointed. The newspapers reported hordes of office seekers and their supporters in front of the mayor's office in City Hall, forcing Bingham to retreat to quieter places from which to carry out the city's business. For example, Rev. E. L. Powell, pastor of the First Christian Church, urged the appointment of a friend as building inspector. An attorney asked for a job with the promise to support Bingham if he ran for mayor. The Brotherhood of Locomotive Engineers pressed for an appointment of one of their leaders as superintendent of the street cleaning department. Of course, the Building Trades' Union asked that one of their own be named building inspector; and so on. Through all of this turmoil Bingham consulted with close friends and supporters about appointments and reforms in early July.[9]

The Board of Public Safety and the police department immediately became targets of reform for the Bingham administration. Here Bingham could make immediate changes because of the strong administrative position of the mayor in Louisville's governmental system. First he named Davies as chairman of the board of safety and appointed as members of the board John Stites, president of the Fidelity Trust Company, and former county judge James P. Gregory. The board of safety became the most important of all Bingham's appointees because of that agency's control over the police and fire departments, major sources of patronage and electoral fraud in the past, and the public-health facilities of the city. Rumors spread that Bingham would fire every policeman connected with the Grainger and Barth administrations.[10]

The "old gang" expected a crackdown in the police department, and it was not long in coming. After two weeks in office Bingham replaced Police Chief Gunther with Colonel J. H. Haager. In a public announcement the mayor declared that policemen and firemen would be removed from the political arena. In late July the mayor and board of safety moved against the offending policemen who had participated in the election fraud of 1905. This reform started with a "shake-up" of personnel, reducing in rank six police captains and one major. The board promoted several officers who had been reduced in rank during the Grainger administration. In addition, fusionist William Marshall Bullitt initiated charges against fifty-two policemen for their participation in the 1905 election-fraud cases. Many of these men resigned before the board could fire them.[11]

The board of safety initiated no shake-up in the fire department, except to replace the secretary of the department. Bingham did not remove Fire Chief Fillmore Tyson, but he made it clear that firemen were to stay out of politics in the upcoming election. When Bingham heard that Tyson gave the *Courier* an unfavorable report about the new administration, he immediately called the chief into his office and explained that he would not allow "insubordination." The new mayor let Tyson off with this warning. As a further move to weaken the machine, Davies ordered policemen and firemen to give up membership in the Mose Green Club, an active Democratic political organization in Louisville.[12]

Chief Haager and Sheriff Bullitt enthusiastically supported Bingham's reforms. They enforced the Sunday Closing Law and took an active role in executing the laws of the city and the county. Throughout July, August, and September, Haager used a "flying squadron" of officers and plainclothesmen to sweep periodically through the "tenderloin" district on Green Street (renamed Liberty Street during World War I). On one such swing through the area the police arrested over two hundred men and women for drunkenness, gambling, and prostitution. In the press Chief Haager advocated arresting "men who live by the shame of women," using proper Victorian argot. Many of these men operated saloons on Green Street. An August raid of the city's saloons netted twenty-two men carrying illegal firearms. The progressives in the city urged a police crackdown on gambling as well. Sheriff Bullitt raided poolrooms, arresting a number of violators who had illegal poker and lottery operations. To accent his support of police efforts to clean up the city, Bingham on one occasion joined an inspection tour with Chief Haager through the "red light" district on Green Street.[13]

While the Bingham administration directed an attack on crime, the *Courier* and the *Times* took little notice of the activities of the Louisville police and the sheriff's department. The *Evening Post,* on the other hand, praised every effort to clean up the city and enforce the law. Editor Knott delighted in running cartoons of his nemesis at the *Courier* on the front page of the *Post.* After the announcement of the filing of charges against fifty-two policemen, cartoonist Paul A. Plaschke illustrated Watterson and Haldeman as demoted, paunchy policemen walking a beat for the first time in a long while. Knott, like most progressives, viewed crime as a serious problem that needed constant attention. He found that Louisville appeared little different from large cities such as New York and needed the continuous "work of regeneration" in its law enforcement.[14]

In other areas the Bingham administration attacked the alleged corruption and mismanagement of previous Democratic administrations. During July, August, and September, Bingham pressed investigations on several fronts. One week after he took the oath of office, he appointed Charles Meriweather to study the account books at City Hall and ordered a review of all city accounts and a special investigation of the City Hospital. The latter study, made by a select committee of physicians, ended in the resignation of Dr. Julius C. Vogt and the appointment of Dr. Jouett Menefee. The committee discovered deplorable conditions in the hospital, particularly citing the "filthy" wards, hallways, and examination and operating rooms. They declared the "colored ward" to be in even worse condition.[15]

Bingham and the board of safety also examined other public-health areas. The board prosecuted Dr. S. A. Bradley, the city livestock and meat inspector, for making false entries and allowing spoiled and diseased meat to go to market. Bingham took personal interest in this case and collected affidavits from businessmen admitting they bribed Dr. Bradley. The board declared Bradley guilty as charged in a preliminary hearing, and a Jefferson County grand jury returned an indictment. Fearing that the case would not be properly prosecuted in the courts, Bingham asked the general council to appropriate ten thousand dollars to pursue the case against Bradley. The city attorney, however, issued an opinion that any such appropriation would be illegal. After Bingham left office, Bradley won acquittal in a lengthy jury trial.[16]

In all matters related to public health, the mayor and the board of safety took characteristic progressive approaches to reform. Davies proposed an ordinance appointing a milk inspector for the Louisville market while working for passage of a state meat-inspection law. Dr. M. K. Allen, chief health officer of the city, supported Davies's efforts. Bingham also asked that the general council approve a separate nonpartisan health board. Progressives usually championed the nonpartisan approach to take all public boards out of the political arena.[17]

The *Courier,* however, found only ulterior political motives in the proposed reform, claiming that Bingham designed the nonpartisan board to protect Dr. Allen from a hostile board of safety if the Democrats swept back into power. Bingham let the matter drop when he could not muster enough votes for passage in the general council, declaring that he wanted a completely nonpartisan health board or "none at all." Even under the suspicion of partisanship and the fear of political reprisals, Dr. Allen proposed far-reaching reforms such as regulation of milk transport, stringent control of veterinarians' licenses, and regular health examinations of schoolchildren and school envi-

ronments. But Bingham could not reverse in four months the tradition of poor health regulations in Louisville.[18]

Bingham's administration continued exposure of the old machine's
activities throughout the summer months. Rumors and charges of
corruption among public officials had been adrift in Louisville and
Jefferson County for years, but nothing surfaced or reached the courts.
The reform element rejoiced when Chief Haager arrested former
county clerk William J. Semonin on charges of embezzling over forty-
eight thousand dollars in county and state funds. These charges again
turned into an editorial donnybrook between the *Courier* and the *Post,*
with the former defending Semonin as being falsely accused and the
latter deploring a cover-up of corruption. After a few weeks of uncertainty, Semonin made a settlement with the state and county for accounts due from collections, claiming to have delayed in making the
payment only until he knew the full extent of the debt. The prosecu-
tion allowed the court to dismiss the case.[19]

The reform administration also investigated city contracts and the
Louisville Water Company. At Bingham's insistence the general council hired out-of-state auditors to go over the old account books of the
water company. Bingham praised Sebastian Zorn's current leadership
and emphasized that he was interested in surveying the period only
before 1905. The preliminary report indicated "belated entries" and
"irregular vouchers," but no proof of criminal intent or action.
Bingham also questioned the profits of several Louisville corporations—particularly the steel-construction company of former Mayor
Grainger and the cement business of former Mayor Barth—that had
contracts with the city. The reform mayor hoped that the full report
of this study would cite specific instances of corruption in the affairs
of the Water Company. Bingham now came up against the machine,
whose last boss had been Grainger.[20]

Grainger, who served as mayor from 1901 through 1905 after having temporarily wrested control of the Louisville Democratic party
from the clutches of John Whallen, named Barth as his successor in
1906. When Bingham became mayor, Grainger sat on the board of
waterworks and also served as a member of the state racing commission. Bingham claimed that the state constitution limited a public official to only one such post. Helm Bruce and William Marshall Bullitt,
members of an important law firm in the city, backed Bingham's assertion that Grainger could hold only one public office. As usual the

Evening Post supported Bingham and the progressives. Knott charged that a conflict of interest existed because Grainger's company had large contracts on the filter-plant facilities then under construction. Grainger, however, refused to resign either post. He defended his position on both boards as being within the confines of the state constitution, because he received no direct compensation for either job.[21]

Keeping up the pressure, Bingham asked for an opinion from Kentucky attorney general N. B. Hays. The attorney general ruled that Grainger had indeed vacated the directorship of the board of waterworks when he had accepted the place on the state racing commission, but Hays declined to pursue the case because his term of office had nearly expired. Furthermore, he preferred not to stir up any difficulties for Beckham, whom he supported in the upcoming senatorial contest. County attorney Page filed suit against Grainger, but with no success. The final report on the water board's activities, issued a few days after Bingham left the mayor's chair, listed inferences of corruption, charging the board with "incorrect bookkeeping," "loose" business methods, and "carelessness." However, these alleged irregularities did not warrant indictments, and the Bingham administration again failed to prosecute successfully an official of the Democratic machine.[22]

Bingham knew any reform would be short-lived if the "old machine" returned a pliable Democratic mayor to office in November. Governor Beckham's ambitions for the United States Senate depended on the return of heavy Democratic majorities in the Kentucky General Assembly as that body, prior to passage of the Seventeenth Amendment, elected the commonwealth's two senators. He did not want to alienate the Louisville machine because of the important Democratic vote in the city and county. A key to settling the problems of the Democratic party in Louisville depended on whether the governor would be willing to support the reformers or remain neutral and allow the machine to resume control.[23]

To make the political picture even more confusing, a brief movement surfaced in July to develop a fusion ticket similar to the one that had united Republicans and independent Democrats in the election of 1905. The Republican City and County Committee met with the City Club, a group of reform-minded Louisvillians on 5 July. It appeared that these groups would again cooperate. In a separate meeting the City Club voted to put the same ticket on the ballot again, with

J. T. O'Neal as their candidate for mayor. Prominent Louisvillians such as William Heyburn, Morris B. Belknap, Basil Duke, Lewis Humphrey, Richard Knott, C. T. Ballard, and Helm Bruce provided leadership for the City Club. Augustus E. Willson, Republican candidate for governor, and Colonel Albert S. Scott, chairman of the local Republican committee, announced that they favored fusion as late as 7 July.[24]

Within two days, however, Republican leaders decided against fusion, reasoning that this would harm their state ticket. While Republicans William Marshall Bullitt and Joseph Seligman praised the fusionist effort of 1905 and the role played by independent Democrats in that election, they and other Republicans believed that they had an excellent chance this time to capture outright control of city hall with their own ticket. They invited independent Democrats to support them. In late July a Louisville Republican convention chose James F. Grinstead as its mayoral candidate.[25]

Bingham wanted to run for mayor, preferring to run on the Democratic ticket. In early July some leaders recommended that Bingham might head a fusion ticket, but Republicans quashed that move by going their own way and nominating Grinstead. A few Louisville Democrats supported Bingham's bid for office. James B. Brown, cashier of the First National Bank and chairman of the board of public works, and others urged Bingham to stay in the race for the nomination. The *Evening Post* gave almost daily support to the nomination of Bingham in its news accounts and editorials. Bingham continued to confer with Beckham, testing the governor's support for his candidacy and the progressive administration of Louisville. A political and business ally from Owensboro, however, warned the Louisvillian "they are trying to fix you for slaughter" and urged Bingham to stay out of the fray.[26]

On a sultry July evening on the rooftop of the Seelbach Hotel, Bingham openly clashed with Grainger in a Democratic caucus. Both agreed that the party's candidate should be chosen in a primary, but the mayor wanted the ballot delayed until just a few weeks before the November general election. The machine packed the meeting with its partisans, who applauded Grainger's speech and "hissed" when Bingham took the rostrum. This activity left little doubt that the machine, this time controlled by Grainger, intended to nominate one of its own for office. Bingham charged that John W. Vreeland, state central committeeman from Jefferson County, directed "so many corrupt primaries in the past" that no honest Democrat had any confidence in him. Grainger publicly denied that he packed the meeting, innocently claiming that the conflict with Bingham "is not of my seeking."[27]

Unable to win control of the caucus, Bingham tried another tack. He sought intervention from the State Central Democratic Committee, asking that it assume administration of the local primary and guarantee an honest election. The state committee, however, decided against coming into the local election for two reasons: first, there appeared to be no clear legal precedent for such a move; and second, the committee feared losing votes in Louisville for the state ticket. The Jefferson County Democratic Committee set 24 September for the primary, adding a ruling that all primary candidates must support the victors in the general election. Bingham refused to enter the primary because he would not accept the latter dictum. Lincoln, Blain, Page, County Clerk Phil Thompson, and several members of the general council also declined to enter the primary for the same reason.[28]

In one last attempt to bring the local primary under control of the state committee, sixty ministers petitioned Judge Henry B. Hines, the state Democratic party chairman, to follow the advice of Bingham. Their pleas went unheeded. Watterson usually took only sporadic interest in local political affairs, but he could not pass up this action without condemning direct participation of the Louisville Ministerial Association in politics. "He that dabbles in pitch," the *Courier* editor pontificated, "shall be defiled." With no opposition on the ballot for the machine candidates, the county committee declared their choices to be the official candidates of the Democratic party in the fall election, including mayoral candidate Owen Tyler.[29]

These setbacks did not deter Bingham from assaulting the Democratic machine. As part of the battle plan, Bingham disclosed some suspicious purchases made by the Barth administration. Strong evidence indicated that Barth condoned the purchase of several horses and mules that either died or disappeared under somewhat mysterious circumstances. Moreover, Barth kept a fine saddle horse ironically named Marc Hanna for his own personal use after he left office. Editor Knott seized this issue as a blatant example of corruption in the Grainger and Barth administrations. In satirical Plaschke cartoons entitled "Pauly and His Horse" and "Diary of a City Horse," the *Evening Post* pressed the attack. After incessant pressure from Bingham and the *Post*, Barth sent the mayor a personal check for $750 to pay for the horse.[30]

The incident appeared to be over, but when Barth did not return home on 20 August, family members went to his office at the Utica Lime Company. They found him slumped in his chair, having fired a "bullet through the brain." The Louisville papers took their usual stances in reporting and commenting on the suicide, with Bingham in the middle of the fray. The *Courier* and the *Times* declared that Barth had been unjustly attacked over what appeared to be only a minor indiscretion. Haldeman in the *Times* blamed the *Herald,* the *Evening Post*, and Bingham for persecuting Barth over an otherwise insignificant error in judgment. Watterson used bitter sarcasm in condemning Bingham. The *Courier* editor declared that he "hoped that the young gentleman who posed as a Reformer in the City Hall, and newspaper and other satellites, who are making such efforts to be spectacular in front of the grand stand, whilst keeping such equivocal company under the cover of darkness, are now entirely happy." The latter reference was to the charge of the Grainger people that old boss Whallen had now joined in league with Bingham to get control of the party.[31]

The *Herald,* on the other hand, did not apologize for its attacks on Barth, claiming that many politicians had weathered more criticism than the former mayor without committing suicide. Bingham responded with a public statement defending exposure of the horse incident as part of an overall program to reform city government. He took the fight to the *Courier* and allowed that his pressure did not lead to the "unbalanced" condition of Barth. The *Evening Post* supported Bingham. Knott declared in no uncertain terms that "the death of Mr. Barth closes a life of business success and political failure. . . . He has paid his last debt." The *Courier* did not relent in turning this episode into an attack on the progressive administration of Bingham. When the police could not handle the large crowd at Barth's funeral, the *Courier* claimed that Chief Haager had purposefully added further insult to a "Victim of Relentless Persecution."[32]

The suicide of Barth undoubtedly weakened the incipient reformist cause in Louisville. Though a convenient target because of his connection with the machine and use of the city-purchased horse, Barth appears to have been a basically honest man caught out of his element by the circumstances of the contested election of 1905 and the reform efforts of Bingham. The attacks on his character broke his spirit. Bingham may have been a bit overzealous in using the "Marc

Hanna" incident to get at more serious problems of corruption, but Barth's supporters, including the *Courier* and the *Times,* did not realistically face the facts of the case. Watterson's elevation of Barth to martyrdom demonstrated his subservience to the local democratic machine in contrast to his lofty national image as political sage. The former city buyer, who purchased the horse, later admitted that Barth knew exactly what he was doing when he accepted use of Marc Hanna and should have immediately paid for the animal when he left office. If the Bingham administration had had more time to let the public furor over Barth's death dissipate, reform of the city might have stood a better chance of success. Bingham's base of support eroded with the death of Barth, and time began to run out on the progressive administration.[33]

With Bingham out of the mayor's race and his administration rapidly drawing to a close, the political scene shifted to the contest between Grinstead and Tyler. This campaign coincided with the race for governor between Willson and Democrat S. W. Hager. The Sunday Closing Law became the major issue in the mayoral election in Louisville. Tyler upheld the premise of home rule and asked for repeal of the Sunday Closing Law. Grinstead promised to enforce that law. The *Herald* and the *Evening Post* supported Grinstead. The *Post* came out for Grinstead on 18 September and for Willson two days later, declaring the Democratic party to be beyond "redemption." Knott argued that Hager should renounce the local Democratic machine, but the gubernatorial candidate supported the "old gang." The *Post* editor drew sharp distinctions between Beckham and Watterson, claiming that the *Courier* editor wanted to "destroy" the governor's career. In early October the City Club offered its support to Grinstead. In the end the Republicans got what they wanted, that is, full support from fusionists, reformers of several persuasions, and independent Democrats without full-fledged fusionist politics.[34]

The regular Democratic forces rallied for a difficult campaign. Bullitt, Lincoln, Thompson, and Page finally came out for Tyler in early October. Bingham, however, did not bend to the pressure, refusing to declare publicly for either side. The *Courier* and the *Times,* of course, lined up in favor of Tyler. None of the Louisville papers at the time, particularly the Haldeman papers, made a pretense of objective reporting. Page-one news stories often read like editorials. In his continuing battle with Beckham, Watterson took occasional sarcastic swipes at the governor's appointees as "The Lord's Anointed" and advocates of the "New Jerusalem." Watterson praised Tyler's stand for home rule against the threatened takeover by the State Democratic Committee. The *Courier* and the *Times* did not adhere to any real issues in the campaign. On one occasion the *Times* reported that Bingham had made a deal to resign and accept a judgeship as a reward for supporting Grinstead. Bingham quickly rejoined that he did not intend to resign before the election of a new mayor.[35]

Side issues continued to cloud the election. The language of the news stories and editorials remained colorful if not always relevant. The Haldeman papers enjoyed taking any slight provocation as an excuse for attacking Bingham and the progressives. For example, during a strike of streetcar employees a citizen allegedly wrote the *Times* and declared that Bingham had cursed the name of Bill Haldeman, editor of the *Times* and commander of the Louisville militia unit. The writer claimed to have heard Bingham refer to Haldeman as "that G—d d———d brute," who wanted evidence of evil intent on the part of the strikers in order to call out his troops to kill the unionists. Watterson accepted the letter as completely authentic and maintained that Bingham had embarked on a campaign of "hatred and revenge." The *Times* published a cartoon of Bingham as a petulant child having his mouth washed out by Judge Lincoln, who had often used this punishment in juvenile cases.[36]

The *Evening Post,* of course, rushed to Bingham's defense and questioned the "sincerity of the Reverend Mr. Watterson and the Reverend Mr. Haldeman, when with palms downward and eyes upward rolling they censure Mayor Bingham for certain profane language." Knott asserted that Bingham's reformist activities, not his language, terrified his foes. This incident demonstrated one of the tragicomic features of Kentucky politics as editors and politicians alike wasted their finest rhetoric on useless side issues.[37]

If Bingham could not institutionalize reform on the Louisville political scene, he and Chief Haager could guarantee an honest, peaceful election. They issued proclamations warning police and fire personnel to remain neutral. The Board of Public Safety worked around the clock on the day before the election and on election day. Sheriff Bullitt guarded the ballots before the election, and the ballot boxes on election day, against tampering. Chief Haager gave special instructions to be on watch for "repeaters" allegedly brought in from Indianapolis.

Grinstead and Willson ran well together. With the polls closely guarded and with support from Republicans, reformers, and independent Democrats, Grinstead won the mayor's race by forty-five hundred votes. Willson carried his home county handily and the state by over eighteen thousand votes in the governor's race. The Republicans made gains in the state legislature and won a majority of the races in Louisville and Jefferson County. Beckham thereby lost his chance of easily winning the senate seat in the first meeting of the newly elected general assembly.[38]

Bingham's brief tenure as mayor demonstrated the tenuous nature of progressive reform in Louisville. The Democratic machine resisted attempts at reform in the city and the threatened takeover by the state committee. Bingham held office for too short a time to develop a power base from which to unseat the machine. He quickly became a lame-duck mayor and without power after he refused to enter the Democratic primary. The success of a fusion or progressive candidate depended on the cooperation of the Republicans, who exhibited no desire to again leave the GOP. Traditional party affiliation remained too strong in Kentucky for success of a reformist third party during the national Progressive Era.[39]

Bingham could expose alleged wrongdoing, but he could not prove the corruption of the Democratic machine. Yet it would be an injustice to claim that his administration failed. He and his progressive supporters gave the city a brief respite from the manipulations of the machine, ensured an honest election in 1907, and established a tone that gave Mayor Grinstead a head start on an honest administration of the city. Even crusty old Watterson admitted editorially that "there was a need for a Democratic house-cleaning" and he grudgingly forecast that the "party will be the best for it." In a personal letter to Bingham the old editor declared: "nothing has happened which leaves the slightest unfriendly impression on my mind." Perhaps the vitriolic rhetoric had been just for effect after all.[40]

When the Republican administration came into office in late 1907, Bingham held no office for the first time in four years. In two years the Democratic machine, this time under the thumb of Whallen, swept back into city hall with the election of William O. Head as mayor. According to Bingham, the election of Head returned "the old corrupt and vicious Democratic ring" to power and the "conditions are now as bad, if not worse, than they have ever been." The young progressive decided once more to enter the political fray against the machine.[41]

Still interested in reform, Bingham cooperated with local Republican leaders in forming a limited fusionist effort to win a seat on the state's highest court, the court of appeals. He agreed to run on the Republican ticket for the Fourth District seat, but only if the party emphasized that his candidacy was nonpartisan in nature. U.S. senator W. O. Bradley lauded Bingham's public spirit. Prominent Republicans William Heyburn and Andrew Cowan placed Bingham's name before the local GOP convention, and the party faithful accepted the renegade Democrat as their nominee by acclamation. In his acceptance speech Bingham declared his continued membership in the Democratic party and faith in the idea of a nonpartisan judiciary. Some reform-minded Louisvillians proposed that an informal fusion ticket had been formed. Shackelford Miller, the Jefferson circuit judge who ruled against the fusionist cases, became the Democratic-party nominee.[42]

Bingham moved into this campaign with the knowledge that he faced the well-tuned Whallen machine, but he believed his chances for victory were good. "This fight here must be made," he declared, because "Louisville is in worse condition than it has ever been, and unless there are some left to fight for better things here, the city is doomed to years of base and contemptible servitude." In typical righteous progressive certitude he argued:

> It is not only political conditions, but business conditions, and not only that but moral conditions, that are in desperate case here. Yet if we can win this battle we shall gain a foothold to win others. The struggle for clean, decent politics cannot be decided in one fight, nor in one campaign. It is really a war, and in this war I have not enlisted as a sixty-day volunteer, but I am entered for the war.[43]

Bingham's optimism did not diminish throughout the campaign. In a campaign rally at Phoenix Hill auditorium attended by over three thousand partisans, he appeared to have the support of the Republican rank and file as well as the leadership of the party. The former mayor urged Republicans and Democrats to "throw off the yoke of political machines," and he returned to his favorite theme in condemning "boss rule" in Louisville. He wisely praised the "moral influence" of former president Theodore Roosevelt in political affairs and declared the need for such standards among Louisville politicians.[44]

The former mayor appealed for support to the same reform-minded group that had won only partial victories in the past. The men who responded to a Bingham campaign circular letter demonstrated a strong sense of public service that characterized progressivism. For example, a ministerial student at Southern Baptist Theological Seminary, then in downtown Louisville, perhaps best expressed the religious fervor of many progressives as he praised Bingham for fighting "the mighty host of political corruption in this town." Many other supporters voiced similar thoughts, using terminology associated with religion.[45]

The Democratic machine resorted to its usual ploys during the campaign, emphasizing the Negro issue as it had in 1907 and 1909. Editor Watterson, in an early indictment of the Republican party in the campaign, averred that "the Negro vote in Kentucky is largely a fungus vote carrying with it neither moral nor the pressure of any intelligent, independent public opinion." At the precinct level the machine kept Negroes from registering. In another ploy aimed at harming the Bingham candidacy, someone inserted anti-Bingham tracts into issues of the popular *Saturday Evening Post* on the newsstands in downtown Louisville. Bingham finally traced the culprit to a distributor for the Curtiss Publishing Company, but not before some damage had been done. A supporter predicted that Bingham would win the election, but was "skeptical of the returns being made correctly."[46]

With the Whallen-Head machine in control of the electoral process and the law-enforcement agencies, Bingham lost the 8 November 1910 general election to Miller by sixteen hundred votes. In a speech at Republican headquarters he proclaimed: "I am glad I have made this fight and I believe that it has not been in vain. I have neither excuse or apology to offer. The fight was made for principle and not for office, and for a principle which sooner or later must prevail. . . . This fight is not ended, but only begun." Bingham maintained that the machine used "intimidation, bribery," and other corrupt practices to defeat him. "It was necessary to rob me of over 5,000 votes to compass my defeat," the Louisvillian charged. In a repeat of the methods used in the 1905 mayoral race, the Democratic machine took yet another election by corrupting the electoral process.[47]

However, if Democratic-machine politicians thought that they were now free of Bingham, they were mistaken. As soon as Miller resigned from the Jefferson Circuit Court to take the seat on the state court of appeals, Governor Willson appointed Bingham to fill out Miller's unexpired term. Congratulations poured in from the elite of Kentucky progressivism. William Marshall Bullitt, Charles C. Stoll, John Stites, Temple Bodley, and George C. Norton, representing the cream of Louisville law and commercial enterprises, cheered the appointment as a vindication for the fight that Bingham had recently made for the court of appeals.[48]

Taking over a court docket that had a large backlog of cases, he resigned after ten months, having reduced the cases to a more normal level. He chose not to run for a full four-year term on the bench in 1911. Some of his friends later asked that he consider running for mayor in 1913. "I have, however, no political ambition whatever, and I cannot consider becoming a candidate for any office," the Louisvillian demurred. Although Bingham appeared to have had enough of the turmoil of party politics, he relented in 1917 and ran for a county commissioner's seat on the Democratic ticket. He lost by less than three hundred votes as Republicans swept nearly all Louisville and Jefferson County races.[49]

Bingham's commitment to progressivism remained constant in the period from the late nineties through his appointment to Jefferson Circuit Court. He typified the middle-class ethos so dominant among progressives in Kentucky and other regions of the country. Though he failed in the end to reform the local Democratic Party, Bingham publicly exposed the blatant bossism so rampant in that party in Louisville and Jefferson County. However, in so doing he ended forever his own political career. After 1917 he never again sought elective office.

chapter four

Founding a Dynasty

Great wealth brings responsibilities to those who possess it.
—Mary Lily Flagler, *New York Herald*, 6 November 1916

AFTER BINGHAM LEFT THE chancery bench, he resumed his law practice and dabbled in business ventures with his old friend Will Davies. He how had more time to spend with his wife and children. Family ties with the Millers were strong.

In late April 1913 Eleanor Miller Bingham planned a Sunday outing with her children and her brother, Dennis Long Miller, at his PeWee Valley summer residence east of Louisville. "Judge" Bingham, as he was now being called, did not accompany his family, having planned to take an afternoon train to Cincinnati, where he had a Monday morning court appearance. Barry recalled years later that he dozed off and on in his mother's arms as the Miller auto wound its way out of Louisville. All seemed so peaceful and calm on that spring afternoon as a light rain began to fall. After stopping to clean his glasses at an interurban railway crossing at O'Bannon, Miller drove his six-cylinder automobile across the track, his vision obstructed by a barn and other buildings near the crossing.[1]

Moments earlier an interurban car left the nearby station. Cradled in his mother's arms, Barry remembered hearing only her startled cry as an interurban slammed into the Miller auto and drove it across the adjoining railroad track. Miller and the two smallest Bingham children,

Henrietta and Barry, received only minor injuries. Franklin M. Callahan, Barry's older cousin, received a serious head injury, being thrown from the car. Eleanor received the most serious injury of all, a blow to the head. The injured received treatment on the spot and at a nearby house by a physician before being placed on an interurban car for the ride to Norton Memorial Infirmary. The staff of the hospital immediately identified Eleanor's condition as "hopeless." On his way to Cincinnati, the Judge's train passed the accident site on a parallel railroad track; he hurriedly returned by rail when he received word of the accident. Only twelve hours after being taken to the infirmary, Eleanor died, never having regained consciousness. Sallie Bingham suggested that her grandmother committed suicide and that a conspiracy has since covered up that tragedy, but there is no evidence to warrant such a jejune assertion.[2]

Three Bingham children survived their mother, who was forty-three at the time of her death. Robert Norwood (his middle name was later changed to Worth, making him Robert Worth Bingham, Jr.), the oldest, was barely sixteen; Henrietta Worth, twelve; and George Barry, seven. The anguish of his wife's death did not pass easily for the Judge. In the next few years he would sometimes rent a small downtown movie theater during the off hours. There he watched a home movie of him and Eleanor dancing together in happier days. On the flickering screen he would again see his wife smile as they swirled to the silent music. Only slowly did he come to grips with his irretrievable loss.[3]

Bingham found some relief from the grief of his wife's death and the added burden of caring for his children in his law practice and business ventures. By middecade his firm had become one of the largest in Louisville by combining the partnerships of Stanley E. Sloss, George Cary Tabb, and Arthur H. Mann. Emanuel Levi became the junior member of the firm. Bingham maintained business interests outside of his corporate law practice. Business relations with the Millers and Longs continued after the death of Eleanor, particularly in league with Dennis Long and Company and the various waterworks companies. However, the Louisvillian still found time for annual pilgrimages to Great Britain and the continent, increasing his circle of English friends while enjoying his passion for hunting.[4]

Bingham's personal life changed with the meeting again of an old acquaintance in the summer of 1915. Over two years after the death of his first wife, Bingham renewed an old romance with Mary Lily

Kenan Flagler, the widow of multimillionnaire Henry M. Flagler. Mary
Lily had been known by the Bingham family for some time, as Robert
Worth's sister Sadie had been her classmate at The Peace Institute, a
finishing school in Raleigh. Robert Worth and Mary Lily had first met
in 1890, at the University of Virginia. Apparently they dated for a
brief spell but then parted. Meanwhile, Mary Lily first lived with and
then married Flagler, one of the founders of the Standard Oil Company, in 1901. Josephus Daniels, a fellow North Carolinian, remembered Mary Lily as having "a lovely voice" in her youth. Will Davies
also became acquainted with the vivacious Mary Lily, who belonged to
one of the most prominent and wealthy North Carolina families.[5]

Mary Lily's liaison with Henry Flagler, builder of the Florida East
Coast Railway Company, began shortly after they first met in
Wilmington, North Carolina, in 1891. By that time his second wife,
Ida Alice Shourds, suffered from severe mental problems. For several
years Flagler and Mary Lily, none too secretly, kept company with each
other. Deciding to divorce Ida Alice, whom he had declared legally
insane, the old entrepreneur ran into the difficulty of there being a
prohibition on divorce in both New York and Florida except in cases
of adultery. Flagler used friends in the Florida legislature to pass a law
making "incurable insanity" legal grounds for divorce. One week after the divorce cleared the courts of Florida, the betrothal of Henry
Flagler and Mary Lily Kenan appeared in the press. They married on
24 August 1901; he was seventy-one and she thirty-four.[6]

Flagler lavished his wealth on his young wife, reportedly purchasing a priceless string of pearls as well as other jewels. Moreover, he
built for her a $2.5 million marble mansion in Palm Beach, known as
Whitehall, a project completed in only eight months with no consideration of expense. The third Mrs. Flagler enjoyed giving lavish parties and apparently fancied "expensive wines" and may also have developed a taste for stronger liquor during this time. The Flaglers lived
together for over a decade until Henry's death on 20 May 1913. Soon
thereafter, Mary Lily received property, jewels, cash, and the bulk of
the Flagler fortune in a trust fund, estimated to be worth as much as
one hundred million dollars, depending on the market value of Standard Oil and other securities. She annually received one hundred
thousand dollars cash from a trust fund.[7]

The Bingham-Flagler romance blossomed again after their meeting in Asheville. The couple kept each other company for a few months,

with Bingham traveling to New York City on several occasions to be with Mary Lily and meet her friends. No doubt after some discussion of financial arrangements, Bingham and Mrs. Flagler announced their plans to be married. Mary Lily specifically answered rumors that she was marrying beneath herself, reporting to the press that it was a "very brilliant match," one "of the heart, and what can be more brilliant than that." She also explained that she and Bingham had known each other quite well two decades before and had enjoyed a brief, but intense, romance, "one that you might call 'an affair.'" Mary Lily also told a visiting *New York Herald* reporter that her niece, Louise Wise, would inherit the bulk of the Flagler fortune when she died. "Great wealth," she explained, "brings responsibilities." She believed her twenty-year-old niece had the character to "possess it." The press contained no announcement about prenuptial agreements concerning Mary Lily's fortune.[8]

On 15 November 1916, more than a year after the renewal of their romance and with only a few close friends and relatives in attendance, Robert Worth and Mary Lily exchanged marriage vows at the home of Mr. and Mrs. Pembroke Jones in New York City. Louise Wise attended the bride while Dr. Hugh Young served as best man. The Reverend Doctor George Morgan Ward, for whom Henry Flagler had constructed a chapel in Palm Beach, Florida, performed the marriage ceremony for the couple. The new Mrs. Bingham was forty-nine years of age and her husband forty-five. To celebrate the wedding, Mary Lily gave $125,000 to the St. Augustine Hospital, a favorite charity of her first husband.[9]

Mr. and Mrs. Robert Worth Bingham moved into the Seelbach Hotel in Louisville. In May 1917 they rented the W. R. Belknap estate, Lincliffe, located east of the city on the bluffs above River Road. Then the Binghams began to entertain in a more elegant fashion. The Bingham children did not immediately move into Lincliffe. They were off at school, and Barry, thought to have tuberculosis, stayed at the Bingham School in a specially prepared room paid for by his father.[10]

In early May 1917 the couple traveled to Wilmington, North Carolina, for the wedding of Mrs. Bingham's niece, Louise. A week later they attended the annual Pendennis Club Derby dinner. Hannah Bolles, an old friend of Mary Lily from Wilmington, came to visit. Bingham began to direct at least some of his wife's business affairs, handling, for example, some of her property. Meanwhile, America's participation in World War I commanded an increasing amount of the public's attention. The Judge contemplated applying for an officer's commission. He also became deeply involved in important litigation within the Haldeman family, the owners of the *Courier-Journal* and the *Louisville Times*, in mid-1917.[11]

All appeared to be going well in the Bingham household, but in mid-July Mary Lily became ill. The press reported she had taken to bed because of a long-standing heart condition. Three doctors attended her bedside but could do nothing to improve her condition, identified as myocarditis, an inflammation of the myocardium, the muscular substance of the heart. After nearly two weeks of declining health, she sank into unconsciousness.[12]

On 27 July she died; the cause listed on the death certificate was swelling of the brain contributed to by myocarditis. The press described the death, in more simplified laymen's terms, as "acute heart disturbance." At her bedside were her husband, his old friend W. W. Davies, Mrs. Bingham's brother, William Rand Kenan, her sister Jessie Kenan Wise, and Hannah Bolles. In three days Mary Lily Bingham was buried in the Oakland Cemetery in Wilmington, North Carolina. The nation's press reiterated that Mrs. Lawrence Lewis, née Louise Wise, would be the principal heir to the enormous Flagler fortune. A family friend sent her condolences to the widower with the thought that "I shall always think of her, as she was at her wedding, young, radiant and full of life."[13]

Not long after the funeral a dispute broke out over the cause of death of Mary Lily. In the coming weeks the Kenans would consider contesting the will of their sister, and the states of Kentucky and New York would fight over the rights of probating the will and thereby collecting inheritance taxes of several million dollars. More important, Bingham would be charged with contributing to the death of his wife. This controversy continues to the present day with Bingham's biographers of the 1980s essentially charging him with murder.[14]

The press as well as the gossipmongers had a field day after the public announcement that a codicil, penned by W. W. Davies at the request of Mary Lily and witnessed by Dr. M. L. Ravitch in his office six weeks before Mrs. Bingham's death, bequeathed five million dollars to Robert Worth Bingham. That document and the circumstances of its signing so near the death of Mary Lily brought the Kenan heirs into the fray, but only after finding out about the codicil and hearing rumors from disgruntled Louisvillians. The latter charged that Robert Worth Bingham withheld competent medical treatment from Mary Lily and possibly plied her with drugs in order to obtain the bequest in the codicil. The press speculated that more controversy was in the offing.[15]

In Mary Lily's will, dated 23 September 1916, and revalidated on 8 December, no provision had been set aside for Bingham, essentially removing his dower rights by his assent to that document. Later, under cross-examination at a probate hearing, Davies testified that Mary Lily told him that Bingham deserved a reward for not asking for a prenuptial bequest. Therefore, she added a five-million-dollar codicil to her will for her husband. At the time of her death the Judge received a substantial income, rumored to be at least fifty thousand dollars a year from a fund of nearly seven hundred thousand dollars set aside for him in securities.[16]

At the probate hearings to determine the validity of the codicil, Bingham's old progressive political ally Helm Bruce represented the Kenan family in Louisville, while Alex P. Humphrey stood for the Judge. Part of these proceedings concerned which banks would handle the administration of the estate. Bingham and the Kenans agreed that the Fidelity and Columbia Trust Company should be sole administrator, but Jefferson circuit judge Charles T. Ray decreed that that duty should be shared with the Louisville Trust Company. The Kentucky Court of Appeals later overturned Ray's ruling, favoring the choice of the Kenans and Bingham.[17]

Under cross-examination by Bruce, Davies explained the circumstances of the writing and signing of the codicil. He said that "tentative" drafts written by him with the guidance of Mary Lily resulted in the codicil presented to the court. "The handwriting is mine, but the language is mostly hers," Davies explained. Bruce asked if the wealthy heiress had been under the influence of drugs administered by Dr. Ravitch; Davies replied no and stated that Mrs. Bingham appeared to be in good health and mental state. Mary Lily wanted to reward Bingham for his "noble spirit," the Louisville lawyer affirmed. When asked why the document had been signed in a doctor's office rather than in that of a lawyer, Bingham's old friend stated that Mary Lily said she wanted to avoid the "public eye" as much as possible. Some of Bruce's questions indicated that he was probing for an opening to invalidate the codicil, such as, Did Davies know about alleged drug

injections administered by Ravitch on Mrs. Bingham? Davies, however, denied any such allegations. Stanley Sloss, a law partner of
Bingham, and Emily Overman, the Judge's personal secretary, confirmed the republication of Mary Lily's will and Bingham's assent to
that document on 8 December 1916 at the Seelbach Hotel. County
Judge Samuel W. Greene on 14 September 1917 validated the will
and the codicil, but the controversy was only beginning.[18]

The Bingham and Kenan interests hired private investigators to
look after the affairs of their clients. Bingham retained the services of
old college chum Shepard Bryan to represent his interests in
Wilmington, North Carolina. Adding more controversy, Dr. Ravitch
reported that drug records had been stolen from his office. Speculation about those records reverberated throughout the local papers.
The press surmised that the Kenans wanted to break the codicil by
proving that the Judge had used drugs to force their sister into signing. Moreover, the Kenans promptly charged that they had not been
properly notified at the onset of Mrs. Bingham's illness.[19]

Rumors of a secret autopsy encourged more sensationalism in the
press. Scarcely two weeks after the probate hearing ended, the press
reported the "exhumation and evisceration" of the remains of Mary
Lily Bingham. In front-page headlines the *Courier-Journal* reported
"BODY SECRETLY EXHUMED AND AUTOPSY HELD LAST TUES-
DAY" with the "vital organs" of the deceased removed and sent to
laboratories in Boston, Baltimore, and New York for pathological study.
Speculation about the findings of the pathology reports increased each
day. When the results were not released after several days, the press
became impatient, asking for a complete report as soon as possible.
An exasperated Will Davies replied to a reporter's query: "All I know
is what I see in the papers." The tension mounted after Dr. Charles
Norris of New York City told a reporter that the autopsy report would
soon be published.[20]

Meanwhile, the Louisville press and several friends unswervingly
supported Bingham. The *Courier* decried the "beggars on horseback"
who made an "accusation of murder" against a leading citizen of Louisville. "Truly, big money bringeth a multitude of evils," the editorialist intoned. Cross-town rivals the *Louisville Herald* and the *Evening Post*,
echoed the same sentiments about the "Lawlessness of Great Wealth,"
claiming to see a conspiracy emanating from the Standard Oil Company. Friends like Emily Dawson claimed that she, like many of

Bingham's acquaintances, "believed nothing of the unpleasant and mischievous stories" about the death of Mary Lily. "I am deeply grateful to you for writing me as you did about the hideous scandal which I have had to endure," Bingham replied to one such letter, "The undivided loyalty of my friends and acquaintances has been more to me than could ever be expressed."[21]

The results of the autopsy were never made publc, adding to the debate of late and leaving many questions unanswered. Did the results indicate that Mary Lily was indeed an alcoholic and/or drug addict, or that she had been poisoned by her husband? All or part of the pathology reports may have revealed information unfavorable to the case of the Kenan family or something about their sister that they did not want revealed and publicized, such as that she may have died as a result of alcohol abuse. Or did she have "cardiovascular syphilis," transmitted to her by Flagler, as suggested by Susan E. Tifft and Alex S. Jones in *The Patriarch: The Rise and Fall of the Bingham Dynasty*? On the other hand, the autopsy may have revealed nothing anomalous at all, and the Kenans, not wishing further embarrassment or publicity, simply allowed the matter to drop.[22]

More important, did Bingham play a role in the death of his wife? There is no evidence or "smoking gun" to indicate that he did so, as indicated by Sallie Bingham and David Leon Chandler, and to a lesser extent by Marie Brenner. Moreover, Bingham and Chandler charged that Robert Worth had infected Mary Lily with syphilis during their North Carolina days and that he carried this malady to his grave. They cite his continual trips to Johns Hopkins for treatment, and to Dr. Michael Ravitch locally. Medical records at the Johns Hopkins archives, however, indicate otherwise. Bingham suffered throughout his lifetime from "neuroeczema," for which he received periodic treatments from Dr. Ravitch. Radiotherapy at Johns Hopkins in 1921 for this ailment may have eventually contributed to his death. Several tests at Johns Hopkins in the 1930s proved conclusively that Robert Worth Bingham had never had syphilis. The charges of Bingham's granddaughter, Chandler, and Brenner are those of creative writers with fertile and misguided imaginations.[23]

However, there is evidence that something was amiss at the Bingham mansion on River Road. About the time that Mary Lily took to bed with her final illness in mid-July 1917, a letter from Reverend George M. Ward, her former pastor in Florida, to her husband indicated something wrong in the Bingham household. "I know what you are going thru," Ward wrote. But there the trail ends as the problem is not identified. The letter probably referred to Mrs. Bingham's longstanding problem with alcohol. Over the years the public's perception of Bingham's callousness toward his second wife, based on rumor and gossip in 1917, developed into a legend that follows the Bingham family to the present day. The results of my own study of Robert Worth Bingham for over a decade and a half indicates a person who may have been ambitious and covetous of some of the Flagler fortune, but who in no way displayed a character so flawed as to have committed murder or to have willfully contributed to the death of Mary Lily Kenan Flagler Bingham. And there is solid evidence to prove his innocence.[24]

Recently surfaced documents, produced by Dr. Hugh H. Young after Mary Lily's death, effectively counter the charges of foul play made against Bingham. Young claimed that both he and the Judge made a strenuous effort to change Mary Lily's substance abuse. Unfortunately for Bingham, Young was in Europe when Mary Lily died and the Baltimore doctor could not directly offer his advice and services in defense of his friend. In 1933 Young wrote a memorandum and placed it in the Johns Hopkins medical archives. That document asserted that Bingham had discovered, soon after his marriage, that his new wife had a serious drinking problem. These episodes often extended for days at a time, during which she would "lock herself up and drink many bottles of gin." "As a result of this her health had rapidly declined, she was already in a very serious condition," Young explained, "and Judge Bingham implored me to see if medical aid could not be secured in curing her of this terrible habit."[25]

These binges unnerved Bingham, and he conspired with Young to lure Mary Lily to Johns Hopkins for treatment. She rebuffed any and all suggestions or attempts to seek treatment for alcohol abuse. Owing to the difficulty of getting Mrs. Bingham to accept medical aid, they organized a ruse on the premise that Bingham was about to be appointed to Herbert Hoover's food conservation administration and would relocate to Washington, D.C., thereby moving Mary Lily closer to Johns Hopkins. However, before the plan could be implemented, Young went off to Europe during World War I. Meanwhile, Mary Lily died, according to Young, "as a result of one of those terrible sprees."[26]

When Young returned from Europe in 1919, he interviewed three pathologists, one of whom was a colleague at John Hopkins. He discovered that the wealthy heiress had indeed died of alcohol abuse and not by "poisoning or foul play," that is, by the administration of drugs or other poisons. Young claimed he tried to force the Kenans to recant their charges against Bingham by threatening to make public this information. He even argued with the Judge over initiating a possible multimillion-dollar lawsuit against the Kenans. However, both parties allowed the matter to rest because neither Bingham nor the Kenans wanted a public pronouncement of Mary Lily's alcoholism. Apparently, the Kenans were willing to live with the rumors but not a public announcement of their sister's addiction. Bingham accepted the burden that malicious gossip would follow him the rest of his life, tainting discussion of his life and family even today. Many in Louisville and around the state have heard the tale about Bingham allegedly pushing Mary Lily down a flight of stairs. One of the more ridiculous scenarios suggested that Bingham and Mary Lily plotted the death of Flagler and then waited for a proper number of years before marrying.[27]

After preliminary wrangling over the codicil and the subsequent autopsy, the Kenans, for whatever reasons, decided not to contest the bequest to Bingham. Negotiations continued for several months over the precise proportion of the inheritance in cash and securities and side issues, such as whether the Judge should receive interest on his bequest from the date of Mary Lily's death. Alex P. Humphrey handled Bingham's negotiations with the Kenan and Standard Oil lawyers. The Kenans allowed a million-dollar note as an advance to Bingham. In the final settlement the executor of Mary Lily's estate transferred large blocks of stock to the Judge, the majority of which was several varieties of Standard Oil securities. Bingham noted on at least one occasion that "Kenan is trying to hold out on us," for some minor expenses involved in the transfer of stock, but they soon settled the matter. At the end of the required probate year in Kentucky, the Louisvillian received his bequest of five million dollars. The bitterness of the Kenan family toward Bingham never ceased in his lifetime.[28]

Other legatees and governments also obtained their shares of the Flagler wealth. Louise Wise Lewis received an income of two hundred thousand dollars a year cash stipend until she was forty from the estate in trust and then claimed five million dollars plus valuable property, while the two sisters and brother of Mary Lily claimed substantial, though lesser, amounts. In her will Mary Lily identified Louise as someone with "a sunshiny disposition and a wealth of common sense." The will also established the Kenan professorships, most of which are endowed at the University of North Carolina at Chapel Hill, a bequest suggested by Robert Worth Bingham and his father. For over three years the governments of the United States, Kentucky, and Jefferson County belabored the legal system in pursuit of their largesse from the Flagler fortune. Lawsuits filed in New York and Kentucky finally settled the issue that Louisville, Kentucky, should be the "taxing situs" where the taxes would be collected.[29]

As soon as Mary Lily died, attempts to estimate the wealth of this lady reputed to be one of the wealthiest women in the United States flooded the press. Not a few Kentuckians applauded the fact that a collection of over three million dollars would be more than enough to pay off the revolving state debt. Appraisals of jewelry purchased by Henry Flagler caused some speculation, as did rumor of an alleged million-dollar pearl necklace that never materialized. While the federal government soon collected its six-million-dollar share of the Flagler fortune, court suits over estimation of the total worth of the holdings and disposition of the estate taxes in Jefferson County and Kentucky clogged the state's courts for several years. Prominent political figures in the state became involved, including Governors A. O. Stanley and E. P. Morrow, two of the commonwealth's most colorful politicians in this century. In the end the state government and several educational institutions received nearly $3.33 million, including road, general, sinking, and common school funds and smaller shares for the University of Kentucky, and the Eastern and Western state normal schools.[30]

A Richmond lawyer and judge perhaps best summed up, rather callously, the whole episode for many Kentuckians when he told Bingham: "At the time, I had no idea that that important event, to wit; your said marriage, could possibly mean as much as it now seems it will mean to the State of Kentucky and its taxpayers." In a very cynical way the life and death of Mary Lily Kenan Flagler Bingham became lost in a flood of litigation as the Kenans, Wise, Bingham, and the various levels of government claimed their share of her fortune. As Mary Lily said in the interview just before her marriage to Bingham, "Great wealth brings responsibilities to those who possess it." Robert

Worth Bingham automatically became one of the wealthiest and most influential men in Kentucky when he received his bequest a year to the day after the death of his second wife. It did not take long for him to find a way to use part of his newfound fortune.[31]

Like many Americans, the steady drift toward participation in World War I caused Bingham no end of soul-searching. He witnessed the beginning of the war in August 1914 while on his annual vacation in England. For many progressives, and most certainly for Woodrow Wilson, the role of the United States in that event appeared the crowning touch of their movement. The Judge desperately wanted to become involved in the war and offered his services before the declaration of war, the death of Mary Lily, and the tumultuous events of summer and fall of 1917. However, the War Department turned down his request because of his age, forty-six, and lack of formal military training. Several of his best friends and closest business associates went off to Europe. Will Davies left his law practice and served as a Red Cross ambulance driver in 1918. Dr. Hugh Young became a U.S. Army surgeon attached to General Pershing's headquarters. Bingham's young law partner, Emanuel Levi, left for an army camp in September 1917.[32]

Arthur Krock, a native Kentuckian who later went on to attain considerable power as chief Washington columnist for the *New York Times,* maintained in his *Memoirs* that one day in mid-1917 he had found a despondent Bingham staring out a Pendennis Club window. He explained that he had been rejected for military service and could think of no better way to serve his country than by following his basic southern instincts for army life. At the time managing editor of the *Courier-Journal* and *Louisville Times,* Krock said he brought up the subject of purchasing the papers as an even better way to perform "a great public service," in the event that the Haldemans could not work out their problems. According to Krock, it did not take Bingham long to grasp the significance of the opportunity.[33]

While this assertion was disputed by Barry Bingham, Sr., there appears to be some evidence that Krock did make the initial contact for the *Courier* and *Times* owners, perhaps even making the suggestion as he stated. A letter from Krock to Bingham indicates that the suggestion may have been made as early as mid-1917 with "the little idea I whispered into your ear." Was that the suggestion of buying the newspapers? Perhaps. Undoubtedly, others also had Bingham's ear and he understood that a breakup of the Haldemans and Watterson could open the way for someone to purchase the papers. Deeply involved in litigation between the owners of the newspapers, Bingham also would have known that if no settlement in the courts could be reached between the Haldemans, they might consider a sale to break the impasse.[34]

Since before the turn of the century, the Haldeman family and Henry Watterson had held control of the *Courier* and *Times*. Walter N. Haldeman had led the two papers since before the Civil War, taking part in their consolidation. After he died in 1902, ownership passed to his two sons and a daughter. W. B. Haldeman edited the *Times* while his brother Bruce acted as president of the newspaper company. Sister Isabel took no active role in the companies but still controlled a major block of stock. In the nineties the *Courier* lost considerable circulation among the state's Democrats because of Watterson's anti-Bryan and pro–gold-standard editorials. The *Times* carried the companies financially for several years as the *Courier* slowly built back its circulation at its location on the corner of Third and Green streets.[35]

But friction between the ownership and Watterson soon surfaced. Beginning in 1914 Bruce Haldeman and Watterson argued over editorial policy on the war in Europe. Watterson's increasingly anti-German writings did not suit Haldeman, who feared the loss of advertising revenue from Louisville's substantial German-American community. On 3 September 1914 a Watterson editorial declared "To Hell with the Hohenzollerns and the Hapsburgs." He would win two Pulitzer prizes with later World War I editorials. To complicate matters even further, the papers faced increasingly stiff competition from the *Louisville Herald* and the *Evening Post*.[36]

The split in *Courier* and *Times* leadership lined up W. B. along with sister Isabel and Henry Watterson against Bruce in a series of lawsuits argued all the way to the Kentucky Court of Appeals. Bingham represented W. B. during the summer of 1917; both sides fought not only in court but in their papers. Bruce Haldeman defended himself as "indecently treated" by his brother and sister in being "ousted," or outvoted on the boards of the papers. After Bruce received an injunction blocking his brother and sister from taking control of publication and editorial policies, Kentucky's highest court overturned that decision, effectively eliminating the former president of the companies from any further control over the papers. In the meantime, Mary Lily died and the codicil controversy soon engulfed her husband.[37]

When it became apparent that Bingham would receive his bequest, he and Krock began talking about a possible sale of the papers as the Haldemans' differences became irreconcilable. Bingham was given an option lasting for two months to purchase the papers, paying only five dollars for that privilege. In a few weeks negotiations completed the sale of the controlling two-thirds interest in the papers to Bingham. He paid Watterson $186,000 for his 12.5 percent. W. B. Haldeman and his sister Isabel each received $433,900 for their respective 29 percent shares.[38]

On 7 August 1918 Bingham took over direction of the papers. In his first public announcement Bingham pledged that the *Courier* and *Times* "will continue to espouse the principles of the Democratic party, and, above that—as always—the principles of human freedom and public weal." Bruce Haldeman at first refused to sell, but Bingham persisted in his desire to become sole owner of the *Courier* and *Times* properties. On 30 April 1920 he fulfilled an option on Bruce's stock and completed purchase of the newspapers, paying $418,500 for the remaining 29 percent of shares outstanding.[39]

At the beginning of the transition to new ownership, Watterson agreed to remain in a semiretired role, becoming editor emeritus while retaining his ten-thousand-dollar yearly salary. On 7 August 1918 the *Courier-Journal* published its first issue with the name of Robert Worth Bingham on the editorial page as publisher. Watterson wrote a vale-dictory editorial as full-time editor entitled "Fifty Years of Independent Journalism," highlighting his career at the paper. After completing control of these properties the new publisher declared his purpose to make the papers "more and more effective instruments for public service, champions of uprightness in public affairs, [and] advocates of justice and fair-dealing everywhere." From that day forward Bingham and Watterson clashed.[40]

Numerous prominent citizens from Louisville and Kentucky and across the nation rushed to congratulate the new publisher-owner of Louisville's largest papers. Kentucky progressives like Clarence A. Woods and J. A. Sullivan of Richmond viewed the Bingham takeover as a vindication of their ideals. Alluding to the reformist zeal of Bingham as mayor in 1907, one vowed his support of efforts to "clean out, clean up and keep clean" both city and state governments. Louisville religious leaders such as E. Y. Mullins, president of the Southern Baptist Theological Seminary, expressed confidence in Bingham. E. L. Powell, minister of the First Christian Church, declared: "Man alive! What an opportunity." Several correspondents praised the character of the new owner. A prominent Louisville Republican said the same for the honesty of Bingham. A staunch Democrat reported that the party would be better served now that Bingham was at the helm.[41]

Other editors and publishers also expressed their confidence in the Judge. Desha Breckinridge, editor of the *Lexington Herald,* declared that he knew the papers "will be used only for the uplifting of the best sentiment of Kentucky and the South." W. H. Bagley, owner of the *Fort Worth Record,* congratulated his distant cousin on the opportunity presented by purchase of the papers. Another writer summed up the thoughts of not a few when he exclaimed: "What a calamity it would have been if this property had fallen into the hands of a man like Hearst." Roger Burlingame of the *New Orleans Picayune,* who had served as a reporter for the *Courier-Journal* in 1907, expressed his hope that Bingham could restore prestige to the "old lady on Green Street," as the paper was affectionately known.[42]

The new publisher entered a volatile field where change had become the norm; the number of daily newspapers declined as consolidations continued into the era of World War I. Media magnates such as William Randolph Hearst, Joseph Pulitzer, and Edward Wyllis Scripps stayed their courses of developing large empires while Adolph Ochs tried to save the old *New York Times* from bankruptcy. Josephus Daniels, Henry Watterson, William Allen White, and a few others developed national reputations while leading the editorial offices of regional papers. The *Courier-Journal* and the *Louisville Times* had already found a niche as the leading papers in Louisville, in Kentucky, and in the surrounding region. Press associations and syndicated features had become commonplace by the time Bingham entered the newspaper field. World War I placed strains on the staffs and budgets of America's press. In the twenties new competition came with the development of the movie industry and radio.[43]

When Bingham took over the papers, Krock controlled the day-to-day activities of both papers, with Harrison Robertson in charge of the editorial pages, and Robert E. Hughes general business manager of both companies. Bingham immediately made his imprint on the papers—too much so for Krock, who charged that the appointment of Wallace T. Hughes as executive assistant of the papers undercut his authority. When the peace conference began at Versailles, Bingham assigned Krock to cover the meetings. The latter maintained in his *Memoirs* that prior to his departure for Europe, Bingham's hand at the helm "was beginning to prove onerous to me." When Krock returned from Europe, he found that he had been placed in charge of the *Times*, to him an unmistakable demotion from managing editor of both papers. However, Krock's critique in hindsight belied the fact that in 1923, when he left the Louisville papers for a position with Will H. Hays's Motion Pictures Producers' Association, he accepted a large gift of money from Bingham to pay off his mortgage, fawningly "seeking readmission to your confidence and approval." Although Bingham felt some regard for an anti-Kenan editorial by Krock in the *Times* in his preownership days, he finally gave up on Krock. "He is hopeless. I have worked on him for five years, nearly," Bingham said in 1923, "and it is no use. He is just crooked and I can't straighten him out."[44]

Bingham left no doubt about who controlled the papers and immediately interjected himself into the determination of publication policy, most of which demonstrated his progressive ideals. Not long after purchasing the papers he became an active member of the National Press Club. Although having no newspaper experience, he had precise ideas about how the papers should be operated. For example, he changed the policy of the papers toward the Louisville Churchmen's Federation, promising not to be antagonistic to that group's attempt to break up prostitution in Louisville. He pledged support of Sebastian Zorn, president of the Louisville Water Company, "in reconstructing and rehabilitating" that municipal public utility. When a strike of Louisville Railway employees threatened to spread throughout the city in 1919, Bingham quickly supported the efforts of the Employer's Association of Louisville.[45]

The new publisher also took full control of the business side of the papers. For a while he considered adding a farm journal to his publications, but decided against such a venture, fearing that the journal would make no profits. Not long after Bingham took control of the papers, he raised the price of street sales from a penny to two cents per copy for the morning *Courier* and the afternoon *Times* and from five cents to seven cents for the Sunday *Courier-Journal*. In the short run, sales increased slightly as Bingham tried to bring publication costs into line with revenue. The longtime debts of the papers also decreased slightly in the early twenties.[46]

During Bingham's first months as publisher the greatest challenges to his authority came from Watterson and Krock. The latter considered himself the "professional protégé" of the elderly editor and eventual heir to the editorship of the *Courier-Journal.* A strain in the Bingham-Watterson relationship developed almost from the beginning of the Judge's assuming control as publisher. As editor emeritus, Watterson had no specific duties except to write occasional editorials and, of course, lend his considerable national prestige to the masthead of the *Courier.* Bingham expressed the hope that "Marse Henry," as he was known throughout the country, "is going to radiate in the Courier-Journal for many years to come." However, Watterson and Bingham parted ways on three specific issues: prohibition, women's suffrage, and the Versailles Treaty. Krock supported his mentor implicitly.[47]

Upon becoming publisher, Bingham directed that the papers support the prohibitionist amendment then up for adoption in the states. Dry Kentucky progressive Democrats, in particular, immediately praised the new stance of the *Courier.* Many prohibitionists in Kentucky had long associated the state's liquor interests with Democratic-machine politics. Watterson never had a kind word for any form of temperance or prohibition effort. Although Watterson did nothing publicly to attack the publisher's new directive, Krock committed what he called a "small treason" by encouraging another *Courier* editor to publish antiprohibition letters. "In expiation of my use of [Editor] Coghlan as the guinea pig for demonstrating the lunacy of the directive," Krock explained, "I promptly recommended him for a job as an editorial writer on the [St. Louis] *Post Dispatch.*" Apparently, Krock took some satisfaction in periodically secretly undermining the control of Bingham and sniping at his directives.[48]

Bingham's support of a second progressive reform, women's suffrage, further widened the breach with Watterson. Not long after the change of ownership, the *Courier* published "Votes for Women," an editorial fully supporting women's suffrage. Mrs. Bruce Haldeman, wife of the part owner who had held out the longest against Bingham ownership, praised Bingham for the editorial. Ida Husted Harper, chairman of the department of editorial correspondence of the Leslie Woman Suffrage Commission, and Carrie Chapman Catt, president of the National American Woman Suffrage Association, rejoiced that their old nemesis Henry Watterson, whose editorials had been "abrasive and vindictive," appeared to be on his way out.[49]

To Senator Park Trammell, Bingham explained that "as a southern man, I am not unmindful of the reasons which have influenced many southern representatives, but, from opposing woman's suffrage outright, I have come to believe in it not only as a matter of principle and as truly Democratic, but also to believe that it will be an advantage, and not a disadvantage to the distinctly southern states." Support of the amendment could also possibly work to the advantage of those who championed that cause. Mrs. John Glover South, president of the Kentucky Equal Rights Association, explained to Bingham: "Kentucky women will ever remember gratefully the man who struck the most telling blow for their cause at the hour of greatest need."[50]

Bingham's support for ratification of the Versailles Treaty and formation of the League of Nations eliminated any hope for his continued association with Watterson. The younger southerner's support for the League came from a general desire to aid the administration of Woodrow Wilson. Joe Tumulty and the president himself expressed their gratitude for the turnabout in *Courier* policy. In the early days of Bingham's ownership, Tom Wallace, *Times* Washington chief, conferred with Tumulty on several occasions about strategies to bolster the Wilson administration in the columns of the Louisville papers. This new tack offered quite a contrast to the antiadministration course so often followed by Watterson and Krock in the past. Bingham had clearly decided that his paper would take a partisan stand in politics.[51]

In early 1919 the League issue heated up throughout the country. The day after publishing a special "Marse Henry Edition" of the *Courier,* Bingham and Watterson openly clashed. Showing his predilection for quoting or paraphrasing holy scripture to stress a point, Watterson telegraphed Bingham: "Now letteth thy servant depart in peace." Bingham had to decide whether to print Watterson's proffered anti-League editorials or Harrison Robertson's pro-League editorials in the *Courier.* "I feel deeply hurt to find that you are opposing the League of Nations," Bingham explained to the old editor, "for I had hoped that the Courier-Journal would have the benefit of the support of its Editor Emeritus on a question of such grave public concern." He continued, "I hope you will forgive me for asking you, therefore, not to request us to publish articles by you combatting the League of Nations, for I do not wish the paper to appear as assailing its distinguished former editor and present Editor Emeritus."[52]

Bingham expected Marse Henry to retire. A few days later Watterson explained to Bingham the precise reason for his decision to leave the *Courier.* "Your purpose to make [the *Courier*] an organ of the Wilson administration is especially odious to me," Watterson exclaimed. With one final request he severed his forty-one-year relationship with the Louisville paper: "I will thank you, therefore, to take my name down as Editor Emeritus . . . ." On 2 April 1919 the *Courier-Journal* announced the retirement of Watterson. Although the Bingham-Watterson relationship soon returned to one of "warm sentiments" according to the older man, the young publisher had firmly established his control over the papers as well as making a break with the long-standing Watterson philosophy and style.[53]

In less than two years Watterson died, and soon thereafter his protégé Krock left the Louisville papers. Members of the Wilson administration and others supporting the League of Nations expressed their strong support for the change of editorial policy at the *Courier* and *Times.* To the president in France, Bingham cabled: "I have no doubt people firmly behind you in your work for humanity, and that opponents in Senate wholly misrepresent American sentiment."[54]

If Watterson and Bingham parted ways on the specific issues of prohibition, women's suffrage, and the League of Nations, on another issue close to the hearts of southerners, that of race, they differed not so much in substance as in nuance and style. Significantly, the issue of the *Courier* dedicated to the four-decade-long influence of Marse Henry included a special "Hambone" cartoon, done by J. P. Alley of the *Memphis Commercial-Appeal,* showing a stereotyped black tramp making his own comment about the end of the reign of Watterson. The caption read in white interpretation of black dialect: "He Gwins alluz Be De Marster o'Evy-thing roun 'im!!"[55]

Although of different generations, both Watterson and Bingham ascribed to a more enlightened and benign form of race prejudice than did southern rabble rousers of this era, like Georgian Tom Watson. Watterson also associated Republicanism and the black race because of his Civil War and Reconstruction experiences. Although he would valiantly oppose lynching on occasion, he could never believe that Negroes could be elevated much above the way he saw them in Louisville. His views of race as part of the New South ethos almost exactly fit

those of Colonel Robert Bingham, a member of his own generation
of Civil War–era southerners. The younger Bingham, on the other
hand, took a more enlightened view of white-black relations than Marse
Henry, one that coincided with that of most other southern
progressives of his generation. Overall, the progressives' record on
race is perhaps the most deplorable part of their agenda.[56]

In the first decade of the Judge's control of the Louisville papers,
he assumed an ever larger role in the life of his city and state, none
more so than in his leadership in racial matters. The underlying racism of the papers continued under his direction. The cartoon
"Hambone" endured as a daily feature in the *Courier* in the twenties. If
publicly outlawed in the papers, Bingham used "nigger" in his private
correspondence with his daughter. *Courier* cartoonist Grover Page
sometimes turned to race-oriented offerings in his daily drawings. For
example, the 28 March 1920 Sunday *Courier* magazine contained a
cynical Page cartoon, typical of the age. A small white boy stands by a
wagon as a young black boy repeatedly offers items in order to ride in
the wagon. Finally the black youth ends up pulling the white in the
wagon with the caption: "Den, White Boy, I'll Be De Boss."[57]

That cartoon represented the racial views of most white people in
Louisville as described in George C. Wright's *Life Behind a Veil: Blacks
in Louisville, Kentucky, 1865–1930*. Wright maintained that though
Louisville race relations were generally more peaceful than in the Deep
South, overall they were just as oppressive. But individuals like Bingham
meliorated a racial climate that could have been much worse. As a
member of the local branches of the Urban League and the Commission on Interracial Cooperation, the Louisville publisher worked for
improved housing for Negroes and better race relations. For a while
in the twenties Bingham served as chairman of the Louisville Urban
League. He helped hire J. M. Ragland, a Detroit African American, as
executive secretary of that group in 1923.[58]

Throughout the twenties Bingham downplayed the issue in state
politics while steadfastly opposing the resurgent Ku Klux Klan in that
decade. "I am absolutely opposed to the modern fake Ku Klux organization," he told a Louisville friend. However, he retained a belief in the
old "redeemer" myth about the Klan of his father's generation: "In its
day the genuine, old organization absolutely saved the women and children and the civilization of the South." The Louisville publisher
contributed to most worthy black causes such as the Lincoln Institute

of Kentucky in nearby Shelby County. To Henry Luce of *Time* magazine, Bingham concluded that in the twenties the "racial relations here
are on a fine basis." According to Wright in *Life Behind a Veil,* that
translated into peaceful coexistence between the races but little actual economic and social progress for Louisville blacks.[59]

Bingham's support of prohibition, women's suffrage, and the
League of Nations continued through the conclusion of the Wilson
administration and the fading of the Progressive Era. Passage of the
Eighteenth and Nineteenth Amendments institutionalized the first
two of these causes. Both the *Courier* and *Times* ardently supported
the League and continued that tack well into the twenties. "I believe
that the campaign of education with reference to the Treaty and the
League will result finally in their adoption by this country," the Judge
maintained. He expressed great hope for the world at the conclusion of World War I and vowed to use his newspapers to work "constantly and consistently" for world peace. On things over which he
had more control, Bingham's influence on several levels increased
because of his wealth. The Louisville papers became an extension of
the Judge's determination to influence the affairs of his city, state,
and nation.[60]

Not long after taking over the papers, Bingham moved into a new
estate two miles from Lincliffe on River Road in the Glenview development, originated by the Fincastle Club on a trotting-horse farm that
had once belonged to wealthy meat packer James C. McFerran. Trad-
ing his Cherokee Park property for Bushy Park with Charles Ballard's
widow, Bingham renamed it Melcombe Bingham after an estate in
England where some distant ancestors had once lived. He combined
two properties, each with a house, the larger constructed in 1910–11
and the smaller, known as the "little house," built for the daughter of
Judge Alex Humphrey in 1916. Over the next two decades the Judge
made Melcombe Bingham into a showplace.[61]

Becoming one of the wealthiest men in Kentucky did not radi-
cally change Bingham's lifestyle, but only increased the volume of
his business investments and the size of his contributions to charity.
His investments became less speculative, with more funds diverted
into such areas as the Liberty Loan Drives, government bonds, and
corporate bonds. He became part of a group of Kentucky businessmen who managed the fortune of John C. C. Mayo's widow and her

considerable interests in the Appalachian coal fields. As oil exploration expanded into several areas of Kentucky, Bingham became a director of such corporations as the Swiss Oil Company. He indulged his tastes for art, began purchasing rare manuscripts and books, bought fine automobiles, but could still quibble about the cost of building a monument at Eleanor Miller Bingham's burial lot in Cave Hill Cemetery.[62]

Bingham also expanded his philanthropy. It seemed that nearly every worthy cause in Kentucky and the region asked for his aid, including numerous religious groups. He carefully chose which causes to support. Following the business progressive's predilection toward organizational efficiency, he supported the efforts of the Louisville Federation of Social Agencies to systematize support for various philanthropic organizations in that city. The Kentucky Children's Home Society remained one of his special favorites. Moreover, in the early twenties, upkeep of the Bingham School in Asheville took an increasing amount of his support each year as that institution faced financial crisis. He contributed to other causes as well. For example, he gave five thousand dollars to help finance the flight of William Byrd over the South Pole in 1928.[63]

Purchase of the Louisville papers gave Bingham access to the political power structure that he had never had before. Though after 1917 he denied any desire whatever for political office, from the first day he took control of the papers a year later, the Judge determined to use his newfound power to push for the causes he believed would benefit the people of the state. "I am interested in principles rather than in persons," he explained, "and expect to conduct the Courier-Journal and the Times on that plane." In a more practical vein he would use his fortune to directly support like-minded candidates running at the local, state, and national levels. Nominally a Democrat, he had proved to be independent of party on more than one occasion in his early political career. He very soon became leader of a faction in the Kentucky Democratic party headed by himself, former governor J. C. W. Beckham, and former adjutant general Percy Haly. The latter became Bingham's personal political liaison with state and national Democratic party leaders. Robert Worth Bingham supported the Democratic party with more than editorials. During the congressional elections of 1918, for example, he donated at least ten thousand dollars to the Democratic National Committee.[64]

In the latter part of the Progressive Era, the inheritance from the Flagler estate altered Bingham's life. Purchase of the *Courier-Journal* and the *Louisville Times* paved the way for nearly two decades of influence over local, state, and national affairs. During the 1920s Bingham became an active participant in Democratic-party affairs in an era in which that party suffered continued losses at the national level. Through it all the Judge supported the party at the national level, while maintaining independence in Louisville and Kentucky politics. Control of important regional newspapers and the remainder of the Flagler bequest made it possible for Bingham to expand his influence outside the bounds of the Commonwealth of Kentucky. His role in the farm cooperative movement in the early twenties thrust him into the effort to solve the serious marketing problems of the nation's farmers. This became the first outstanding demonstration of the influence of the new publisher of the *Courier* and *Times*.

chapter five

"My Great Plan"

A Case Study
in Business
Progressivism

PROGRESSIVISM LOST ITS VITALITY as the nation moved into the Jazz Age. Historians often cite disillusionment with the results of World War I, or the sheer exhaustion of the moral crusades of the Wilson years, as the cause. Many progressives, particularly southerners, considered the Eighteenth Amendment as the sine qua non and finale of reform. With the failure of the United States to join the League of Nations, and the election of Warren G. Harding in 1920 to the presidency, the nation turned once again to the right, toward conservatism and isolationism.[1]

However, there is another argument that progressivism "did not disappear in the 1920s." George Brown Tindall described "The Metamorphosis of Progressivism" in *The Emergence of the New South* as a transformation into new lines of endeavor. Economic development, efficiency, and "good government" became the primary themes of southern progressive types as they continued to search for a fulfillment of "The New South." At the state government level, "business progressives," "stressed economy and efficiency," exemplified by such governors as Cameron Morrison in North Carolina, Austin Peay in Tennessee, and Harry Flood Byrd in Virginia. Southern businessmen and professionals adopted this line of thought as necessary for the benefit of both the region and their own lives. Good roads, better education, and public health became the rallying cries of many southern progressives. As a lawyer, businessman, investor, and publisher,

Bingham demonstrated many of the ideals of business progressivism in the twenties.[2]

The general farm prosperity caused by World War I soon ended for most American farmers in the fall of 1920. All farm commodity prices by 1921 fell to an average of two-thirds their market value of the previous year. This farm depression struck especially hard in the South. Cotton sold for less than half of its old value as the boll weevil worked its way inexorably across the lower South. Most southern farmers never tasted the full prosperity of the war years. The large rural population of the South suffered from depression conditions long before the stock-market crash of October 1929. Many sharecroppers and tenant farmers began migrating to new land or abandoned agriculture entirely.[3]

Complete disaster struck Kentucky tobacco farmers on Black Monday, 20 December 1920. Burley markets in Kentucky opened with bids of less than half the previous year's average. Most markets closed abruptly, reopening two weeks later on 3 January 1921. In Lexington the largest tobacco market in the nation closed that day after only one hour of sales. Critics observed that buyers reverted to their old practices of "seesawing," or alternating their purchases, and not competing with each other for the individual farmer's crop.[4]

Unrest spread to other parts of the state. North, in Covington, authorities called out the sheriff's department to quell a disturbance. In Carlisle fifteen hundred unruly farmers surrounded a warehouse after opening sales averaged only nine cents per pound, far below production costs. Wild rumors swept through the Burley Belt. Central Kentucky congressman J. Campbell Cantrill called for stern action against the tobacco companies. Prominent tobaccomen and editors asked for calm and a "cut-out" of the entire 1921 crop. Many remembered the lawless night-riding period of the previous decade in western Kentucky, an era immortalized by native son Robert Penn Warren in his first novel, *The Night Rider* (1939).[5]

With less than two years of experience as owner and publisher of the *Courier* and *Times,* but with the power of his wealth and the newspapers behind him, Bingham considered promoting farm cooperation as a solution to the problems of Kentucky tobacco farmers. He applied the optimistic "can-do" spirit that business progressives carried into the 1920s to the practical problem of organizing farmers.[6]

Early on the *Courier-Journal* editorialized that "careful management and the application of sound business principles should insure results for both the producers and the consumers." Bingham assumed a role of national influence in the farm cooperative movement. He took up the cause with some knowledge of its previous history, having studied the success of agricultural cooperation in California. He received early and valuable support from Bernard Baruch, the southern-reared "speculator" and millionaire who dabbled in economic policy as well as politics. President Frank L. McVey of the University of Kentucky, an economist, dedicated himself and the staff of the university's farm-extension service to organizing a tobacco cooperative.[7]

No one, however, had more influence on Bingham's view of cooperation than Aaron Sapiro, a San Francisco lawyer who spearheaded cooperative organizations across the nation. Sapiro captivated Bingham with his knowledge of the details of cooperation, his devotion to the organization of all commodities produced in America and Canada, and his sheer vitality in encouraging cooperation.[8]

In the twenties Bingham and Sapiro maintained a close personal and working relationship as their names became synonymous with cooperative organization. Bingham adopted Sapiro's grand scheme of monopolistic, centralized marketing for the entire production of a given commodity, rather than only through local organizations. Initially, Bingham depended heavily on Sapiro's knowledge of cooperation and organizational skill in developing tobacco cooperation. "Sapiro is the greatest brain I have ever seen, a fire and a force without equal, in my judgment the most valuable individual asset America has today," the Louisvillian confided to his daughter.[9]

Bingham accepted a role of leadership at a critical time in the history of cooperation, in general, and the marketing of tobacco, in particular. To a Lexington banker he claimed: "I believe you know that I have no political ambition for myself or for any one else." However, he expressed a determination "to try to improve conditions in our state," now having the platform and the wealth to influence events immediately in his state and beyond.[10]

Bingham first decided to concentrate on organizing the Burley Belt and, if successful, to carry the process on into the Black Patch, the dark-fired tobacco area of Western Kentucky. Cooperative organization represented "The Right Road," according to one of the frequent

Courier-Journal editorials. After laying the foundations by using his papers, Bingham orchestrated a speaking tour for Sapiro before meetings of bankers in several key Kentucky locations in late May 1921. At a Lexington meeting of bankers, warehousemen, and businessmen, Sapiro received a "rising vote of thanks" after his presentation. Desha Breckinridge, editor of the *Lexington Herald,* admitted to skepticism about the plan at first. However, he too soon fell under the spell of Sapiro's oratory and wholeheartedly supported the tobacco co-op as "the beginning of an era of far greater and permanent prosperity."[11]

Initial enthusiasm for burley cooperation cooled somewhat during the summer of 1921 as the crop matured in the fields. The threat of low prices again spurred the movement in early October as auction warehouses prepared for annual sales. Bingham boldly took the responsibility for financing the organization of what would become the Burley Tobacco Growers' Cooperative Association. Sapiro returned to the state for extensive campaigning. Additionally, Joseph Passoneau, an aide to Sapiro, came to Kentucky to work for the cooperative. Bingham personally paid his salary and travel expenses.[12]

Large growers and tenant farmers alike joined the movement. As might be expected, substantial growers and agribusinessmen assumed leading roles in the effort, because they had the most to gain from higher prices and market stability. Besides Bingham, who chaired the organizational effort, such prominent warehousemen and growers as Ralph M. Barker of Carrollton, James C. Stone of Lexington, James N. Kehoe of Maysville, John B. Winn of Versailles, and Bush W. Allin of Harrodsburg provided early leadership and later became chief officers of the co-op's executive committee.[13]

The marketing agreement that circulated in the Burley Belt showed Sapiro's strategy of monopolistic cooperation. In order for the pool to go into effect, those growers who represented at least 75 percent of the 1920 crop had to sign the membership roll. Those who signed up also pledged not to sell outside the pool for a period of five years, agreeing to an "ironclad" liability for legal action if they broke their promise. This represented the essential part of the agreement. However, from the beginning most farmers thought more about the immediate impact on prices than the long-term benefits of cooperation.[14]

By mid-1921 Bingham devoted almost all his time to the tobacco cooperative effort. To his daughter at this time the Louisville publisher confided words that revealed self-confidence as well as a haughty sense of noblesse oblige bordering on arrogance: "This tobacco thing can be put over but it will take every moment of my time, and I can't see it fail when we are so near success. It could be a dreadful blow to thousands of people if we don't put it over & yet we who have no personal interest in it must work prodigiously to get the poor things to accept their salvation."[15]

After a flurry of old-fashioned speech-making and politicking in mid-November, farmers pledged about 84 percent of the burley belt's crop to the cooperative. When Bingham made the announcement at an organizational meeting in Lexington, the crowd rose in a thunderous ovation. Then they settled down to the difficult task of organizing a cooperative with the largest membership in the nation.[16]

With the 1921 crop already in the barns and auction sales within days of opening, key committees set to work on publicity, sales plans, and developing warehousing and grading policies. The cooperative promised farmers partial payments when they turned their crops over to the co-op for grading and storage.[17]

Bingham set about finding funds for the venture. He negotiated with the War Finance Corporation, headed by Eugene Meyer, Jr., who agreed to loans to store the burley tobacco after it had been processed, or redried. But stopgap financing had to be arranged quickly to make the initial payment to farmers. When a preliminary arrangement with the largest regional banks fell through, Bingham stepped in with a personal guarantee of one million dollars. Within days major banks in Louisville and Cincinnati pledged 2.5 million more, and smaller banks in the region offered several hundred thousand dollars. With these funds the cooperative completed the first part of its task. Individual farmers turned over their tobacco to the co-op and, more important, received a check for about 40 percent of their crop's value. Without Bingham's loan guarantee the Burley Association would never have successfully organized in 1921.[18]

The burley group hurriedly organized to carry out its function. Bingham continued to lead, becoming a member at large of the board of directors and the all-important five-man executive committee. The board elected Stone as president and general manager and appointed other officers. Passoneau stayed on as field service chief. With tobacco as collateral the cooperative secured loans from the War Finance Corporation to buy storage facilities. If all went well, these loans would be retired in five years by selling securities and charging a small fee to farmers for storing the tobacco. To keep members informed, *The Burley Tobacco Grower,* a monthly organ, began publication in May 1922.[19]

Bingham also became involved in pushing for legislation protecting cooperative organization. The burley group in Kentucky initially organized under a North Carolina statute in 1921. In 1922 Congress passed the Capper-Volstead Cooperative Marketing Act, and the Kentucky General Assembly authorized the Bingham Act. Other state legislatures soon adopted this latter "model" act, written by Sapiro. In brief, this law skirted the problem of organization without capital stock by a nonprofit marketing group. A test case later came before the Supreme Court, with Bingham and Sapiro collaborating on the defense briefs. The nation's highest court decreed that a producer could be penalized for not fulfilling a vow to market all his tobacco with the cooperative and, consequently, declared the Bingham Act to be constitutional.[20]

The Louisville publisher followed the same procedures in organizing other cooperatives, initially in the Black Patch area of western Kentucky and Tennessee. Farmers in west Tennessee proved to be a particularly hard sell, but here too Bingham and Sapiro finally won out, forming the Dark Tobacco Association by late 1922.[21]

In the midst of organizing the tobacco cooperatives, Bingham joined the national cooperative movement in several leadership capacities. He chaired the first meeting of the National Council of Farmers' Cooperative Marketing Associations in mid-December 1922, in the nation's capital. The National Council soon opened offices there for the purpose of coordinating the movement nationwide. Walton Peteet, former director of the American Farm Bureau Federation's Cooperative Marketing Bureau, became secretary of the council.[22]

By late 1923 Bingham and other leaders in the cooperative movement could be proud of their accomplishments. After all, they had formed three large tobacco cooperatives based on Sapiro's centralization schema and a national coordinating council. Bingham played a lesser role in organization of the Tobacco Growers' Cooperative Association of Virginia and the Carolinas, or Tri-State Association, and the much smaller tobacco co-ops in the Connecticut Valley and in Wisconsin. However, even in these regions he completed exhaustive speaking tours. Nationwide, more than three-fourths of the 1923 tobacco crop fell under pool contracts. Local opposition and the power of the major tobacco interests always stood in the way of cooperative success.

Yet within less than two years tobacco cooperatives triumphantly pulled together diverse political, social, and economic interests into functioning organizations. Now came the real trial, testing farmer cooperation, the viability of business progressivism, and the leadership of Bingham, Sapiro, and others involved in the cooperative movement of the 1920s.[23]

Tangible signs of success immediately surfaced in most tobacco-growing areas. Some farmers grumbled because they received only a portion of their crop's worth, but the majority appeared satisfied with a general rise in overall market prices. The Burley Association controlled a larger share of its type than did the dark tobacco or Tri-State co-ops, and its members reaped the benefit in higher prices. Final settlement of the 1921 burley crop came to over twenty dollars per one hundred pounds. The figures jumped to over twenty-five dollars per hundred for concluding sales of the 1922 crop. With economy measures in operation, the profit for the co-op farmer per pound appeared substantially higher than that of the "outsider," who sold his burley tobacco at the auction market in those crop years.[24]

Bingham, Sapiro, and others exulted over their apparent success in the burley belt. Words of praise poured in from other sources. From the War Finance Corporation, Eugene Meyer sent congratulations, as did the secretaries of the Departments of Commerce and Agriculture. Numerous Kentuckians, ranging from Jim Stone, president of the burley pool, to semiliterate farmers praised Bingham's efforts. Having offered his skills and resources to the organizational fight, and with apparently selfless motives, Bingham emerged as the most popular, and possibly the most powerful, figure in the Commonwealth of Kentucky in 1922.[25]

However, within months the tobacco cooperative movement weakened. The fate of the co-ops became a topic of general conversation throughout the region. A bitter joke began circulating in western Kentucky in which two local wags tell about their recent sentences for committing crimes. When one cites the sixty days his neighbor spent in jail for having a moonshine still on his farm, the other tops him by claiming: "Well you got worse than that. You got five years in the pool."[26]

It was one thing to organize the tobacco cooperatives and quite another to keep them functioning smoothly. Right from the start outward appearances of success had been misleading even in the burley belt. Co-op leadership overemphasized large membership rolls as a symbol of progress and strength. While the number of burley contracts grew from 55,000 in 1921 to 109,000 in 1926, the percentage of the total crop handled by the cooperative plummeted from nearly 70 percent to only 41 percent by middecade. The Dark Tobacco and Tri-State co-ops broke down even sooner. Similarly, as their membership figures rose, the percentage of the total crop actually received fell. For example, in 1925 the Tri-State Association marketed only 15 percent of that year's bright-leaf crop even as its membership tally expanded.[27]

In general, producer cooperatives failed to fulfill their promise of coordinating marketing in the 1920s. The successes and failures of the tobacco pools illustrated the crisis of cooperative marketing in that decade. Four conditions contributed to their downfall: First, the volatile nature of the marketplace placed farmers at a disadvantage. Second, farmers contributed to their own cooperative dilemma by their lack of confidence in forming such groups. Third, Bingham, Sapiro, and other leaders applied inappropriate strategies to the movement. Fourth, rivalries among farm interest groups, led by the ascendancy of the American Farm Bureau Federation, weakened the cooperative effort.[28]

What role did the market play in the failure of the tobacco cooperatives? The simplest answer lies in the fact that the American Tobacco Company, the nation's largest buyer, completely refused to negotiate with the pools. ATC and other buyers were obviously guilty of "collusion," as later indicated by a Federal Trade Commission study. R. J. Reynolds, and Liggett and Myers, bought sparingly from the co-ops, but their purchases were more than offset by the reluctance of the Regie, or European national monopolies, to buy from the pools. Even a well-publicized trip by Bingham, Stone, and other tobaccomen to several European capitals in mid-1924 failed to garner large international purchases. American Tobacco and other corporations could always purchase enough tobacco from outsiders to do more than meet their needs in the short run. Believing that the pools would fail just as they had after the turn of the century, the major tobacco-purchasing corporations knew they had time on their side.[29]

Farmers themselves contributed to the failure of the tobacco cooperatives. They generally followed the lead of prominent men in the community, some of whom did not always have the best of intentions.

Like most American farmers, tobacco producers tended to expand too rapidly, and overproduction meant a sacrifice in quality. Low quality played into the hands of the buyers. Psychologically, farmers were not prepared for the discipline of successful cooperative effort over the long haul in the early twenties. A single cash-crop mentality pervaded in the tobacco belts. Most farmers did not place enough faith in the promise of future payments. They had bills to pay, and, particularly for tenant farmers, payment of those debts made it possible to remain on the land for another year. Moreover, illiteracy made it difficult to communicate with a large number of farmers, many of whom lived in isolated rural communities. Communication and singleness of purpose became even more difficult considering the racial mores of the day. A large percentage of black tenant farmers and sharecroppers in the dark-fired area added racial tensions to the competitiveness among local farmers.[30]

Shortsighted cooperative leadership added the decisive element in the failure of the movement. The strategies of Bingham and Sapiro contributed to the defeat. Their plans included more than organizing limited numbers of farmers into cooperatives. Sapiro's driving ambition to organize along the lines of horizontal integration into centralized national cooperatives for all commodities failed. Bingham expanded this vision and schema into an even more ambitious plan. A firm Wilsonian internationalist, the Louisvillian advocated development of a North American wheat cooperative as the entrée for closer economic ties with Great Britain and Western Europe. He hoped this would eventually lead to full American membership in the League of Nations. Although in early 1923 Bingham could claim that "my great plan is working spendidly," these overarching schemes reached too far.[31]

If the grand strategies of Bingham and Sapiro failed, so did their tactical application in organizing the tobacco cooperatives. Emphasis on signing up a nearly complete producer monopoly for each type of tobacco proved unwieldy. Smaller tobacco cooperatives, like those for other products in California, survived because of their limited numbers and tighter discipline. The three tobacco pools never had control of their large unruly memberships because of the problems of distance and communication.[32]

Organizational strategy also failed in one other key aspect: too many co-ops formed in too short a period of time. In early 1924 Bingham sensed that cooperative leaders overreached their grasp, and he urged Sapiro to halt organizational activities. "The failure of one cooperative already organized will do the whole movement great harm," the Judge warned, "much greater harm, in fact, than would result from delaying the organization of new cooperatives." He further encouraged Sapiro to embark on a campaign to "revive" the "religious fervor" among the existing co-ops, particularly in the lagging dark tobacco cooperative area. As predicted, the weakness of one cooperative induced others to fail. In the end the tottering Dark Tobacco Association pulled down the stronger burley co-op.[33]

Leadership also failed in other ways. The very success of Sapiro's ubiquitous, evangelistic approach in winning converts to the cooperative cause also contributed to the defeat. Bingham and others also relied on impassioned oratory to sway large public gatherings into signing marketing agreements. After the initial successes of 1922–23, however, this enthusiasm wore thin as production rose and prices plummeted. Bingham later admitted that member education had been the real key to success. For a variety of reasons the tobacco co-ops failed this vital responsibility. Without adequate time and financing, the cooperative effort repeated the mistakes of earlier attempts to forge grower awareness and cooperation in the late nineteenth and early twentieth centuries.[34]

On other matters Bingham perhaps had no control at all, particularly over conflicting personalities within the cooperative movement. For example, local political rivalries between contending groups weakened the cooperative effort. In western Kentucky charges of nepotism were made against one prominent member of the dark tobacco cooperative board. Others claimed that cooperative executives Jim Stone and R. M. Barker profiteered at the expense of other members.[35]

Conflicting personalities also played a role. Sapiro and Passoneau warred over development of cooperative policy and eventually came to physical blows. After a strongly worded argument over plans for combining the dark and burley cooperative papers, Sapiro told Bingham that Passoneau suddenly arose "and punched me a perfectly good swat in the jaw." Passoneau soon left employment in the Bingham-sponsored cooperatives and wrote damaging letters to farm leaders throughout the country. Bingham assumed that Passoneau's efforts were "doubtless being financed by interests hostile to cooperative marketing," hinting that somehow Henry Ford was behind it all.[36]

Another controversy involving Bingham, Sapiro, and secretary of the National Council Walton Peteet, ended with that Washington office being closed amid charges that Peteet sold out the farm cooperative movement to the American Farm Bureau Federation. If that were not enough, the fact that Sapiro charged a forty-eight-thousand-dollar fee for his services in behalf of the cooperatives inflamed anti-Semitic passions among not a few Kentucky cooperative members. All of this evidence of internal strife worked to the detriment of the cooperatives, and in the end Bingham could do little to solve these basic problems of leadership credibility.[37]

After being totally immersed in organizational activity for several years, Bingham lost his earlier enthusiasm for cooperation. While he continued to serve as a board member of the burley and dark tobacco pools, and as chairman of the National Council of Farmers' Cooperative Marketing Associations, his ardor noticeably cooled by late 1923. Like Sapiro, Bingham intended to organize the co-ops and then allow others to take over the more mundane task of running them on a day-to-day basis. The Louisvillian made several attempts to resign from the burley and dark tobacco directorships, finally doing so in mid-1924 by claiming that it had become impossible for him to attend meetings of the boards. Bingham had ambitions beyond that of successfully organizing farm cooperatives. Although he always denied any desire for public office, the Judge had other political ambitions. Through the use of the papers he could influence a variety of issues. His editorial policies demonstrated a broad range of national and international interests. Like Sapiro, Bingham spread himself too thin, having neither the time nor inclination to devote himself fully to the farm cooperative movement over the long haul.[38]

For a brief span in the early 1920s both the wealth and personality of Bingham held the cooperative movement together. He used his fortune to support several cooperative efforts outside of the tobacco belt, ranging all the way from Maine potato farmers to Kansas wheat producers. Eventually, he lost several hundred thousand dollars from failed cooperative ventures. By late 1923 he determined to cut his losses and no longer risk his fortune on unworthy co-ops. Moreover, personal conflicts and rivalries within the cooperative movement took up much of Bingham's time, requiring his attention that could have been better spent elsewhere.[39]

Sapiro's style and ethnic background caused no end of problems, but Bingham constantly supported him in the twenties. Eventually, Bingham ended as the stronger of the two, on occasion loaning large sums of money to the Californian. Moreover, Bingham supported Sapiro in a libel suit against Henry Ford for columns printed in the *Dearborn Independent*. Ford had been one of the most outspoken anticooperative critics in the early twenties. "I'm sorry I've been so frequently a source — unintentional or otherwise — of any trouble to you," Sapiro apologized to Bingham. "You've been the one most glorious friendship I know."[40]

When farmers refused to ratify a new burley marketing agreement in 1926, the other tobacco pools had already collapsed. A few burley-belt leaders suggested a total "cutout" to limit supplies of the leaf, but that idea quickly died as most farmers rushed to overproduce in order to eke out a living. A nearly complete demoralization swept across the tobacco belt in the upper South. Other cooperatives throughout the nation also failed to survive the mid-twenties.[41]

The farm cooperative movement began to gather strength in the late nineteenth century, particularly in Wisconsin and California. Continuing successes during the Progressive Era gave cause for the high expectations of the early 1920s. Hope had turned to bitter frustration by the middecade. Most of the Sapiro-inspired and Bingham-backed monopolistic cooperatives outside the state of California suffered the same fate as that of the tobacco co-ops. Bingham's application of business progressivism to farm cooperation could not sustain the movement. The ideals of organization, efficiency, and discipline could not be translated into a workable form for the greater benefit of the tobacco farmer. However, valuable lessons came from these experiences — ones that could be applied to government direction of agriculture a decade later. In the New Deal era federal sponsorship of farm cooperation proved workable. Out of the agricultural disasters of the twenties, the American Farm Bureau Federation solidified its position as the political arm of American agriculture.[42]

Meanwhile, Robert Worth Bingham pursued other avenues of interest, influence, and power in the twenties. He set his own agenda.

From the time he purchased the papers in 1918, he took a strong interest in influencing Kentucky politics. Critics claimed that Bingham became the real power, the money man, behind the Beckham-Haly faction, and that he overused that control. He had strong, progressively inclined convictions that he would apply to the direction of the *Courier-Journal* and *Louisville Times* in the twenties.[43]

chapter six

The 1920s

Publisher,
Businessman,
Father

THE FARM COOPERATIVE CRUSADE represented only one part of Robert Worth Bingham's life and career in the twenties. Other challenges came in his roles as publisher of "the Bingham papers," a businessman of some influence, and a father of three children who came to adulthood in the twenties.

Bingham came to the newspaper business with no experience. From the beginning he understood that he would need to depend heavily on the personnel already in place. However, he had his own ideas about how the *Courier-Journal* and *Times* should be operated, and set about to establish his own mark on these properties. In reorganizing the staff of the papers, he alienated Arthur Krock in the process, eventually forcing that editor out of any consideration for a continuing high-level position with the papers. Bingham brought Emily Overman, whom he trusted implicitly, from his law firm to the publisher's office as his personal secretary. Completely loyal to her boss, she served him throughout the twenties and thirties.[1]

Once Bingham got a feel for the papers, he made personnel changes to suit his managerial style. Tom Wallace, longtime reporter and former Washington chief of the *Louisville Times,* took over the editorial chair of that paper in 1923, adding his own unique imprint on the afternoon paper. The new editor of the *Times,* who favored short, pungent editorials in contrast to Watterson's long-winded essays in the *Courier-Journal,* humorously told his young writers that he wanted their work to be no longer than a pencil, and a short one at that. Wallace took an increasing interest in conservation as well as Latin American affairs as he settled into the editorial positon. His efforts on behalf of forestry conservation in Kentucky increased in the twenties and thirties with Bingham's full support.[2]

The masthead of the *Courier-Journal* soon identified Bingham as editor and publisher, and Harrison Robertson as chief of the editorial staff. Robertson often demonstrated not only the writing flair of his mentor Henry Watterson, but also an independent streak that occasionally clashed with the policies of his publisher. Though physically handicapped, the crusty old Robertson insisted on walking up steps to his office even after the newspaper building added an elevator. He also wrote several novels that indicated a writing flair outside of his usual tightly written, though sometimes florid, editorials. Indeed, insiders hinted that Robertson wrote some of the editorials credited to Watterson in the latter days of Marse Henry's tenure at the helm of the *Courier-Journal*. When promoted to full charge of the editorial page, Robertson declared his "unswerving devotion to the interest of your great paper (I think of it as our great paper) and of yourself."[3]

Reorganization continued well into the twenties. Emanuel Levi, the young law partner of Bingham, rounded out the executive staff as vice-president and business manager of both papers, and immediately set about to find more advertising revenue for the papers soon after the purchase. Bingham demanded complete loyalty from his employees and fired them if he thought necessary. For example, he tried to let Robert E. Hughes down easily, hoping "to wound you as little as possible," explaining that Hughes had not demonstrated the ability to run his department. But the publisher could also show some compassion. When a former employee developed a problem with alcohol, Bingham assured him that he would help pay for the young man's medical treatment. The Judge could not forgo delivering a Victorian/ Progressive-inspired homily, averring that: "You are now the victim. You are now a slave. You have prostituted your character and your ability and you have temporarily betrayed your natural endowments of both mind and heart." Bingham also declared high standards for himself and allowed the papers to print personal items about his family. For example, when arrested for speeding in his automobile, the *Courier* ran a brief notice of his ten-dollar fine.[4]

The publisher also kept a tight rein over the staff. If an occasional editorial displeased the Judge, he usually reprimanded the writer quickly. For example, an offending piece by editorial writer Anthony Woodson in the *Times* in mid-1924 charging that all state-asylum personnel had been appointed because of patronage brought a quick response from Bingham, who served on the board of this institution at the time. Although Bingham expressed his general support of Woodson's work on the editorial page of the *Times,* he ordered the editor to mend his ways immediately. Bingham also had definite ideas about how other employees of the papers should relate to their jobs. While he accepted unionism of the printers, in 1923 he told them on one occasion that if they walked out, they would automatically be replaced. There was no strike. Moreover, the publisher refused to accept newspaper guild organization for reporters and editorial staff.[5]

Lorenzo Martin and Ulric Bell, who served as heads, respectively, of the separate and competing *Times* and *Courier-Journal* bureaus in Washington, became confidants of their publisher. On national and international affairs Bingham depended heavily on the insights of Martin and Bell and used them as well for political contacts. The publisher could be as rewarding to his employees as he was demanding. When Bell complained about the fact that the Washington competition made more money than he, and could therefore afford to belong to important clubs, Bingham promptly raised the *Courier* Washington chief's salary and provided funds for club memberships and entertaining news sources in the capital.[6]

In the 1920s Bingham adjusted to both the needs of his papers and the changing economy, technology, and culture of that decade. He used his wealth to expand the services of the papers, adding more news services and features to both papers and purchasing badly needed modern printing machinery. The papers continued to depend heavily on the Associated Press, the only cooperative news service in the country. Bingham also joined the North American Newspaper Alliance, becoming a member of the board of directors of that group in the mid-twenties. Relations with other newspaper people, particularly in the South, strengthened in the twenties. Josephus Daniels, who called on the Judge for a substantial loan to keep afloat the *Raleigh News and Observer,* shared similar newspaper, regional, and political interests with the Louisvillian.[7]

Bingham proved to be both flexible and innovative in operating his papers. For example, WHAS radio, another Bingham enterprise, began operations in the early twenties as one of the first radio stations in the nation. On 18 July 1922 Credo Harris, a longtime *Courier* and *Times* reporter who took over direction as manager, announced: "This is WHAS, the radio-telephone broadcasting station of the *Courier-Journal* and the *Louisville Times* in Louisville, Kentucky." After the playing of "My Old Kentucky Home," Bingham spoke, surely rather esoterically for most of his audience: "Now, tonight, we inaugurate this necromancy of the electric air, the radio." At the time all radio stations in the country operated on the 360-meter band, and signals often overlapped. While the station followed the commercial and entertainment trends common in the fledgling radio industry in the twenties, Bingham also visualized a higher purpose for the operation of his new business.[8]

Very soon WHAS began beaming public-service educational programming developed by the University of Kentucky. The Bingham papers advertised free radios such as "The Aeriola, Jr." and "The Etherian" in exchange for a few subscriptions to the papers. By the mid-twenties the station broadcast from early in the afternoon into the late evening. News, weather, and sports announcements became regular features, as well as afternoon baseball games in the summertime. An expanding audience heard about the fatal ordeal of Floyd Collins's entrapment in Sand Cave near Mammoth Cave. Skeets Miller, a young *Courier* reporter, helped the paper win a Pulitzer Prize for his colorful coverage of the tragedy. WHAS also sought closer ties with the outlying parts of Kentucky, particularly in the Appalachian region, where the station established listening centers at well-located post offices and general stores.[9]

Bingham grasped the fact that radio could be used to communicate with people either unwilling or unable to read a newspaper. He determined not only to exploit the financial benefits of such an endeavor, but also to provide the listeners with educational, uplifting programming. WHAS became a successful operation in the twenties and, no doubt, increased the circulation of the *Courier-Journal.* Moreover, merchants soon learned about the range of the broadcasts. For example, one advertiser who gave away free cigars to everyone who heard his ad on WHAS and came into his store soon thereafter had to cancel the commercial because he ran out of cigars.[10]

The Judge also allowed the papers and radio station to use other popular promotional gimmicks of the 1920s. Alvin "Shipwreck" Kelly,

one of the most famous characters in that decade of unforgettable
zaniness, sat on a 112-foot high, ten-inch wide flagpole atop the *Courier* building for one hundred hours in mid-May 1928. Not long after
beginning his stunt, Kelly complained about the acrid coal smoke
coming from nearby office buildings and industries and asked for a
gas mask. In order to fortify the intrepid Kelly against the elements,
some employees of the papers "hauled moonshine liquor" up the pole
on a rope. During the daylight hours substantial crowds stood on the
streets below watching the irrepressible Kelly. Other promotions included inviting girls to compete in the "Flossie Flirt" doll give-away
competition with the *Louisville Herald-Post* and sending genuine Alas-
kan reindeer and an Eskimo along with Santa Claus (played on one
occasion by Kentucky author James Tandy Ellis) to visit area schools
and children's groups during the Christmas season. On a higher plane
of public service, the papers sponsored a national spelling-bee
competiton for schoolchildren until the early 1940s.[11]

As Bingham became more active in publishing circles, he naturally
gravitated toward the anti-Hearst publishers in the country. In the
mid-twenties William Randolph Hearst, who already owned the International News Service and the Universal Service, tried to gain access
to the Associated Press, perhaps thinking of adding that enterprise to
his string of media holdings. Frank E. Gannett, another newspaper
magnate, also entered the fray when he attempted to obtain AP membership for his Rochester newspapers. The editor of the *New York
Evening Journal,* a Hearst paper, declared that Gannett, and not his
publisher, was behind the troubles of the AP. In the end Hearst obtained an entrée into the Associated Press by purchasing three papers
that already subscribed to that news service. Perhaps William Allen
White of the *Emporia Gazette* best summed up this power play among
the nation's publishing elite in a letter to Bingham: "I believe the evidence entitles me to the opinion that Mr. Hearst does not play our
game," the Kansan said. "The ideals of the Associated Press, as I understand them, do not seem to interest him." Throughout this controversy Bingham supported the leadership of the Associated Press.[12]

Louisvillians witnessed a more competitive newspaper market with
the purchase of the *Louisville Herald* and the *Evening Post* by financier
and Democratic party boss James B. Brown in 1925. For many years
these papers had operated as progressive Republican papers. Though
neither had the circulation of the *Courier* and *Times,* they made their

presence felt beyond the confines of Louisville and Jefferson County. When Brown took control, he consolidated the papers into the *Herald-Post,* built a new printing plant, and changed their editorial orientation to his own peculiar brand of Democratic-party factionalism. As president of the National Bank of Kentucky, the largest bank in the Commonwealth, Brown wielded considerable economic and political power in the twenties. Moreover, he served in the inner circle of the Democratic party in the state and fully intended to use his newspapers as a foil against the Bingham press.[13]

Ironically, for several years prior to 1926, Bingham and Brown had rather close business ties and interests. At one time a substantial portion of the Bingham fortune and investments was held in Brown's bank. A short while before Brown entered the newspaper business, Bingham pulled his money out of that bank, investing in Liberty National Bank. Meanwhile, Brown persisted in developing his own empire. He consolidated his business interests, competed with the Bingham papers on a daily basis, and continued his political plotting. With all the skill, charm, and luck, at least for a few years, of one of the nineteenth-century robber barons, Brown manipulated such companies as the Kentucky Wagon Company into bankruptcy, all the while extracting substantial assets for himself. For the remainder of the twenties the Bingham papers and Brown's continued what amounted to a "war" for advertising dollars and circulation numbers in the Falls City area. The politics of the state reverberated in the pages of both Louisville newspaper empires in the twenties.[14]

Throughout that decade Bingham adhered to his own specific agenda and well-defined policies quite separate from the orthodox Democratic party of Kentucky. He continually declared his intention to remain separate from direct connection with either party and to publish "Independent" newspapers. For example, in 1920 he supported James Cox in his bid for the presidency as a member of the "Pro-league Independents." Moreover, he claimed to avoid investing in businesses that "might give the appearance of bias in any position" in the *Courier* and *Times,* but kept the substantial holdings in the Standard Oil stock he had received as part of the settlement of Mary Lily's estate. Bingham proved to be an activist in both the publishing and the political realms. He reacted to most issues of the 1920s.[15]

Although the Eighteenth Amendment and Volstead Act apparently sealed the fate of alcohol in that decade, everyone soon realized that neither the liquor interests nor the individual tastes of millions of Americans had been changed by government fiat. Bingham allowed editors Robertson of the *Courier* and Wallace of the *Times* more leeway on this issue than any other that came under their editorial direction in the twenties, because he understood the complexity of the matter. Whereas Robertson completely opposed the "noble experiment," Wallace proved to be more sympathetic to prohibition in both principle and practice. On several occasions this gave the appearance of a "divided mentality" in the leadership of the papers at Third and Liberty streets. In more than one instance the publisher had to defend and apologize for the "jocular nature" of some of Robertson's offerings to dry advocates. Yet through most of the decade the leadership of the Anti-Saloon League of Kentucky praised the Bingham papers. A. C. Graham, superintendant of the ASL in Kentucky, heralded the Judge's fight for "Civic Righteousness and Christian Citizenship" through the mid-twenties.[16]

Although Bingham supported national prohibition "heartily and strongly," he believed that the amendment had gone into effect with too much whiskey on hand, contributing to subsequent corruption and bootlegging. Moreover, he declared that foreign ships should not be forced to comply with an American law, and he declined to contribute to the ASL until that group stopped pressuring foreign shipping. Prohibition remained an important issue in both state and national politics. As will be discussed in the following chapter, the Bingham-Beckham-Haly faction among Kentucky Democrats held firm against the liquor interests.[17]

However, prohibition did not represent a clear personal break with alcohol to Bingham. He was not above the normal amount of hypocrisy shared by not a few upper-middle-class Americans in supporting prohibition publicly while personally taking an occasional drink. The use of alcohol, of course, had become an expected part of social discourse at many functions, even in the nation's capital. For example, in planning for a *Courier*-sponsored party to be given after a 1926 Gridiron Dinner in Washington, D.C., Bingham agreed with Ulric Bell that supplying "some ammunition" (alcohol) would be appropriate for the occasion.[18]

Religious issues often came before the American public in the 1920s. Throughout his life Bingham remained a strong Protestant, first as a Presbyterian of the southern variety, and later, after his first marriage, as an Episcopalian. He attended church services regularly, contributed to the church coffers, and gave most of the outward appearances of religiosity expected of a gentleman of his southern and Victorian background. "In our news and editorial columns," he boasted to a Catholic who voiced disapproval of the paper's stance on Ireland, "we know neither Jew, Protestant nor Catholic." The *Kentucky Irish-American*, an old-fashioned ethnic paper edited by John J. Barry in the 1920s, often attacked its larger Louisville competitor for alleged anti-Irish editorials. However, these assaults usually resulted from the *Irish-American* editor's propensity for hyperbole rather than from real *Courier* and *Times* bias on either the Irish question or attacks on Irish-Americans in this country.[19]

On another matter touching religion, the teaching of evolution, Bingham and the Louisville papers played a prominent role in the defeat of proposed legislation in 1922. In that year the Kentucky legislature became the first such body in the nation to deliberate anti-evolution legislation like that passed in the famous Butler Bill in Tennessee in 1925. After a well-coordinated campaign by antievolutionists in the state, and an appearance by William Jennings Bryan before a joint session of the Kentucky General Assembly, antievolution bills came before Senate and House of Representatives committees. J. W. Porter, a Lexington Baptist minister, and Victor I. Masters, editor of the state Southern Baptist paper the *Western Recorder*, led the effort to arouse public opinion in favor of antievolution legislation. A coalition composed of E. Y. Mullins, president of the Southern Baptist Theological Seminary in Louisville; E. L. Powell, pastor of the Louisville First Christian Church; and Frank L. McVey, president of the University of Kentucky, led the forces against restricting the teaching of evolution. The Bingham papers editorially opposed passage of the Kentucky antievolution bills. Robertson, in particular, wrote several forceful editorials.[20]

During the same period, the early months of 1922, the *Courier* serially ran H. W. Van Loon's evolutionist-inspired book, *The Story of Mankind*. Pastor Porter attacked both the editorial stance of the Bingham papers and the publication of Van Loon's book. "I differ wholly from you," Bingham personally replied to Porter's charges, citing the importance of academic freedom and scientific inquiry. This first episode in the antievolution crusade of the 1920s ended when both houses of the Kentucky General Assembly rejected restrictive bills.[21]

For the remainder of the twenties the Bingham papers gave full coverage to religious stories and issues. In May 1923, for example, the papers received high praise for their "full reports" of a Billy Sunday evangelistic meeting in Louisville. E. Y. Mullins credited Bingham for his support of moral issues in the papers.[22]

Race, the intellectual and cultural solvent that more closely connected Robert Worth Bingham with his father and the southern mystique than any other, often arose in the 1920s as an issue of consequence. In that decade lynching continued to blight the South. Moreover, a resurgent Ku Klux Klan became important in state and national political races in the mid-twenties. In Kentucky in 1923, for example, some Democrats associated with the candidacy of William Fields for governor raised the specter of race against the Republicans. A year later Klan influence in the Democratic party became a central issue in that party's national convention in New York City. That same week a crowd of several hundred hooded celebrants paraded down Richmond's streets in daylight and concluded their festivities that evening with a cross burning and public-speaking event that drew an even larger audience. Bingham forthrightly opposed the Ku Klux Klan in the twenties, and the papers editorialized against Klan activities throughout the country. To the transplanted North Carolinian, this was something quite different from the Klan of his father, Colonel Robert.[23]

According to George C. Wright in *Life Behind a Veil*, the "Louisville Way" consisted of the mild reactions of both whites and blacks to the racial strictures of the day. Bingham gave both time and money to several interracial organizations that followed this path. However, racial affairs never ranked high on Bingham's list of priorities. He recognized that African Americans needed better educational opportunity, health, and housing. Similar to many old-line progressives, he placed the greatest hope for both poor blacks and poor whites in education, agreeing with George Colvin, state superintendent of public instruction, that black youth needed "practical courses," that is, vocational and domestic-service training, in order to find their economic niche in America. For that reason Bingham supported the Lincoln Institute in Shelby County and the African American college in Frankfort. In the same vein he also continued his contributions to Berea College, a school that assumed the responsibility of educating and uplifting poor white Appalachian youth.[24]

After being a member of the board of the Louisville Urban League for several years, Bingham resigned in the early twenties, citing the increasing difficulty of attending meetings. He claimed the same cause for resigning from the board of the Booker T. Washington Community Center at Ninth and Magazine in Louisville. Clearly, Bingham saw his role in racial affairs as that of an enlightened, benevolent, and paternalistic southerner. He never got close enough to the problem of racism in America to believe that anything other than a semi-moderate approach would suffice. The racist "Hambone" and "Joe, Asbestos and the Horses" cartoons continued to be prominent fixtures in the daily *Courier* in the twenties. Both relied on stereotypically Negro characters for comic effect, expressing the general racial mores of the community and of Bingham as well. "In the main, I think that the negro [*sic*] is better off in the South than anywhere else," Bingham explained to a fellow southerner. Although he might soften the hardest edges of the rampant racism of his day, he lacked the imagination and inclination to tamper with the racial mores of his time and community.[25]

Bingham did not lack concern for his fellow man. Slowly in the twenties his views of labor unions altered to the conclusion that some union organization was necessary in order to raise not only workers' expectations but their real income as well. However, he never entertained the possibility of allowing guild organization at his newspapers.[26]

After the decline of the farm cooperative movement in the mid-twenties, Bingham kept up his support of the nation's farmers. However, similar to many other insightful farm leaders, he had no quick fix for the ills of agriculture, understanding that American farmers needed nearly revolutionary programs, such as cooperation, in order to solve their problems. He cautioned against a "cutout" of the 1925 tobacco crop, because of the fear that violence would break out in the tobacco belt. When tobacco prices plunged again in 1927, the Judge urged farmers to join in pooling their crops to ward off the continued low prices that the market would force upon them. He never supported the McNary-Haugen bills and applauded each time President Calvin Coolidge vetoed that legislation. In 1927 he accepted an appointment to the Business Men's Commission on Agriculture sponsored by the National Chambers of Commerce and the National Industrial Conference Board to study the agricultural problems of the United States. However, little of a substantive nature was done by anyone as the agricultural depression of the 1920s deepened long before the Great Crash and onset of the Great Depression.[27]

On foreign-policy issues Bingham and his papers adhered to a strict Wilsonian internationalism in the twenties. Bingham's early support for the Versailles Treaty and the League of Nations never wavered. When he first took over the papers, he assumed that Wilson's ideals of internationalism suited the spirit of the times. As antitreaty sentiment intensified in the United States Senate, Bingham made his first direct effort since becoming editor to influence national afffairs by sending telegrams to all members of that body asking that they support the treaty. He urged that Democrats, in particular, not join the "Borah battalion of death" in assaulting the only means for lasting peace available. Colonel Edward M. House and the peripatetic Bernard M. Baruch, two of the most important Democratic-party power brokers in the interwar period, had a profound influence on Bingham, particularly the former. After Wilson left office, Bingham retained his reverence for the former president and helped found the Woodrow Wilson Foundation.[28]

Bingham's partisanship on the League issue led to his support of groups championing that goal in the twenties, and he never gave up on the hope that one day the United States would join the League of Nations. His financial maintenance of the "Pro-League Independents," of which Irving Fisher served as president in the early twenties, revealed the Judge's belief that such organizations had continued viability. Consequently, when the American Defense Society turned against League ratification, Bingham quickly severed his connection with that organization. Membership in the more liberal Foreign Policy Association in the early twenties coincided with Bingham's views of a stronger international role for the United States. The association included such prominent internationalists on its board of directors as Carlton J. H. Hayes, John Dewey, Felix Frankfurter, and Reverend John A. Ryan. Bingham also believed that the United States should become a member of the International Court of Justice. The most important League advocacy group, the League of Nations Non-Partisan Association, received the full support of Bingham, who assumed the chairmanship of the Kentucky branch and assigned a *Courier* employee, Claud Perry, to organize county committees across the state. From its New York City offices, the leaders of the Non-Partisan Association always found a sympathetic supporter in the Louisville publisher, who contributed often and generously to their national treasury.[29]

Although hundreds of miles from the ocean and living in a part of the nation that often did not concern itself about foreign affairs, Bingham became firmly convinced that the United States and the English-speaking world should develop closer ties, including lowering their tariff barriers. "Indeed I believe the future of civilization," he explained to a Canadian friend, "depends largely upon a cordial, continuous understanding and co-operation between Great Britain and her great self-governing colonies and the United States." Annual trips to the United Kingdom and a widening circle of English friends convinced him even more of the need for cooperation. In the twenties Bingham corresponded on a regular basis with Colonel Hugh B. Protheroe-Smith, Sir Campbell Stuart, Sir John Frazer, the Reverend R. W. Paul, and other British friends. Their exchanges stressed the need for Anglo-American dialogue on world issues. Bingham also accepted a role in trying to improve relations with the U.K. For example, he served as a founder and later as secretary-treasurer of the Kentucky branch of the English-Speaking Union.[30]

As part of Bingham's efforts on behalf of closer ties with Britain, he helped sponsor a trip to Louisville of former prime minister David Lloyd George in the fall of 1923. Lloyd George, on an extended speaking tour of "the states," agreed to make a brief stopover in Louisville without making a major address. At the same time Bingham also tried, unsuccessfully, to persuade the Englishman to use his influence with the British Imperial Tobacco Company to purchase cooperative tobacco stockpiles in America. On 20 October 1923 Lloyd George arrived from St. Louis and received the honor of being the first guest to sign the register at the recently opened Brown Hotel at Fourth and Broadway, built by Louisvillian J. Graham Brown. "CITY HAILS LLOYD GEORGE AS OUR SON" ran the bold headlines in the *Courier-Journal.* During his two-day visit the prime minister received a royal reception. He played golf at the Louisville Country Club, made a pilgrimage to the Lincoln Memorial at Hodgenville, and attended a banquet in his honor. After moving on to Indianapolis, Lloyd George personally thanked Bingham for his hospitality. These events only reinforced Bingham's attachment to things English and would soon bring charges of his being an Anglophile.[31]

Family remained at the center of Robert Worth Bingham's life in the twenties. On 20 August 1924 he married Aleen Muldoon Hilliard, his third wife, in a ceremony at St. Margaret Church, Westminster, in London. The widow of Louisville stockbroker, Byron Hilliard, who died in early 1922, the new Mrs. Bingham was herself wealthy. In an agreement made before their marriage the third Mrs. Bingham gave up "all her interest" in her husband's estate in return for a one-million-dollar settlement. As part of that arrangement three hundred thousand dollars was given to her before Bingham's death and the remainder from his estate. Only a few members of the family, including children Robert, Jr., Henrietta, and Barry, and some close friends, attended the wedding in London. The couple immediately left for a tour of England and the continent.[32]

The Judge's relationship with his father continued to be one of increasing responsibility as the old colonel entered advanced age. Robert Worth made one final expensive effort to save the Bingham School in the twenties and honored his father with buildings in his name at the University of North Carolina at Chapel Hill and the Richmond Presbyterian Seminary in Virginia, and paid to have the colonel's name included on the Stone Mountain Confederate memorial in Georgia. Colonel Robert's health declined abruptly in the early twenties and he spent his remaining years as an invalid at the school. His son saw to it that his days were spent as comfortably as possible.[33]

On 8 May 1927 Colonel Robert Bingham died. After funeral rites at the Asheville First Presbyterian Church, he was buried at the nearby Riverside Cemetery. Although the physical link between the Old South generation of the elder Bingham and the New South generation of Robert Worth had been broken, the younger Bingham's life continued to radiate the southern mystique. The Bingham School, however, soon closed its doors forever.[34]

The Bingham children came of age in the early twenties, but not without problems. Robert, Jr., the eldest, battled alcoholism, while Henrietta, the middle child, fought her own battles with alcohol, as well as against authority and convention. Only Barry, the youngest, lived up to his father's expectations.

Young Robert's addiction tainted all the family. While working at the *Courier-Journal*, he fell into periodic drinking bouts with Robert "Bum" Callahan, the son of staunch Catholic prohibitionist P. H. Callahan. Robert Worth Bingham resorted to attempts at closeting and keeping an around-the-clock watch on young Robert, whose binge drinking he compared with that of the late Mary Lily. During the height of the effort to organize farm co-ops, Robert's condition worsened. "I think much if not most of the fault is mine," Bingham wrote his daughter. The Judge bought what became the Standard Gravure Company in hopes that by working there Robert would change his life. But the drinking worsened. Robert could not "take hold" of the family business, according to his brother. Eventually, Robert left Louisville, moving to England, where he married and worked for a London firm.[35]

Henrietta also received the best of opportunities and squandered most. She graduated from Louisville Collegiate School then went off to study at Stuart Hall in Staunton, Virginia. She attended Smith College but did not graduate. From an early age she showed an interest in the arts and, for a period in the late twenties, worked to organize publication of the *Theatre Arts Monthly*, serving briefly as editor, and all the while receiving a substantial monthly stipend from her father. For a short while in the twenties she and Edith Callahan operated the Wilderness Road bookstore in Louisville. But for most of the twenties and thirties she lived in England, moving back to the United States permanently only after the death of her father. Her father financed her every whim and could not control her rebelliousness.[36]

While in England, Henrietta became "a fringe member of the celebrated Bloomsbury group," a famous literary circle of the twenties. In *Love in Bloomsbury*, Frances Partridge reminisced that Henrietta, "a glamorous femme fatale," openly practiced bisexualism and drifted from male to female companions with some abandon. "Henrietta had nothing to say for herself," Partridge explained, "but managed by her meaning silences and her husky singing of negro [sic] spirituals to a guitar, to break many hearts belonging to both sexes." Apparently Henrietta suffered from some mental distress and traveled to the continent for psychoanalysis. Like Robert, Jr., she abused alcohol and drifted from one unfulfilled venture to another.[37]

The Judge's last hope for his children's success came in his youngest child, Barry. If Henrietta and Robert, Jr., tried the patience and taxed the fortune of their father, Barry appeared to be just the opposite. "He is really wonderful, the most brilliant, exhilarating, lovely boy in the world," the Judge wrote his daughter, who could not have taken such praise of a sibling lightly. Barry "is . . . his mother over again," he continued.[38]

Barry, who attended the private Patterson-Davenport School and the Richmond School in Louisville in the primary grades, spent one term at the Bingham School and graduated from the Middlesex School in Concord, Massachusetts, a "very starchy New England" preparatory school. At the latter he came in contact with young men of backgrounds quite different from those of the southerners of Kentucky and North Carolina he was more familiar with as he prepared for admission to Harvard University. When Barry's grades in mathematics lagged a bit, his father arranged for special tutoring from professors at the University of Louisville. Barry, like his sister, demonstrated a predilection for the theater and the arts—in his case, for prose and poetry. When the youngster wrote a volume of poems, the elder Bingham had it published in 1923. Later that year Barry entered Harvard. Before he left for his first semester, the Judge demonstrated his regard for Barry in a letter to a cooperative associate. "My lovely Barry is at home now," the proud father exclaimed, "he is filling this house with sunshine and I am having a very happy time."[39]

After Barry finished his four years at Harvard with a major in English, he took a year off to write a novel, "Battle in the Dark," one that he himself found to be "very turgid" and unpublishable. With no word ever being spoken, he understood he would eventually return to Louisville and the newspapers. Consequently, after that year away from Glenview, he came back to work as a continuity writer for WHAS under the tutelage of Credo Harris, who "was more like a benevolent uncle than a boss." He soon moved over to the newspapers, becoming a city reporter for the *Louisville Times,* where he picked up valuable experience in the businesses that would one day come under his direction.[40]

The elder Bingham's lifestyle in the twenties befitted a man of his wealth, power, and influence. Bingham added to his memberships in prestigious clubs by joining the Metropolitan Club in Washington, D.C., and the Louisiana Gulf Coast Club. He could afford an expensive yacht anchored in Jacksonville, Florida, and a bronze bust of himself for his home.[41]

That home itself and the surrounding property received an infusion of Bingham money in the twenties. A tennis court, swimming pool, and immaculate gardens and grounds added to the comforts of "Melcombe Bingham," named after an ancestral home of the English

Binghams whom the Judge claimed as ancestors. Bingham's attachment to things British became more pronounced in the selection of
improvements in his mansion. The addition of a billiard room and
palm room to the "Great Hall" followed the English manor style. Moreover, a set of iron gates produced in England added that special old-
country touch over an archway that still contained the ornamental *B*
from the time when Charles Ballard owned the estate. A well-designed
amphitheater served the artistic tastes of the younger Binghams. Local theatrical groups began producing plays there in the summertime.
Along with thirteen other industrialists, lawyers, and other professionals, the inhabitants of Glenview created their own separate sphere, a
compound for the wealthy, far different from any other community in
Kentucky.[42]

Wealth and the financial success of the papers allowed Bingham to
indulge two of his passions—hunting and travel to the United Kingdom. Annual trips to England and Scotland became longer in dura-
tion and more extensive in the 1920s. Bingham often rented Guthrie
Castle in Scotland, a two-thousand-acre estate, for three months in
the late summer and early fall. There he hunted to his heart's content, even using "beaters" on occasion to increase the kill by driving
more game toward the hunters.[43]

In the early 1920s he and a few other investors began buying up
southwest-Georgia farmland near Newton and formed the Bedess Pecan Company, the area becoming known as the Pineland Plantation.
Although the land was originally purchased for investment, Bingham
drew his greatest pleasure from having exclusive rights to hunt over
several thousand acres. On one occasion he and a few friends were
indicted "on charge of shooting doves in a baited field" at Pineland.
The charges were later dropped for lack of evidence.[44]

In addition to his love of hunting, the Louisvillian also developed a
liking for fine hunting dogs and spent considerable sums for their
purchase, breeding, and upkeep at the Pineland location. By the mid-
thirties he had over seventy-five purebred hunting dogs at Pineland.
With members of the Juniper Hunt Club of Louisville and such national groups as the Delta Duck Club, he traveled to other southern
locations for hunting. Moreover, this recreation kindled a keen interest in state and national legislation affecting hunting.[45]

Bingham's health continued to be of concern in the 1920s. Periodic
problems with eczema brought him to the Johns Hopkins University

Hospital for "radiotherapy" in 1921. He suffered another setback necessitating an emergency appendectomy in late July 1925 and compounded his health problems by his incessant cigarette-smoking habit. His wealth allowed him the advantage of the best health services and medical facilities in America.[46]

Wealth and the continued prosperity of the Bingham companies also permitted him to increase his support of charities. He received a multitude of requests from individuals and organizations each year and established an annual amount that he subscribed to such needs. Kentucky institutions received the largest benefit of the Bingham fortune. Berea College counted the Louisville publisher among its trustees and benefactors, even naming a cow "Courier-Journal" in his honor. Hindman Settlement School in Knott County also received continuing Bingham support. The Kentucky Children's Home Society, where Bingham served as a longtime board member, remained one of his key charitable interests; he donated twenty-five thousand dollars in the mid-twenties to build "The Eleanor M. Bingham Memorial Hospital" at that facility. His institutional support also included the University of Louisville, the Masonic lodge, Alpha Tau Omega fraternity, and the Gimghouls, and he even donated occasionally to small churches in the state.[47]

Although he preferred to donate to institutions rather than to individuals, Bingham sometimes directly supported persons he deemed worthy. Those donations ranged from paying doctor's expenses for a widow, to sending a needy student to nursing school, to paying for a poor tenant farmer's subscription to the *Courier-Journal*. When Henry Watterson's widow needed money, owing to her husband's disregard of finances during his lifetime, Bingham signed five thousand dollars in notes at James B. Brown's National Bank of Kentucky to care for her needs. Although Bingham believed he had a "duty to give away" a portion of his fortune, he established firm guidelines for his philanthropic stewardship.[48]

After concentrating on the reorganization of the papers in the early 1920s, Bingham branched out into additional business interests in middecade. He got caught up in the economic optimism of that decade, and he played the market with some relish. Yet he never plunged into the market to join the speculative frenzy of the "Jazz Age." James C. Wilson and Company of Louisville, as well as other brokers in that city and New York, handled most of his business. The Judge became more interested in oil stock in the 1920s and kept his large holdings in Standard Oil. Along with old law partner W. W. Davies, he invested in such southern companies as the Bedess Pecan Company of Georgia and the American Tar Products Company. In Louisville he bought into such firms as the Frank Fehr Cold Storage Company and the B. F. Avery Company.[49]

For the most part Bingham's papers and other investments did well in the 1920s, with a one-thousand-dollar per day gross in mid-1923 for the *Courier* and *Times*. In 1922 he paid three thousand dollars to lawyer Elwood Hamilton, an old progressive ally, for preparing his income taxes, a sum indicating the size of the Bingham income and the health of his inherited fortune. Bingham, like most American citizens, complained a bit about federal income taxes and as late as 1924 employed another Louisville lawyer to pursue the return of a portion of nearly twenty-two thousand dollars he had paid to the federal government in 1918.[50]

One Bingham financial venture in partnership with the widow of John C. C. Mayo, James B. Brown, and Percy Haly, eventually failed. The formation of the Standard Petroleum Company became more complicated when Brown purchased control of the *Herald* and *Post* while his National Bank of Kentucky held loans for that company. After sinking several thousand dollars down a dry well near Tucumcari, New Mexico, Bingham suggested that he and his fellow investors "dissolve the corporation, go out of business and . . . digest our losses as best we can." The directors of Standard Petroleum did just that in 1926. Bingham's speculation never exceeded his rather conservative limits on such ventures; he tempered his financial advice to others with paternalism. For example, when stock values in the Swiss Oil Company, another Bingham investment and the forerunner of the Ashland Oil Corporation, fell suddenly and caught short a young investor who could not stand the loss, Bingham bought back the stock at the original price.[51]

Most of Bingham's business dealings in the 1920s, in one way or another, came into eventual conflict with the enigmatic James B. Brown, his financial, publishing, and political competitor. Brown, who liked to work in the middle of the night and gamble at French Lick Springs in southern Indiana and Churchill Downs, took increasing dictatorial control of the BancoKentucky in middecade. After serving as a director of the National Bank of Kentucky through early 1924, and using that institution to service a note for $440,000, Bingham resigned and sold nearly $34,000 in stock when Brown became a newspaper competitor. Moreover, the publisher of the *Courier-Journal* and the *Louisville Times* had increasing reservations about the political manipulation and financial scheming of Brown.[52]

The case of the Inter-Southern Insurance Company of Louisville in the twenties demonstrated the tenuous nature of many American businesses in the "prosperity decade." Owing to poor management, Inter-Southern entered middecade in a deep financial crisis, as did numerous companies in the nation at the time. Brown, Bingham, and other Louisville movers and shakers involved themselves in an effort to save the company in 1926. Lee L. Miles, president of the Louisville Taxicab and Transfer Company; Attilla Cox, lawyer and director of the Fidelity and Columbia Trust Company; and Dinwiddie Lampton, president of the American Life and Accident Insurance Company of Louisville, served with Bingham and Brown as directors of Inter-Southern.[53]

Bingham and the other directors worked to keep the company from falling completely into the hands of Brown, whom they deeply distrusted. The *Courier* and *Times* publisher tried to place Inter-Southern into what he considered the "good hands" of Rogers Caldwell, a Nashville financier, whose Caldwell and Company held top rank as the leading holding company in the mid-South. Bingham dispatched Emanuel Levi to "dicker" with Caldwell in mid-March 1926. The Tennessean finally agreed to take control of the company while leaving its main offices in Louisville. Bingham received seventy-thousand dollars for his shares of stock and appeared relieved that Brown had again been checked. To Bernard Baruch the Louisvillian exulted that "we finally whipped Brown," and turned the company over to Caldwell, who "is always as good as his word." Ironically, it would not be long before Brown and Caldwell formed one of the most unusual alliances in American economic history, one that played a prominent role in Louisville's severe banking crisis of early-depression days in 1930.[54]

chapter seven

Politics in the Twenties

The "Damnedest" Again

IN ADDITION TO BINGHAM'S cooperative efforts, re-organization of the newspapers, and family responsibilities, he took an avid interest in local, state, and national politics. "I shall never in any circumstances be a candidate for any political office," he explained in the twenties. Critics charged that he tried to manipulate the Kentucky Democratic party and political events using his wealth and the power of his papers.[1]

"Independent" is the way Bingham often described his political course in the 1920s. In that decade he did just that in local and state races while supporting the Democratic party in presidential elections. "I am entirely independent and am operating my newspapers on that basis," he told a fellow member of the North American Newspaper Alliance. To another political confidant he haughtily proclaimed that "patriotism is above party affiliation, and I believe that a firm stand on this principle by men who have no political aspirations, but who have the real interest of the state and country at heart, is likely to have a continuing beneficial effect." While the southern mystique never lost its hold, he began to take a more national and international perspective with the purchase of the papers. Furthermore, Bingham declared an educational role for himself and his papers. "We are trying very hard to give the people of Kentucky facts unadorned and unembellished," he explained, "both with reference to the deplorable situation for our state and its fiscal education and other matters of grave concern."[2]

In the national political arena Bingham's support of the Democratic party contrasted with his more independent tack in local and state politics. A protégé of Colonel Edward M. House, Bingham remained forever a devotee of Wilson as the ideal southerner turned internationalist. In the first national election after purchase of the Louisville papers, Bingham established his pattern of total support of a Democratic candidate for the presidency during the campaign of 1920. Of course, support of women's suffrage appeared to him the logical result of progressivism's quest for justice and democratic reform. He viewed the election of 1920 as the first test of the new political order and a referendum on the League of Nations. He was to be disappointed.[3]

Pondering the possibilities for the presidency in 1920, Bingham first considered supporting Illinois Republican governor Frank O. Lowden, a particular favorite among the farm bloc in the Midwest. However, he never used his papers to start a boom for the governor. Early that year Bingham refused to become personally involved in Democratic-party organizational activity, but he assured one Democratic leader that he would support that party in his papers as long as it stood for "strong, intelligent, patriotic action." When Homer Cummings, chairman of the National Democratic Committee, toured Louisville in the spring, Bingham acted as his host. On the other hand, Bingham praised a Louisville speech made by Will H. Hays, chairman of the Republican National Committee, as one that raised "the whole standard of political discussion." Bingham looked for a high-minded purpose as the premise of the American democratic system. "I hope that the politicians and office seekers in both parties may be educated or clubbed into taking the same position," he told Hays, "because the result will be beneficial to our country, and it is our country which I know you and I hold first in our hearts."[4]

After the nomination of Governor James M. Cox, Bingham joined in support of the Ohioan. "I shall take pride and pleasure in supporting you as forcefully and effectively as possible," the Judge explained. When Cox asked that the Louisvillian make some speeches on his behalf in Kentucky, Bingham declined, claiming that newspaper publishers should make few if any speeches of a political nature. However, he offered advice, service, and money. First, he suggested that Cox make full use of the services of James B. Brown, who "exerts influence in many directions" and who would bring out the "Irish" vote in Louisville. Second, he assigned Arthur Krock to work full-time for the Democratic National Committee and paid his salary. Third, the Judge contributed at least ten thousand dollars to the coffers of the national committee and nearly as much to the state committee.[5]

In the 1920 general election, incumbent Senator J. C. W. Beckham, a longtime Bingham political ally and the first popularly elected senator in the Commonwealth, stood for reelection against Republican Richard P. Ernst. As usual, factionalism in the state worked to the disadvantage of both the state and national Democratic candidates. The Stanley and Beckham factions' struggle for control of the state Democratic organization hurt Cox's national race. Bingham supported Beckham and Cox with both words and money. The *Courier* editorialized that the election of Cox meant "going in" the League of Nations and the fulfillment of American aims in World War I. Just before the election old progressive ally Lewis Humphrey of the *Louisville Evening Post* congratulated Bingham and his papers. "You have made a clean-cut, logical, temperate, and intelligent campaign," Humphrey announced, "not one whit inferior to that presented by the great Democratic morning journals of New York City."[6]

On election night a festive crowd estimated at nearly five thousand gathered outside the Third and Liberty Street offices of the *Courier* to hear the results. They did not have long to wait as Cox conceded the presidential race at eleven o'clock P.M. The results of the campaign proved to be disastrous to Democrats. While Beckham lost to Ernst by less than five thousand votes and Cox took the state by a small majority, Warren G. Harding's "normalcy" campaign carried the nation with a landslide 60 percent popular majority. State Democratic leaders claimed that election fraud in the heavily Republican mountain areas of the commonwealth added to the GOP poll and the defeat of Beckham, but nothing substantive came of the charges. The Republican sweep included Jefferson County and other areas of the state as well. Republican Edwin P. Morrow of Somerset held the governor's post in Frankfort, having defeated Governor J. D. Black in 1919. The nation entered the "Prosperity Decade," with Republicans entrenched in the nation's capital and with more support in Kentucky than since before the turn of the century.[7]

Kentucky politics for the remainder of the twenties turned into competition between the Democratic party, with its two prominent factions, and the generally united Republicans. On occasion several

Democratic and Republican leaders would unite in a so-called "bi-partisan combine" to defeat a reform-minded Democratic-party candidate. The Kentucky Jockey Club, an organization that controlled the state's racetracks, "the coal crowd," and occasionally whiskey and textbook interests, joined in a cabal of political intrigue that matched any political machine in the nation. Maurice Galvin, a northern-Kentucky Republican state legislator, and Billy Klair, a Lexington Democratic ward heeler and state legislator, served as the nominal leaders of the combine, with the aid of U.S. representative J. Campbell Cantrill and former Democratic senator Johnson Camden. By controlling blocks of urban voters, the "combine" wielded considerable power from time to time.[8]

To counter the Stanley faction in the Democratic party and the machinations of the bipartisan combine, Bingham united with former governor and senator Beckham and his longtime ally, Percy Haly, into a political combination that represented old-fashioned Democratic-party progressivism. This "triumvirate," according to James C. Klotter in *The Breckinridges of Kentucky,* consisted of "the publicist, the boss, the politician," who "viewed themselves as the reform element and made moral issues their chief target" in the twenties. Bingham considered himself a reformer, albeit self-righteously according to his political enemies.[9]

Kentucky progressives in the twenties, like their cohorts across the nation, fought a rear guard and often losing battle against the antireform tide of the decade. Many Democratic progressives associated their reformist idealism with Beckham, Bingham, and the Wilsonian tradition. Elwood Hamilton, a law partner of Beckham; Alben Barkley, Democratic congressman from the first district in far western Kentucky; Helm Bruce, a Louisville lawyer; and Harry Sommers, editor of the *Elizabethtown News,* typified Kentuckians who still believed in the idealism of progressivism in the twenties. The Kentucky progressives of the Bingham-Beckham-Haly variety supported national prohibition and other reformist ideals of the prewar years. They viewed themselves as bearers of light in a world of political darkness, that is, a world of corruption and self-seeking officeholders. Their idea of "real politik" differed substantially from that of other Democrats in the state.[10]

Former governor and senator A. O. Stanley, who presided over the most progressive legislative years in the state's history during the era of World War I, and editor Desha Breckinridge of the *Lexington Herald,* represented progressivism of another variety, particularly on the subject of prohibition. "I do not think you and I are very likely to disagree on principles," Bingham announced to Breckinridge, "though we might disagree sometimes on the best method of securing the results which we should both like to attain." Stanley and Breckinridge would often be at odds with the Bingham-Beckham-Haly faction in the 1920s, and on occasion, contrary to the Louisvillian's assessment, the conflict would be over principles and other substantive matters.[11]

Bingham aggressively pursued the role of political activist in the twenties. Eventually his views and those expressed in the papers under his direction merged into a singular philosophy. In Louisville he ran into the resurgent Republican party led by local bosses J. Matt Chilton and Chesley H. Searcy, who enjoyed attacking the personal record of Bingham. However, Bingham had both respect for and personal rapport with Republican senator Richard P. Ernst and former GOP governor Augustus E. Willson (1907–11). During the Republican administration of Governor E. P. Morrow in the early twenties he even found a good word for that old political figure, elected on the inane promise of freeing "old dog Ring" in order to ensure himself of the support of Kentucky mountaineers. But Morrow also promised to take the state Board of Charities and Corrections, a special interest of Bingham, out of the political arena. His early record in this area received the glowing support of Bingham.[12]

The Louisville publisher held greatest contempt for members of his own party, including the aforementioned Klair, Cantrill, Camden, as well as Charles I. Dawson, Judge Allie Young, and Eli Brown. These men he condemned as either leaders or pawns of the bipartisan combine and the antiprogressive faction in the Democratic party. Moreover, he viewed Stanley as a fellow traveler who had abandoned his earlier progressive predilections. If Bingham appeared to eschew the idea of running for political office, he nonetheless had no qualms about using his newspapers, money, and any other means at his disposal to influence decisions of a political nature. For example, he suggested names for judicial appointments and even occasionally lobbied with judges in an attempt to sway their decisions. Moreover, he encouraged the political activities of *Courier-Journal* Frankfort reporter Vance Armentrout, who carried out the Judge's agenda in the state capital. According to Bingham's code of conduct, all this was permissible and lofty in purpose as long as the people of the state were better served in the end.[13]

With prohibition in force, women voting for the first time, and American entry into the League of Nations nearly a dead issue, race-track gambling and the political influence of the Jockey Club became the primary Kentucky issues that struck a moralist nerve with Judge Bingham in the 1920s. Robert F. Sexton, in an article about "The Crusade Against Parimutuel Gambling" in that decade has suggested that the movement against racetrack betting "was, first, a truly significant issue in Kentucky and secondly, that it was a significant part of the reform movement in the twentieth century." It became important in gubernatorial primaries and general elections in 1923 and 1927. Moreover, it provided a classic example of an issue of a state-wide nature that united many old progressive "good government" reformers in a decade that is often pictured as the nadir of reformism.[14]

From the Louisville Churchmen's Federation, founded in 1910, came the Kentucky Anti-Pari-Mutuel Gambling Commission, headed by Baptist minister M. P. Hunt at the beginning of the 1920s. The commission included several prominent citizens such as Helm Bruce; William Heyburn, a wealthy businessman and president of the Belknap Hardware Company; C. C. Stoll, operator of the Stoll Refining Company; and Patrick Henry Callahan, president of the Louisville Varnish Company and an active Catholic layman. "Our Motto: Race Track Gambling, Kentucky's outstanding disgrace must go," became the ambition of the commission in a state that prided itself on the breeding of thoroughbred stock, the Kentucky Derby, and the Old South milieu associated with the Kentucky colonel, mint juleps, and the sporting blood. At the time, Kentucky represented one of only a few states in the nation that allowed racing but on-track betting as well.[15]

Bingham did not join the early organizational efforts of the anti-gambling crusaders. He came to their way of thinking after determining that the Jockey Club, led by Colonel Matt Winn, Thomas J. Combs, Maurice Galvin, James B. Brown, and Johnson N. Camden, dabbled too much in the politics of the state. As late as September 1922 Bingham took no exception to the activities of the Jockey Club, but early the next year both he and Alben W. Barkley began questioning the power of the racing crowd. The Louisville publisher became convinced that the leadership of the Jockey Club and of the Kentucky Coal Operators Association acted as one in attempts to control the state legislature. He encouraged his friends to sever their ties with the Jockey Club and soon convinced William F. Bradshaw, a fellow leader in the tobacco cooperative effort, to resign as a director of that organization. Bradshaw told James B. Brown that he could not "approve the methods that I have since found are employed by the Club in the matter of participating in State politics." Several religious leaders applauded Bingham's coming over to the anti-racetrack-gambling crusade, like one Henderson minister who exclaimed: "It is in fact, a source of keen satisfaction to note that you are backing every moral, political, and industrial effort that makes for the progress of our state."[16]

In the Democratic gubernatorial primary of 1923, the Bingham-Beckham-Haly faction coalesced into a potent political force. Bingham by this time had given up on supporters of Senator Stanley, whom he found to be little different from the bipartisan crowd. Bingham kept his word that he would never run for political office, perhaps having learned a lesson from the career of William Randolph Hearst, and refused to consider running for the governorship that year. Editor Desha Breckinridge of the *Lexington Herald* urged that Bingham get into the race for governor. However, Breckinridge and his Louisville competitor soon joined opposite sides in the 1923 primary.[17]

As spring came, two major candidates emerged in the race for the Democratic-party nomination. Congressman J. C. Cantrill of Georgetown, a force in the state legislature and the apparent candidate of the bipartisan combine, entered the primary against ten-term congressman Alben W. Barkley. Elwood Hamilton, law partner of Beckham, became the state chairman for Barkley. The western Kentuckian had a record of support for prohibition, and for that reason picked up the Beckham people.[18]

Barkley, after receiving Haly's counsel, adopted anti-race track gambling and a severance tax on coal as the cornerstones of his campaign. These positions struck directly at the heart of the bipartisan combine and the racetrack and coal interests. Some historians assumed that Barkley never wanted the govenorship, having set his sights on the U.S. Senate race in 1926. He wisely foresaw that a race for governor would give him the visibility, the contacts, and the creation of a statewide organization necessary for a later race. The congressman's campaign in 1923 established him as a capable statewide campaigner, the "iron man" who could make five speeches or more in a day.[19]

In mid-April Bingham began his campaign to find a candidate to oppose Cantrill and did not totally commit himself and his papers to Barkley until late June. However, in an editorial entitled "Mr. Cantrill and 'the Interests,'" the *Courier* left no doubt that it opposed the nomination of the machine candidate. Later in the summer Bingham declared to several political confidants that "Barkley is the better man." "I am not interested in individuals or in parties, but in principles," the Judge explained. "I am convinced that Mr. Barkley represents now the principles which I believe should be put in force if we are to have progress in Kentucky," being "the only hope of the decent people of the state." To Barkley-supporter lawyer Alice Lloyd, a Maysville political activist and prohibitionist, Bingham maintained that he had no "ulterior motives," having only a "disinterested" desire to better the state.[20]

Whether serious or not about winning the primary, Barkley fought hard against an entrenched Democratic machine. Never personally attacking Cantrill, Barkley railed against "the system." "Woodrow Wilson drove the crooks and corruptionists out of New Jersey," he declared, "Governor Pinchot is driving them out of Pennsylvania, I propose to drive them out of Frankfort."[21]

In the early-August primary Cantrill won, as Barkley's efforts to "combine moral and anti-trust crusades" failed. Cantrill won by nine thousand votes statewide and carried Louisville by twelve thousand, while receiving nearly 80 percent of the tally in Billy Klair's Lexington stronghold. A modified rural-urban split apparently divided the Democratic party. Barkley carried the rural areas in central and western Kentucky, and Cantrill took bipartisan strongholds in the urban areas as well as the mountain counties. Bingham, Hamilton, and other Democratic progressives could only console themselves that they had fought the good fight in opposition to the corrupt influences as they saw them in the Democratic party.[22]

The congressman from Georgetown did not live to run in the fall general election, dying in early September from the complications of a ruptured appendix. Some anticombine partisans claimed that Cantrill had been in poor health all along, needing the aid of a "pulmotor" to keep him alive for a time. Although Barkley appeared to be the logical choice to assume the candidacy, he declined. The state Democratic Central Committee chose U.S. congressman William Jason Fields, "Honest Bill from Olive Hill," as their substitute nominee. Fields, the ranking member of the Military Affairs Committee, received the immediate and wholehearted support of Barkley.[23]

In the general election the Bingham papers took no stand on the candidacy of either Fields or the Republican nominee, Kentucky Court of Appeals judge Charles I. Dawson. On election day a Democratic landslide brought Fields into the statehouse, as the Democratic party carried Jefferson County for the first time in seven years. A *Courier* editorial two days after the election declared that "Kentucky is a Democratic State and this is a Democratic year." At least in the short run Bingham took a wait-and-see position on the possibilities of the upcoming Fields administration. Privately Bingham declared that his support of Barkley had been worth the effort and vowed to pursue "the course which I have adopted." That approach would soon run head-on into the administration of Fields and his lieutenant governor, General Henry H. Denhardt. Moreover, the Kentucky Anti-Pari-Mutuel Gambling Commission fully intended to bring its ideas before the upcoming session of the 1924 Kentucky General Assembly.[24]

In the first days of the meeting of the Kentucky legislature, the anti-racetrack gambling group petitioned Fields to push for the removal of legislative approval of wagering. A few days later Fields delivered his opening message to the general assembly; he did not mention racetrack gambling. Instead, he proposed passage of a $75 million highway bond issue, development of teachers' colleges at Murray and Morehead, an increase in the gasoline tax to three cents per gallon, and an effort to pay off the "floating public debt" based on the old state warrant system.[25]

A *Courier* editorial scored the governor's speech, finding fault with the premise of the road-bond suggestion. How could the people trust the old crowd in Frankfort, and in particular the personnel of the State Highway Commission? the paper asked. Moreover, the *Courier* pointed out that an obvious political debt had been paid with the appointment of James B. Brown to the State Tax Commission and suggested openly that the "bi-partisan coalition" was in control. The role of "special interests" in the Fields administration became the rallying cry for its opponents, both Republican and Democratic. For the first time Bingham and his papers took on an administration in Frankfort and tried to mold public policy to the specific liking of the Judge and his political cohorts Beckham and Haly.[26]

Today the conflict between Bingham and Fields appears a bit ironic. As a congressman, Fields demonstrated a rather progressive record. He voted with the Wilson administration, supporting the Federal Reserve System, the Eighteenth Amendment, women's suffrage, and admission to the League of Nations. Moreover, he supported marketing laws and farm cooperation. All the foregoing should have made Bingham less opposed to the candidacy and administration of Fields. Did the Louisvillian oppose Fields because of the defeat of Barkley, or the last-minute choice of Fields by the state committee, or the inability of the Beckham-Bingham-Haly faction to dictate to "Honest Bill" their desires? Quite possibly all of these reasons played a role in the antipathy that developed between Bingham and Fields. However, the primary cause for the conflict came over principles and issues that arose in the first days of the Fields administration and that coincided with the meeting of the legislature. More specifically, Bingham and Fields stood poles apart on the road-bond issue. The aristocratic Bingham and the wily mountain politician Fields also offered a contrast in style and manner as well as on substantive state issues.[27]

Kentuckians divided sharply on the proposition of spending substantial amounts of money—two-thirds of the proposed $75 million bonds—on an improved state highway system. The first step would be passage of enabling legislation in the general assembly, to be followed by a referendum of the people of the state. Organizations formed to push their agendas. The Greater Kentucky Committee of the Kentucky Good Roads Association, chaired by Desha Breckinridge, called for immediate support of Fields's bond issue. Breckinridge and others argued that other states such as North Carolina had already begun ambitious highway construction plans and the need for quick action to catch up with surrounding states.[28]

When first asked to join the Good Roads Association in September 1923, Bingham admitted that the bond issue was a good idea. However, he expressed grave doubts that such a program could be administered fairly in the politically ridden atmosphere in Frankfort. The State Efficiency Commission, given the responsibility of studying the state's institutions and suggesting remedies for improving services to the people of the commonwealth, opposed the road-bond approach.

Governor Fields immediately charged that the efficiency commission's report was "indefensible and inexcusable." Bingham, however, viewed the whole suggestion with suspicion born of his having lived in the state for nearly three decades. "We cannot afford to ask the people of Kentucky to vote for a great sum of money for roads unless we know the money is going to be spent honestly and competently," the Judge argued. Soon a "Pay-As-You-Go" group formed to oppose the Good Roads Association, with Bingham as its principal contributor. He gave as much as five thousand dollars to see the message of the Pay-As-You-Go organization spread across the state in the coming weeks.[29]

With Desha Breckinridge of the *Lexington Herald* championing the road bonds as the beginning of a new day in Kentucky, and the Bingham papers taking the opposite tack, the bond-issue fight promised to be one of great importance in 1924. The eventual referendum vote, if passed by the state legislature, would coincide with the 1924 presidential race and an important senatorial contest in Kentucky. The bonds would not only fund roads but also contribute to maintenance of state prisons, charities, and education, by imposing higher taxes on gasoline and special licenses. The Bingham-Breckinridge debate degenerated into bitter recrimination and sarcasm on the part of the Lexingtonian. Somewhat "facetiously," he predicted that children and others who would be helped by the bond issue would one day be heard "in a plaintive murmur, an almost inarticulate cry toward heaven all of them in one broken voice thanking God again and again for Robert W. Bingham." Another old progressive ally, Lewis Humphrey of the *Louisville Evening Post,* also broke with Bingham and supported the Good Roads Association.[30]

If the Bingham versus Breckinridge and Humphrey conflict added spice to the Kentucky newspaper business, the debate between Bingham and Governor Fields struck much deeper political chords in the state. The Louisville publisher assumed that Klair, Galvin, and others in the bipartisan combine controlled Fields. For the remainder of the 1924 legislative session, the *Courier* allowed no respite for the beleaguered Fields. When the bond-issue bill passed both houses, the *Courier* accused the administration of using bribery to get the bills through. Moreover, the paper charged that investigations of the state's penal and charitable institutions and the political power of the Jockey Club had been mishandled and eventually sidetracked by Fields's henchmen. Even Lieutenant Governor Denhardt came under fire from the *Courier*, which accused him of being an influence peddler for the bipartisan combine.[31]

The Bingham-Fields personal exchange took place in the full glare of the newspaper medium as each let fly with charges and counter-charges. After a February 19 *Courier* editorial scolded the administration for poor appointments to the highway commission, Fields, in a letter published in the *Evening Post*, asked for proof of Bingham's "imputation of corruption against these gentlemen." Bingham replied two days later that the bond issue had no chance for success with the legislature obviously under the control of Galvin and Klair. He charged that "the people of Kentucky cannot hope for a wise and efficient expenditure" of the road funds based on the deplorable situation in Frankfort. Fields shot back in another public letter that "I do not shrink from the contest you and Mr. Haly have forced on me. For myself I care little. But I know the needs of Kentucky." Furthermore, he claimed that Haly also acted as a political boss who dictated political moves to Bingham.[32]

In his own paper Bingham got in the final word in this exchange with Fields: "It is the interlocking bipartisan machine, manipulated by Galvin and Klair and the influences behind them and fostered by you, which is seeking to destroy the penal and charitable institutions, the schools, the roads, the State Board of Health," Bingham charged. "You and your supporters are keeping Kentucky in political mud. We are trying to help Kentucky out of the mud." At the close of the legislative session, the *Courier*, in a final assault on the Fields record, charged that a conspiracy existed in which coal interests wanted to shift any taxes from themselves to the state's farmers. Having already won respect among farmers because of his efforts on behalf of the tobacco cooperatives, Bingham found a willing audience to listen to his assaults on Fields and the bipartisan combine.[33]

He now had an opportunity to affect the state's political system directly. By attacking Fields and the bipartisan combine, he gathered around him willing antiadministration support. Moreover, his contacts in the farm cooperative effort became a valuable network in the anti-road-bond crusade. This support in itself became bipartisan. For example, former Republican Governor Augustus E. Willson praised Bingham and his papers for "rendering yeoman service" in behalf of the people of the state. "You have put your hand to the plow—hold fast—and press steadily on—cut the furrows straight and deep," the old governor intoned. In similar colorful language another Kentucky Republican cursed the influence of Klair on Governor Fields: "No one could pass through the Augean stables, their abode, and come out spotless."[34]

Owing to the domination of the Klair-Galvin clique, bond-issue legislation passed the general assembly, received the signature of a grateful Governor Fields, and went on the ballot for the 1924 general election. By midsummer Bingham developed a smooth-running network of opposition to the bond issue. Scattered across the state, members of the Pay-As-You-Go organization and a host of others agreed with Bingham's fiscal and political ideals. One supporter replied: "I am a Democrat, but your kind, i.e.: I do not vote for a yellow dog simply because he happens to be running on the Democrat ticket." Another respondent praised the effort against Fields: "I very much admire the attitude that you have taken toward trying to pull Kentucky out of the political mire that she is now in and to place her upon the plain of justice and right." R. P. Taylor, a Winchester banker and confidant of the Judge, claimed "to have talked to quite a number of our prominent citizens, and they are more than willing to join in a movement to defeat this bond issue at the polls."[35]

Representatives of the religious community joined the effort, including W. A. Frost, the business manager of the state Baptist paper, the *Western Recorder*. James Tandy Ellis, a noted Kentucky author from Warsaw, supported the antibond forces. These and others agreed with Judge Bingham that the current makeup of the State Highway Commission would not allow for the efficient and honest administration of the bonds. This view corresponded with the widely evident business progressivism in the South in the twenties. "I should like to see a Highway Department in our state which had demonstrated it could spend $9,000,000 a year well before we hand them $50,000,000 in a lump to spend," the Louisville publisher concluded. Throughout the summer and fall of 1924 the debate continued over the bond issue, coinciding with the decline of the cooperative movement.[36]

Meanwhile, the presidential and Kentucky senatorial races grabbed most of the headlines. Bingham did not commit himself to any candidate early on, but preferred the candidacy of Democrat John W. Davis, a Wall Street lawyer born in West Virginia. As time came for instructing the Kentucky delegation, the Judge expressed his hope that an undeclared, uninstructed delegation would be sent to the Democratic

National Convention. However, Brown and Camden gained control of the delegation and favored William G. McAdoo. In the end the Democratic machine dominated the delegation just as it had in previous years. Bingham, being on the outside of the party's leadership, saw little hope of any immediate change. Just before the convention convened, Aaron Sapiro cabled several Democratic-party leaders throughout the country pushing the candidacy of Bingham as a possible "compromise candidate," a sign of his respect for the Judge, but more indicative of the trouble in which the party found itself.[37]

Before the nomination process got under way, Democrats divided bitterly over a proposed anti–Ku Klux Klan plank in the proposed platform. The *Courier* editorially voiced its disapproval of the Klan, giving the appearance of leaning away from McAdoo. The floor battle for the Democratic nomination lasted nearly two weeks. At one time McAdoo came within only twenty votes of the two-thirds needed for the nomination. Davis eventually emerged as a compromise candidate after the McAdoo and Smith forces weakened. After the nomination of Davis on the 103rd ballot by an exhausted convention, the *Courier* declared him to be a "rock-bottom Democrat." To the charge that Wall Street lawyer Davis was a "reactionary," the editorialist found him, instead, to be "an intelligent liberal."[38]

In the choice for senator, Bingham decided early on not to support incumbent Augustus Owsley Stanley. Although the publisher declared Stanley to be "talented and an agreeable companion," he faulted the senator's record in both Frankfort and Washington. Bingham and his papers eventually endorsed Louisvillian Frederic M. Sackett, the Republican nominee, primarily because of that candidate's upholding of prohibition and his previous administrative record. Stanley, on the other hand, represented only the "professional politician," incessantly seeking another office, according to Bingham. A businessman and multimillionaire, Sackett was a native of Rhode Island and a graduate of Harvard Law School. His business success, efforts in behalf of construction of a new Ohio River bridge at Louisville, and work as Federal Food Administrator for Kentucky during World War I won the plaudits of independent Democrats of the Bingham stripe. That record, a spotless reputation for honesty, and adherence to prohibition made it possible for Bingham to bolt the Democratic party once again and support Sackett in the senatorial election of 1924.[39]

However, the candidacy of his fellow Louisvillian placed a severe strain on Bingham. He admitted "this puts me in an awkward position with reference to any contribution to the state campaign because I cannot contribute on behalf of Davis, whom I am supporting, without contributing on behalf of Stanley, whom I am opposing." To circumvent the state committee, Bingham contributed directly to the Democratic National Committee, donating as much as twenty-five thousand dollars in the effort to elect Davis. The nomination of Davis brought the full editorial support of the Bingham papers. "We are happy over your nomination and happy to have the opportunity to do our best for your election," Bingham explained to Davis. The Louisvillian's input into the campaign included information about the deplorable farm situation across the nation, particularly the difficulties of organizing the cooperative movement.[40]

The candidacy of Calvin Coolidge proved overpowering as he swept both the popular and electoral votes with decisive majorities. When officials counted votes in Kentucky, the Coolidge landslide not only carried the state, but pushed Sackett ahead of Stanley by about twenty thousand votes. Bingham took solace in the fact that he had complete confidence in Sackett. "It is particularly fortunate for the state of Kentucky, in my judgment, that he should have been elected over the ordinary type of demagogue politician," the Judge said, "and I hope it is going to teach the politicians in both parties a valuable lesson."[41]

However, Bingham took the greatest satisfaction in seeing the defeat of the bond referendum by about ninety-thousand votes, finding "that we have killed more than one snake when we stopped the bond issue." No longer would citizens of Kentucky have to anticipate that the bond money would be used for corrupt purposes. With no fear of overstatement he proclaimed that: "I have no doubt that our fight in defeating the proposed Bond Issue here was perhaps the greatest contribution to public welfare our papers have ever made." Ultimately, the *Courier* blamed the ineffectual Fields administration for the defeat of Davis in the state poll. Bingham remained an implacable foe during the remainder of the Fields administration.[42]

Bingham also kept up a vital interest in his city in the 1920s as well. He supported the construction of the Memorial Auditorium and served as chairman of the commission that planned, financed, and oversaw construction of the facility. Of course, he took an interest in the government of the city of Louisville, one that had often in the past demonstrated a tendency toward graft and corruption similar to larger cities in the East and Midwest. Attempts to simplify the municipal government with a city commission plan failed to develop in the early twenties when the state legislature did not pass enabling legislation. "We now have enough machinery here to run the British Empire, and to run it badly," an exasperated Bingham charged.[43]

The mayoral election of 1925 proved to be a classic Louisville political donnybrook replete with the usual charges of voter fraud. In this election a special twist came when W. T. Baker, the choice of James B. Brown's Democratic-party machine, turned out to be a member of the Ku Klux Klan. Many local Democrats like Bingham were particularly sensitive to the threat of Klan involvement in their party. The *Courier* helped expose this flaw in candidate Baker's character, and, only three days before the election, Baker withdrew, being replaced by Joseph T. O'Neal, a well-respected local lawyer and judge. This activity only intensified an already heated race. Early returns indicated that A. A. Will, the Republican machine's candidate, won by a small margin. The *Courier* charged that only "Searcyism and [a] solid black vote" carried the day for the Republicans. In a repeat of the 1905 mayoral debacle, disputed election returns went to the courts for resolution, and a Kentucky Court of Appeals decision again overturned the results.[44]

Bingham's interest in state politics continued unabated in the mid-twenties. He and a few others, including Alice Lloyd, a lawyer from Maysville, and Harry Giovannoli, editor of the Republican *Lexington Leader,* began to ask for consideration of state nominating conventions rather than primaries. In a complete turnaround on this old progressive ideal, Bingham charged that political machines in Kentucky had taken complete control of the primaries in recent years. However, repeal of the state primary remained only a pipe dream for old-line progressives in the twenties.[45]

On another matter during the mid-twenties, Bingham also displayed his peculiar form of progressivism. When asked by Josephus Daniels to contribute to the William Jennings Bryan Memorial Association, Bingham refused, citing the fact that he had opposed Bryan from his earliest political days and had never voted for the Great Commoner. However, he admitted that Bryan had served one purpose—that of turning Bingham into a political "independent" because of the Nebraskan's support of free silver in the nineties.[46]

State politics continued at center stage in the late twenties. Alben Barkley bided his time in the U.S. House of Representatives after suffering defeat in the 1923 gubernatorial primary. Having paid his political dues, he ran for the United States Senate in 1926. This time he could count on the support of not only Bingham and his papers but the Democratic party establishment as well. The Democratic members of the bipartisan-combine leadership fell in behind Barkley. Elwood Hamilton again headed Barkley's campaign, a sure sign of the blessing of J. C. W. Beckham. Thirty-one Barkley operatives used Bingham's contribution of ten thousand dollars at a crucial time in the general election. Charged with being a member of the Ku Klux Klan and seeking support of that organization, Barkley skillfully evaded the issue. Bingham and his newspapers stoutly defended Barkley throughout.[47]

On election day "Iron Man" Barkley won by over twenty-two thousand votes over incumbent Republican Richard Ernst. Bingham concluded the obvious: The former congressman from Paducah won because Democrats for once had united behind a candidate without the tampering of the bipartisan combine. The Judge expressed hope that "this election marks the beginning of a new leadership in Kentucky which will bring not only material advancement, but spiritual growth as well." However, Barkley's election was due as much to the nominal Democrats who supported the bipartisan combine as to the more pristine adherents of the Beckham-Bingham-Haly faction. Barkley's election to the Senate allowed him to rise above and move beyond the usual internecine warfare of Kentucky Democratic-party politics. He was glad of it.[48]

In the 1927 gubernatorial race, Kentucky Democrats again returned to their favorite sport of the twenties: cutting each other to ribbons in factional fights. That year Bingham and Haly carefully organized the candidacy of Beckham for the governorship. Beckham took up the anti-pari-mutuel and coal tax crusades again, the same issues that had led to Barkley's defeat at the hands of Cantrill and the bipartisan combine in 1923. In the primary Beckham emerged victorious against "his Combine-supported opponent" Robert Crowe, by dominating the rural vote.[49]

The Republican party countered with Flem D. "Flim Flam" Sampson, an eastern Kentuckian on the court of appeals, the state's highest court, in the fall general election. Beckham and Sampson fought a bitter battle, complete with mudslinging on both sides. Sampson attacked the personal integrity of his opponent by charging that Beckham drank alcohol in quantity on the sly while he himself "never smoked, chewed, drank, gambled—not even bet on an election." A. O. Stanley humorously mused about Sampson, "I wonder if he'd suck an egg?"[50]

The bipartisan combine and Governor Fields tacitly supported Sampson. James B. Brown's *Louisville Herald-Post* pilloried Bingham for his support of Beckham and scored Haly for his bossism. In one *Herald-Post* cartoon Beckham's likeness sat on ventriloquist Haly's lap while Bingham stood nearby saying "I apologize to England for the United States." Throughout the fall campaign the Brown mouthpiece continued the attack on Bingham's partiotism. Meanwhile, rumors circulated that the Jockey Club "invested as much as one million dollars or more in the election of Sampson." The day before the election the *Courier* put the matter simply: Either the "people of Kentucky or the bi-partisan Jockey Club combine" would rule the state.[51]

When the votes were counted, the bipartisan combine again proved formidable. Beckham lost by over thirty-two thousand votes. The remainder of the state Democratic ticket swept into office although Lieutenant Governor James Breathitt did so by less than two hundred votes. The same forces that had defeated Barkley in the 1923 gubernatorial primary, led by the bipartisan combine, triumphed again.[52]

The election of 1928 divided Democrats as never before in Kentucky, and Bingham and his papers did not push an early candidacy for anyone. However, the candidacy of Governor Alfred E. Smith sped the demise of the bipartisan combine. Old progressive political allies like Pat Callahan split with Bingham over the prohibition issue. The religious community of the state also divided over the issues of prohibition and Smith's religion. A Democratic partisan like Union Countian Earle C. Clements, who later became governor and senator, maintained he "caught unshirted Hell" for supporting Smith in a dominantly dry Protestant county. Bingham and the *Courier* waited until the end of August, several weeks after the nominating convention in Houston, to come out for Smith. This delay indicated Bingham's uncertainty about the New Yorker, but once the decision had been made, the *Courier* never looked back.[53]

More important, Smith's candidacy brought Bingham and Franklin D. Roosevelt into closer contact. After declaring for Smith, Bingham wrote FDR that he believed the "Happy Warrior" speech to be "by all odds the best nominating speech that has been made in my time," referring to Roosevelt's stirring message. In a *Courier* campaign editorial in support of Smith, the writer, most likely antiprohibitionist Harrison Robertson, admitted that the "country would be safe" with either candidate. While the *Courier* realized that "he is a wet," it believed that Smith would enforce prohibition as well as Hoover.[54]

By 1928 the Judge convinced himself that prohibition, no matter how laudable as the "noble experiment," could not be successfully enforced. The Catholic issue was irrelevant to the *Courier*. Smith believed in "Jeffersonian principles," and he was closer to the ideals of Woodrow Wilson than Hoover. In a letter to Roosevelt, Bingham declared that his support of Smith again proved the merit of his plan to be "absolutely independent" in political position. In one last editorial before election day, the *Courier* asked: "Is Governor Smith to be crucified because of his religious beliefs?" The candidates and issues in the presidential campaign of 1928 brought out the highest national poll since 1920, a year in which Democrat Cox carried the state. But this time many Kentucky Democrats stayed at home, and Hoover swept the state with a near 60 percent majority, slightly above his national margin.[55]

Within a short time Kentucky and the nation became embroiled in the Great Crash and then the beginning of the Great Depression. Like most predominantly agricultural states, Kentucky already felt the impact of poor economic times in the 1920s. Many farmers lived on the brink of disaster throughout that decade. The beginning of the Great Depression on a nationwide scale struck the industry of Kentucky a near mortal blow. Many industries either shut down or drastically reduced their workforces. Some slashed wages and salaries in an attempt to make ends meet. For example, the Louisville Varnish Company cut everyone's wages, including the salary of president Pat Callahan, but no one was let go and the company survived the depression. The Bingham companies also cut all wages and salaries for a brief spell in the early thirties as advertising revenues plummeted with the onset of the Great Depression.[56]

Kentucky and Kentuckians also could not escape one of the most common disasters of the depression: bank failures. In November 1930

James B. Brown announced that the National Bank of Kentucky, the commonwealth's largest financial institution, would be forced to close its doors. That bank fell because of Brown's poorly advised merger with Caldwell and Company of Nashville. When the Caldwell paper kingdom collapsed, Brown's bank soon followed, and the banking structure of Kentucky stumbled into the depression. In a meeting of the city's leaders, apparently only Bingham showed a willingness to put up some of his own fortune to save the National Bank of Kentucky, and the bank failed. As Christmas neared, Bingham agreed to pay for half of individual Christmas savings in Brown's failed Louisville banks to soften the blow to numerous Louisville families.[57]

Economic and social conditions worsened in the nation and in Kentucky in the early thirties. Rural farm families often survived better than urban families because they could raise their own food. If they had no large debts or a mortgage, farmers made it through the depression. Notwithstanding, studies of childhood nutrition indicated that many Kentucky schoolchildren suffered from dietary deficiency. Several cities in the commonwealth reported unemployment rates exceeding 20 percent. As the Great Depression deepened in the early thirties, many young Kentuckians left the state and went on the road.[58]

With Republicans in the statehouse and the White House, Democrats seized advantage of depression conditions to push the candidacies of their champions. In the 1931 governor's race Bingham and his papers gave lukewarm support to the Republican candidate for governor, William B. Harrison, because of Harrison's progressive record as mayor of Louisville. The bombastic campaign style of his Democratic opponent, Ruby Laffoon, the "terrible Turk" from Madisonville as he was known by many Kentuckians, drew no applause or support from the Judge. But Laffoon won the election, and large Democratic majorities returned to the Kentucky General Assembly. Again, Bingham had an opponent in Frankfort. Kentucky and the rest of the nation now geared up for the presidential election of 1932. Bingham prepared himself for another new crusade, the nomination and election of Franklin D. Roosevelt as president of the United States.[59]

chapter eight

Kentuckian in Knee Breeches

THE UNSUCCESSFUL CAMPAIGN of Al Smith for president in 1928 brought Bingham into personal contact for the first time with Franklin Delano Roosevelt. That attachment grew as the nation struggled with the Great Depression and Roosevelt breathed fresh life into the Democratic party as a highly visible and apparently successful governor of New York. In September 1931 Bingham told Roosevelt: "I have no doubt in my mind that you are the best hope not merely for the Democratic Party, which is a minor consideration, but for our country, which is the major consideration." Bingham predicted success for FDR in 1932. "I believe there is every possibility that you will be elected. My part will be relatively small in both," he explained, "but I expect to devote all of my energy and every resource I have in your behalf." Roosevelt replied that he was "fully convinced that the cycle has swung again after twelve years and that it is our turn next."[1]

Bingham followed up with one of the first large contributions to the Roosevelt campaign chest. Though never in FDR's inner circle, Bingham's influence in the upper South and his fortune became of inestimable value. Like many other supporters he made an obligatory pilgrimage to Hyde Park before the nominating convention, publicly demonstrating his support of Roosevelt's candidacy. In the crucial weeks before the convention, Bingham and other pro-Roosevelt Kentuckians worked to unite the factions in the state Democratic party behind the New Yorker. That being done, for the first time in years a united state delegation traveled to the 1932 Democratic Convention. Bingham backed up his belief in Roosevelt's candidacy by giving more money to party coffers at both the state and national levels. Once nominated, Roosevelt reported to Bingham that "the drive against me seems to be on. All I can hope is that it will not develop into the kind of a row which will mean the re-election of Brother Hoover." Bingham worked hard to keep the Kentucky Democracy in line.[2]

The Bingham papers kept up a steady stream of pro-Roosevelt editorials and articles throughout the campaign. Electing FDR will bring to the White House "the Man of Delivery to supercede the Man of Magic" the *Courier* argued. Once Roosevelt swept into office, he felt obliged to thank Bingham for his support. "You worked hard and faithfully," FDR explained, "and I am more than grateful to you." Just how appreciative became an immediate subject of conversation in political circles, as everyone knew that Roosevelt would soon be making important appointments to this administration. The Binghams, who owned Pineland Plantation in Georgia, visited with the Roosevelts at nearby Warm Springs in late November 1932, and there may have been talk then of a substantive reward for Bingham.[3]

Speculation centered on the probability that the Louisvillian would be appointed ambassador to the Court of St. James's, although there were rumors that a cabinet post was in the offing. Raymond Moley later reported that Bingham, apparently with the support of Colonel House, had been in the running for secretary of state along with Cordell Hull and Owen D. Young. However, this consideration appears not to have been taken seriously by Roosevelt except as a rather playful assertion that this would be a "stiff dose for the international bankers" owing to Bingham's unknown quantity as a diplomat and businessman.[4]

Bingham set his sights on the ambassadorship even before the election of FDR. In late October 1932 he told an old college friend that he would not take a cabinet post, if offered, because it "would tie my papers onto the Democratic Party and inevitably would damage them and their influence." He preferred something "on the outside" that would allow the papers to retain a semblance of independence; he saw no conflict of interest in accepting a diplomatic post while keeping his interests in the newspaper field.[5]

After being out of the White House for twelve years, wealthy Democrats lined up to be appropriately rewarded. Though Secretary of State

Cordell Hull suggested a "50-50" mixture of career men and political appointees for ambassadorial posts, in the end the president followed the time-worn tradition of sending mostly top contributors to the more prestigious foreign posts. Millionaires Jesse I. Straus, Joseph E. Davies, William C. Bullitt, Joseph P. Kennedy, Lawrence A. Steinhardt, and Breckinridge Long were sent abroad at some time during the Roosevelt years as a reward for their support of the New Deal. There were some exceptions to this general rule. Roosevelt appointed his old Navy Department chief, Josephus Daniels, to the post in Mexico. After James M. Cox, Newton D. Baker, and Owen D. Young declined the post in Berlin, he named William E. Dodd, professor of history at the University of Chicago.[6]

Bingham's interest in the appointment to the Court of St. James's came from his genealogical attachment to England, his long association with numerous English and Scottish friends, and his firm belief that the future welfare of the world depended on closer Anglo-American relations. He told an old English friend just before taking up his post: "In my judgment, civilization, as we have known it, is at its greatest crisis. If it is to be saved at all, it can only be saved through the joint effort of the British and ourselves."[7]

The expected appointment by Roosevelt came just after the inauguration, when the president named Daniels, Straus, and Bingham all the same week. Bingham learned of it through Colonel House and *Courier-Journal* Washington chief correspondent Ulric Bell. The president instructed Secretary Hull to inquire if Bingham would be acceptable to the British. "If OK I can appoint him at once & the quicker he goes over the better—don't you think so?" FDR inquired. Hull passed the request on to His Majesty's Government via the American embassy in London. Ambassador Andrew W. Mellon soon replied that the appointment met with the approval of the British government, and Roosevelt sent along word of the appointment to the U.S. Senate for its consent.[8]

The process slowed as questions arose about Bingham being an "Anglophile" and an "apologetic American" who would not represent the best interests of the United States before the Court of St. James's. The isolationist press, led by the *Chicago Daily Tribune*, reported the story gleefully. Such charges went back at least as far as 1927, when a Kentucky political figure attacked Bingham for his alleged pro-British sentiments. The *Tribune* and the *Louisville Herald-Post* misinterpreted a speech given by Bingham at a horticultural fair in Scotland in which the Louisvillian claimed only a general cultural attachment between the United States and Great Britain. Chairman Key Pittman of the Senate Foreign Relations Committee suggested a delay in Bingham's approval after Indiana senator Arthur Robinson asked questions about the Louisvillian's suitability. Old political and personal enemies, including Abraham Flexner, again raised the specter of Mary Lily Flagler Bingham.[9]

After delay of a few days and, no doubt, some pressure from the White House, the committee approved the appointment of Robert Worth Bingham as "Ambassador Extraordinary and Plenipotentiary of the United States to Great Britain." By letter Roosevelt introduced the new ambassador to the king: "My knowledge of his high character and ability gives me entire confidence that he will constantly endeavor to advance the interests and prosperity of both governments and so render himself acceptable to your majesty." *Newsweek* magazine asked the inevitable question directed to all new ministers to Great Britain: "Will you wear knee pants?" Bingham emphatically declared: "I will not."[10]

Without any experience in the diplomatic corps, Bingham quickly sought and received some instruction from the Department of State, where he took a brief orientation course preparing him for the routine matters he would face. To Ray Atherton, a career diplomat and chargé d'affaires in London, Bingham expressed the hope that he would give his utmost aid. "I realize deeply the grave responsibility I am undertaking," the Judge responded. "I can only try my best to measure up to it." Bingham would face numerous obstacles in his role as ambassador, and his tenure would be marked by controversy.[11]

Taking up the post itself proved to be difficult. Recurring health problems plagued Bingham's life until 1933; his remaining years were to be marked by numerous illnesses. Just before Bingham's appointment as ambassador, a "saddle sore" that developed from riding at the Georgia plantation became infected and resisted the best efforts of Dr. Hugh Young. Although specific word of this "wound" never reached the press, it required an operation at Johns Hopkins and never healed properly. He did not leave until mid-May, a delay of two months. Just before his ship, the USS *Washington,* left New York harbor, former governor Al Smith presided over a ceremony in which forty-eight homing pigeons were released, one representing each state. When one bird balked, a bystander quipped: "That's a Republican pigeon."[12]

On his way to assume the ambassadorship, Bingham is pictured with his wife and daughter aboard the USS *Washington*. This photo was taken May 10, 1933. From the Barry Bingham, Sr., Collection. Reprinted with permission of The Filson Club Historical Society, Louisville, Kentucky.

On board Bingham became extremely ill with a painful kidney infection, elevated blood pressure, and swelling of the joints. He recovered enough to appear before the press at the end of the voyage. Upon stepping off the ship at Plymouth, Bingham took the diplomatic offensive and expressed the view that the grave problems of the world could be solved only "by genuine understanding and cooperation between Great Britain and ourselves." When he took up his post on 19 May he was still quite weak. A day later the new ambassador formally presented his credentials to Sir John Simon, the foreign secretary, after riding to Buckingham Palace in a royal state coach.[13]

Even the ceremonial exhilaration of such a venture would not soften the pressures of the years ahead. Throughout his tenure as ambassador, Bingham jealously guarded what he considered to be the prerogatives of the post. As chief representative of the United States government in Great Britain, he objected to the continual flow of special delegations from Washington to conferences in London and other European capitals in the thirties, believing that these detracted from his own diplomatic usefulness. Moreover, he disliked FDR's penchant of assigning two people to work on the same task, so well illustrated by the fiasco that became the London Economic Conference. Keeping the Department of State and the White House informed about other members of the American diplomatic corps took much of the ambassador's time and energy. Sometimes these intrigues proved detrimental to American foreign policy, but more often only demonstrated the whims of individual personalities and the inefficiency of the American diplomatic system.[14]

The duties of an American ambassador, particularly one in such an important post as that of the Court of St. James's in the 1930s, included close attention to ceremonial functions. Attending afternoon levees of the court, in which men were presented to the king, and giving receptions at the American embassy were only part of the duties of the ambassador. It appeared that nearly every young American female who traveled to England in the thirties wanted to be presented at court. Bingham attempted to fulfill their wishes if possible, a chore he declared to be "the most troublesome part of my job." His responsibilities even included mollifying the wounded feelings of the wife of Senator Homer Cummings when one of the London papers criticized the inappropriateness of her dress at an official court function. Writing letters of introduction for British citizens coming to America, giving numerous speeches, attending meetings and formal dedications, sending messages for visiting American dignitaries, meeting many Americans who came through London, and keeping up with the press in Great Britain would not exhaust the list of duties taken on by Bingham in 1933.[15]

The ambassadorship, Bingham once estimated, cost him at least five times the amount of his $17,500 annual salary. Accustomed to living in a grand style, the prestige of serving in such a position must have been more than worth the expense. Moreover, in the earliest days of the New Deal the Department of State slashed its budget, placing an additional burden on the ambassador's pocketbook.[16]

Part of Bingham's job entailed surveillance of the British political scene. He kept up a steady stream of reports on the British government to Secretary Hull. Reporting on parliamentary debates or rumors of a pending dismissal of a minister took up a good bit of the ambassador's time. However, the ceremonial function of the ambassadorship brought Bingham to the brink of rebellion against protocol. Because the American representative to the Court of St. James's did not have an official uniform, protocol required wearing "knee breeches and stockings" for court functions. Old friend and personal physician Hugh Young could joke about his concern for the ambassador's exposing his "seductive calves to the gaze of the English beauties" in knee breeches and stockings, but Bingham thought it an outdated custom and rebelled throughout his tenure against wearing such attire.[17]

These trifles were offset by the perquisites of office, which included receiving honorary degrees from the Universities of Cambridge, Oxford, and London as well as being on the first transatlantic crossing of the SS *Queen Mary*. There were other benefits. Bingham thoroughly enjoyed the English people, whether playing bridge, hunting, or socializing with them in other ways. A steady stream of Louisville acquaintances and other American friends came to the embassy, keeping him in touch with home.[18]

Owing to the depths of the Great Depression, foreign policy took second place to domestic concerns in the early New Deal. During the campaign of 1932 FDR scolded Hoover for blaming the depression on international origins and thereby trying to lift responsibility from his own shoulders. However, Roosevelt soon modified his foreign-policy directives to gain the support of more conservative Democrats. In return for the backing of William Randolph Hearst, Roosevelt dropped his support for membership in the League of Nations. The Democratic candidate, in effect, moved toward isolationism, or economic nationalism, during the campaign, contradicting his Wilsonian internationalist inclination.[19]

After the election the question remained: Would FDR incline toward isolationism once inaugurated, or would he turn back to internationalism? In nominating Representative Cordell Hull of Tennessee for secretary of state, the president indicated his desire for a Wilsonian internationalist in that post. Hull believed that unhindered international trade offered the best hope for world peace; he pushed for the Reciprocal Trade Agreements Act as an expedient measure for attaining that goal. On the other hand, most members of the early New Deal brain trust placed little faith in solving the problems of the depression through international means. They supported such nationalist measures as the Agricultural Adjustment Act and the National Industrial Recovery Act.[20]

Contending internationalist and isolationist forces vied for control of American foreign policy as well as for the mind of the president in the early New Deal. Moreover, FDR had to contend with power broker Bernard M. Baruch, whom Jonathan Daniels identified as a persistent if "benign manipulator." The rumor mill said Baruch controlled the votes of sixty congressmen. Roosevelt had to skillfully handle such a potentially negative force on his administration. There were other considerations as well. The coalition that elected the New Yorker represented numerous ethnic, political, sectional, and economic factions in the country. Each had its own foreign and domestic agenda.[21]

The foreign policy of Roosevelt remains a topic of some debate among American historians. Today most agree there was no clearly defined New Deal foreign policy until the late thirties. The hope of forestalling American participation in world events by the passage of neutrality legislation culminated in the last efforts to negotiate with the Japanese government just before the attack on Pearl Harbor. Some scholars interpret Roosevelt's efforts as Herculean in an attempt to avoid war, whereas others see his peace overtures as only a cover for Machiavellian attempts to lead the country to war stealthily, even suggesting that he maneuvered the Japanese into striking the first blow.[22]

Whether Roosevelt never had a "coherent foreign policy," as some charge, or simply chose addressing domestic affairs before those of a foreign nature, American policy did appear to drift for much of the early New Deal period. One recent critic perhaps best described American foreign policy of those years as "lethargic" and hidebound to the policies of the past. Dominant British and American views of each other further complicated diplomacy in the thirties. The British did not view the United States as a dependable ally, because they saw "the states" as divided between isolationist and internationalist sentiments and preoccupied with difficult economic times. Through the administrations of Prime Ministers Ramsay MacDonald, Stanley Baldwin, and Neville Chamberlain, His Majesty's Government either warily approached any idea of concert with the United States or mostly ignored American overtures. Unfortunately, many British leaders viewed America as "an errant Dominion," an egocentric view among the ruling elite of that island nation. In the early thirties both countries demonstrated ignorance of the other's culture, system of government, and aspirations for world peace and prosperity. Economic rivalry between the two grew after first the United States and then Britain instituted protective tariffs in the early thirties. That competitiveness exacerbated American hostility over war debts and currency stabilization. Many Americans who enjoyed contrasting egalitarian America with allegedly class-ridden England believed the British to be only slightly better than the remainder of decadent Europe.[23]

British political scientist Harold Laski's estimation of Bingham's appointment to the Court of St. James's summed up the ideas of not a few Americans about the English as well as provided a scathing social commentary on his own nation's leaders. Bingham's appointment "will enable our aristocracy to feel that the best Americans are really like themselves," the Englishman explained. "They share the same tastes, they have the same ambitions, they dream the same dreams." Anglophobic representatives of the press such as William Randolph Hearst had a wide audience in the early to mid-thirties, capitalizing on such statements as vindications of their own mind-set.[24]

Bingham sought closer ties with the British and a more prominent role for American foreign policy in European and world affairs. He thought of his function as educational in nature, his primary responsibility being to explain America to the British. In the process he defended Roosevelt and New Deal policy at every opportunity. Significantly, he often appeared ahead of the times. Most of his speeches called for closer Anglo-American relations, often in contrast to official American policy.[25]

In doing so Bingham received heated criticism from both British and American sources. Although officials of the Department of State disliked the candor of these remarks, Roosevelt never repudiated Bingham. In a press conference on 31 May 1933, for example, the president displayed his usual confident control of the proceedings when asked if he agreed with a statement made by Ambassador Bingham about Norman H. Davis and war debts. He replied "off the record" that the ambassador had given a "wrong impression of the American viewpoint" toward disarmament. However, he neither publicly nor privately reprimanded Bingham. In another instance Roosevelt refused to take the bait in a reporter's query about Bingham's urging closer Anglo-American relations, saying that he had not seen the statement when "in fact he had."[26]

If Bingham appeared to be an alarmist on international matters, Roosevelt understood these reactions. Most likely Bingham's responses mirrored those that Roosevelt might himself have made if not constrained by political exigencies. Roosevelt used Bingham, as he did others, to test either the domestic political, or international diplomatic, waters. Some proof of this argument is the fact that Roosevelt apparently never seriously considered replacing his controversial ambassador to Great Britain even after a much publicized and highly criticized anti-Nazi speech by the Louisvillian in 1937.[27]

On the job it did not take Bingham long to show his colors. His first speech, at the annual meeting of the Pilgrim's Society, came only ten days after assuming his post in London and just before the opening of the London Economic Conference. The reading of a telegram from King George V and a personal plea by the Prince of Wales for cooperation between the United States and Great Britain preceded the ambassador's presentation. Though still suffering from a debilitating infection, Bingham delivered a forceful speech, one that not only set the tone for his later speeches but also clearly established the course for his ambassadorship.[28]

"I would have you know that I believe the hope for a stricken world rests largely upon understanding, co-operation and confidence among the English-speaking peoples of the world," the ambassador announced, "and to the task of maintaining and promoting this attitude of mind, I come here resolved to dedicate all that I am, all that I have of mind and spirit." To his audience Bingham described the depths of depression that existed in the United States as Roosevelt took office.

He reported, quite optimistically, that his country had turned the corner of the depression with the advent of the New Deal. Though refraining from criticizing the British for abandoning their free-trade tradition and turning toward autarky (economic nationalism), he explained that his own country had learned a valuable lesson and now accepted the need for lower tariffs. He issued a solemn warning:

> I do not speak to you pessimistically. This is no time for pessimism, but for faith and courage. But I am convinced that our civilization is trembling in the balance. I believe another general war will certainly destroy it. Moreover, I believe that civilization, as we have known and enjoyed it, cannot exist much longer unless the burdens which oppress mankind are lifted soon. The world is in the grip of fear; it is afflicted as if with "the pestilence that walketh in darkness; the sickness that destroyeth in the noonday." Yet I will not believe two nations with our traditions will fail ourselves and mankind in this gravest of emergencies. . . . There is no time for any other thought except "what shall we do to be saved?"[29]

After another warning against cynicism, he repeated the previous theme, that is, "the foundation of hope of our world lies in whole-hearted, concerted action between Great Britain, the great self-governing British Commonwealths, and the United States." Bingham ended his oration by recalling the successful cooperation of these nations in the Great War.[30]

If this speech set the tone for Bingham's ambassadorship, the reactions in Britain and in the United States were also an indication of things to come. On the American side William Randolph Hearst— "always the isolationist," if inconsistent about other matters—allowed his *Chicago Herald-Examiner* to take the offensive with an article entitled "Who Put the Ass in Amb-ass-ador?" claiming that Bingham had already spoken out of turn on several occasions in his brief tenure. "He is a danger to the peace and good understanding which all Americans desire with the people of England," the *Herald-Examiner* editorialist exclaimed. "This country has already had enough of Bingham. We imagine that England has, too." Senator Robinson repeated his earlier attack on the ambassador from the floor of the Congress, whereas the more evenhanded *New York Times* cited Bingham's pronouncement about the need for tariff reduction as a legitimate concern.[31]

On the other side of the Atlantic reactions were also mixed and heated. The *London Daily Telegraph* found the ambassador's pleas for Anglo-American cooperation to have "the authentic ring of sincerity." The *Evening News* proclaimed Bingham to be "the best, the clearest and the most decisive speaker that Washington has sent us as Ambassador for many a year past." However, several papers, like Lord Beaverbrook's *Evening Standard* and the *Daily Mail,* republished the Hearst article and contributed their own critical appraisals of the ambassador. Bingham would later claim that the "Hearst gang in our country and the Beaverbrook gang over here . . . hooked up with each other" in a conspiracy to discredit him. The most eminent Briton, King George V, however, apparently thought well of the new ambassador, at least from his first impressions.[32]

As ambassador to the Court of St. James's, Bingham held a position from which he could readily observe the major diplomatic negotiations in Europe. In Geneva a major conference held forth on the problem of general disarmament. Norman Davis, a friend of Hull and a steadfast Democrat from Tennessee, led the American delegation in mid-1933. Bingham did not trust Davis, whom he believed acted independently of the administration, and their personalities clashed from the start. Mutual suspicions of the nations involved complicated preliminary negotiations. Prime Minister Ramsay MacDonald wanted concrete disarmament agreements, but the United States appeared unwilling to support any form of multilateral agreement. France, fearful of a repeat of the invasions of 1870 and 1914, pleaded for an international assurance of protection. Nazi Germany dashed all hope when it pulled out of negotiations and left the League of Nations on 14 October 1934. Soon afterward a naval conference would convene in London with the purpose of reducing and controlling the size of the world's fleets of warships. It would also end in utter failure.[33]

The London, or World, Economic Conference of 1933 holds a unique place in New Deal history. First planned by President Hoover and Prime Minister MacDonald to stabilize international currencies and thereby attack the problem of world depression from an international perspective, the sessions did not begin until early June 1933. From the beginning Roosevelt determined to surrender no advantages gained by devaluation of the dollar and subsequent inflation in the United States. Owing to deep cuts in Anglo-American trade, both countries appeared primarily concerned about their own individual domestic and international welfare.[34]

Nevertheless, the conference convened with some hope of success. Secretary Hull, who intended to work for lower tariffs, headed the American delegation. One diplomatic historian has found: "To Hull diplomacy was the art of preaching, not of negotiation." Whether true or not, the Tennessean found himself in an almost impossible diplomatic situation in London, one in which the Washington administration appeared to give no direction at all.[35]

Over the next few weeks Bingham became a conduit for information and rumor about political maneuvering both inside and outside the Roosevelt administration. Still suffering from ill health, he worked himself into a state of exhaustion. In his responsiblity as observer of the British government, the ambassador reported to Roosevelt that the British counted on some "tangible achievement" from the conference. He predicted that MacDonald would try to finesse the debt-question issue to his advantage and attempt to get solid agreements on several fronts. Roosevelt instructed Hull before departure that he was to discuss neither war debts nor disarmament. Meanwhile, Senator Key Pittman, who "was drunk all the time," according to one of Bingham's sources, added nothing to the prestige of the American delegation, being interested only in winning concessions for silver producers. In his opening remarks the prime minister declared that war debts must be the first issue to be addressed, followed by a currency stabilization agreement. Bingham immediately recognized that this "would increase the difficulties" of Roosevelt. Although Bingham did not take direct part in the conference, he kept in close touch with Hull, who often talked with him about the negotiations.[36]

Into an already tense situation came special envoy Raymond Moley, an original member of the Roosevelt Brain Trust, who assumed a role as "liaison officer" between FDR and the special delegation headed by Hull. Moley, who served as a sort of Rooseveltian "intense economic nationalist" alter ego, opposed international currency stabilization and tariff reduction. He represented the divided mind of New Deal foreign policy in 1933 and had every intention of scuttling the conference.[37]

With all the hoopla of a Hollywood drama, Moley rushed across the Atlantic by special plane and ship, preceded by word that he would pursue currency stabilization, and apparently carrying the blessing of the president. After landing on the coast, Moley asked for a special plane to speed him to London and then unexpectedly took a train. Failure to use the aircraft, paid for out of Bingham's own pocket, severely strained relations between the two American diplomats from the start.[38]

Moley did not lodge at Claridge's with Hull and the remainder of the American delegation, but accepted the ill-advised, halfhearted hospitality of Bingham and remained at the American embassy. There the ambassador and the special envoy clashed. Moley believed that the Louisvillian owed him support for helping smooth the way for his confirmation by the Senate. Bingham interpreted Moley's hyperactivity as upsetting the embassy's routine and especially disliked Moley's constant use of the code room. Moreover, Bingham visualized a cabal controlled by Bernard Baruch and consisting of William C. Bullitt, Moley, Herbert Feis, and others intent on undermining Hull and taking over the negotiations. During this foray Bingham acted as Hull's chief defender, keeping the secretary and the president informed of the machinations of the opposition. Bingham claimed to have confronted both Moley and Herbert Bayard Swope about taking their cues from Baruch, but both denied the accusation. In the meantime Hull pressed on with his pleas for trade agreements in the face of opposition from Moley and with little, if any, support from Washington.[39]

Roosevelt soon removed all doubt about American intentions when he issued his famous "Bombshell Message" on 2 July 1933. In a telegram from the USS *Indianapolis* to William Philips, acting secretary of state, the president explained that he "would regard it as a catastrophe amounting to a world tragedy" if the conference worked only toward monetary stabilization. "The sound internal economic system of a nation is a greater factor in its well being than the price of its currency in changing terms of the currencies of other nations," Roosevelt demurred. Although seen now as not quite the explosive pronouncement as it appeared in mid-1933, nevertheless the message repudiated Moley and further confused other nations at the conference about America's intentions. The president stated to Hull that stabilization was not a worthy objective while the United States struggled to work out its own internal economic and monetary problems, thereby immediately cutting the ground out from under Moley.

A "chagrined" Moley and his cohorts soon returned to the United States as the conference wound down. Hull fared no better even though he kept up a brave front, apparently retaining the support of FDR.[40]

In Moley's memoirs of his New Deal experiences, he scored Wilsonians like Hull, House, and Bingham, who all appeared to have the ear of the president. "Apparently they are still firmly in the saddle, some of them in person, some of them through protégés, others, career men trained under the old dispensation—all of them the intellectual brethren of the naive Lansing with one foot at Broad and Wall and the other at Geneva," the disgruntled Moley charged.[41]

The London Economic Conference struggled on for several more weeks, vitiated by FDR's "Bombshell" and the incompatibility of the intentions of most of the nations meeting there. Roosevelt agreed to accept token payments on war debts, but this concession only temporarily kept the meetings functioning at a perfunctory level. Bingham put a gloss on things and praised the role of Hull. He reported to the president that Hull "did a really magnificent job here and emerged as the great figure of the Conference, with the respect and confidence of the delegates of all the nations represented here. I know of no finer incident in American diplomatic history than his achievement here." Moreover, he found that the British "have the highest respect for Cordell Hull's character and ability."[42]

Postmortems on the failure of the London Economic Conference varied. Moley blamed the Wilsonians; Walter Lippman faulted Roosevelt; Ray Atherton criticized the self-serving role of Bullitt; and others censured Moley. Several weeks after returning to the United States, Secretary Hull informed Bingham that "it does seem that at this state all international relationships are at an astonishingly low ebb, and if anything, sinking lower." William E. Leuchtenburg has summed up the thoughts of a number of historians by stating that "there is probably no act of Roosevelt's White House years for which he has been more universally censured," and finding the "failure of the London Economic Conference" to be "deplorable." Some other critics have been more charitable, but it is doubtful that the president lost much sleep over the alleged failure of the London Economic Conference. He had his own agenda and kept his own counsel.[43]

For the new ambassador to Great Britain, the combined strain of the conference and lingering effects from infection were almost too much. During the annual Fourth of July reception at the embassy he stopped shaking hands with visitors because of physical weakness. Bingham reported that several people who observed the proceedings of the London Conference suggested he go home and advise FDR about the real story of the conference. His doctors, however, vetoed such a trip in mid-July 1933. In any event Bingham felt relief that the conference had ended without further rupturing Anglo-American relations. However, he believed anti-Americanism more intense in Great Britain than at any time in his experience.[44]

The remainder of Bingham's first few months as ambassador to the Court of St. James's, while not as eventful, proved to be almost as strenuous. In early September 1933 Roosevelt appointed Bingham as the permanent American delegate to the International Wheat Advisory Committee, which had been given the task of working out international production controls. Bingham's interest in agriculture, and his leadership in the cooperative movement during the 1920s, gave him vital experience necessary for this post. Over the next few years the committee met to work out quotas for production and exportation. Although no definitive agreements came from the meetings, Bingham found that most of the participating nations developed a keener appreciation for the internal economic and agricultural problems of the member nations.[45]

Bingham's speech making and public appearances continued without interruption through the remainder of 1933. In a mid-October speech on the British Broadcasting Corporation—introducing a series of programs exploring life in America—Bingham recited his pleas for better understanding between the United States and Great Britain. A few days later he challenged an English-Speaking Union audience to seek peace in the world. At a meeting of the American Society at the Savoy Hotel on Thanksgiving Day 1933, he took the opportunity to educate the British public about America, defending Roosevelt and the New Deal against what he considered to be misunderstanding and misrepresentation in the British press. "In my judgment there will be sadness ahead for those who sell the United States short," Bingham contended. Of course, he also took the opportunity to push for closer Anglo-American cooperation. "In the end, in an anxious world, the greatest cause for thanksgiving today is the fact that the two great democracies, the British Commonwealth of Nations and the United States, seek only peace," he explained, "and thus they stand for the welfare and the progress of all humanity." During the course of the speech Bingham mentioned that the United States had recently initiated a program similar to the British exchange equalization fund. Afterward the British press asked if this meant the United States had established a fund like their own; Bingham clarified that he had referred only to the development of a gold-buying fund for stabilization of the American monetary and economic system, and nothing more extensive.[46]

Bingham's health improved very slowly through the summer and fall of 1933. Ulric Bell from the *Courier*'s Washington bureau expressed the "hope that the time is near when your Excellency will be able to sit on a horse without a qualm." Bingham kept up with most of his appointments and ceremonial duties as ambassador, such as attending the Lord Mayor of London's dinner and receiving an honorary degree from the University of London. Treatments and medical examinations became a regular regimen. By mid-November he appeared to have shaken off the recurring infection, at least to the extent of taking up his favorite pastime of hunting again. Roosevelt assumed this as well and told Bingham that "it is fine to know that you are wholly well again."[47]

Although Bingham kept up a steady stream of communications with Hull in these early months, his correspondence with FDR appears to have been more intimate. In addition to the usual business-like references to foreign affairs, he took the time to initiate a search of British Admiralty records for logs of ships that had shelled Hyde Park, New York, in 1777 and presented the president with a much-appreciated handcrafted rod and reel. He also found the time to indulge the president's passion for philately with fresh British issues.[48]

As the ambassador settled into his post, he began to get a feel for the intricacies of American diplomacy abroad and expressed rather strong opinions about Europeans. Bingham soon developed qualms about developments going on in Nazi Germany and often shared these with the president and others. On a flight from Copenhagen to London in late August 1933, Bingham's plane made a brief stop in Hamburg. Being allowed only to get off the aircraft and smoke a cigarette nearby gave the ambassador a "peculiar sensation" of being in an entirely alien environment. Although Bingham liked Dr. Leopold von Hoesch, the German ambassador in London, he frankly told him that "the American people were skeptical of the intentions of the present

German government," believing that Germany "would probably pre-
cipitate war" if that nation kept on its current course.[49]

Neither did Bingham spare the British, finding them too confident of their position in the world. He warned them individually that
the debt question would have to be dealt with realistically before
America would ever move toward complete cooperation. When an
English admiral privately urged that the United States and Great Britain form an alliance in the Pacific area "to take care of these niggers"
(referring to the Japanese), Bingham explained that the British had
to meet the United States halfway on other issues.[50]

Bingham reacted unfavorably to Prime Minister MacDonald during the London Economic Conference. On one occasion when he
had a meeting scheduled with MacDonald, Canadian prime minister
Richard Bennett suggested that the American "load him up with flat-
tery, as that was all that he was willing to listen to." "Even if I had been
willing to do so," Bingham later explained, "I had no opportunity, for
the Prime Minister began to flatter himself immediately." The first
impressions of King George V still held true toward the end of 1933
when the monarch told FDR that "we all like your Ambassador and
Mrs. Bingham very much and they are very popular in this country,
where he is well known as a good sportsman and an excellent shot."[51]

As much as Bingham desired the appointment to the Court of St.
James's, he valued home even more. Ray Atherton returned from a
vacation in the States in time to take over for the ambassador in December 1933. Rumors immediately circulated that Bingham had been
recalled, a charge he declared to be "totally erroneous." After landing
in New York, the Binghams traveled first to Baltimore, where the ambassador had a complete checkup with Dr. Hugh Young before pro-
ceeding to Washington, where he met with the president. Bingham
recorded in his diary that FDR appeared pleased with his performance.
Moreover, the president did not even ask about Moley or the after-
math of the London Economic Conference, never wasting "time over
matters that are finished." After a three-hour interview with Roosevelt,
Bingham rushed on to Louisville and then to the Georgia plantation
in time for Christmas. For the next few weeks he intended to relax
with family and friends, particularly his grandsons, and learn about the
state of his newspapers and the machinations of Kentucky politics.[52]

chapter nine

A World Closer to War and Battles on the Home Front

AFTER NEARLY TWO MONTHS of rest in America, the Binghams returned to Great Britain in late February 1934. The ambassador immediately resumed his campaign to educate the English people about the New Deal. To English foes of the Roosevelt administration, Bingham delivered what became a stock reply. He blamed the Hearst press in the United States and the Beaverbrook newspapers in Britain for defaming the president and his administration. "The very crowd you are likely to come in contact with, who have the most to lose and who have been saved from destruction by Mr. Roosevelt, are the ones that are knocking the hardest. It shows how stupid they are," Bingham told an Englishman who questioned the early New Deal record.[1]

To American critics of the White House, Bingham used the same approach. "I believe that he [Roosevelt] will succeed," Bingham explained to his first wife's sister, "but if he fails it will be due to the fact that people like yourself, highly intelligent, high-minded and influential, are so blind and so ignorant of the real situation that you would tear down and destroy the one man and the one influence who has rescued our country, revived it, and is the hope for the restoration of real prosperity."[2]

While Bingham kept up his defense of the administration in early 1934, he received censure from two disparate sources. Both the House of Representatives of the Kentucky General Assembly and Eleanor

Roosevelt became incensed by pieces published in the *Courier.* The scolding from the former might have been expected, owing to the anti-Louisville and anti-*Courier* bias of many Kentuckians. In early March 1934 the *Courier* published a letter highly critical of the Governor Ruby Laffoon administration entitled "The Psalm of Politics" signed by "A Member of the House of Representatives." After polling the House and finding no one to claim the letter, that body voted a resolution of contempt against *Courier* reporter and acting editor Vance Armentrout. Bingham completely supported Armentrout, who refused to reveal the source of the letter even under the threat of a jail sentence. In response the House passed a resolution asking for the recall of Ambassador Bingham "for permitting a false and libelous statement." While some of the state legislators might have been deadly serious, neither the president nor the Department of State took any action.[3]

The normally friendly Bingham–Eleanor Roosevelt correspondence became discordant after publication of a *Courier* editorial by Harrison Robertson on a proposed child-labor amendment. Robertson, following a policy opposing a child-labor amendment laid down by Bingham years before, published a "hateful" critique according to the First Lady, which suggested that only socialists supported such legislation. Mrs. Roosevelt's "bitter complaint" did not go unnoticed by Bingham, who apologized for the cutting tone of the editorial. However, he refused to change the policy, maintaining that Congress had no right to "prevent any form of work by any person under eighteen years of age." Other critics of the papers opined that Bingham opposed the amendment only so that he could continue to exploit newsboys and thereby ensure bigger profits for his papers. Notwithstanding, the typically cordial relationship between the ambassador and the First Lady soon returned to normal.[4]

Bingham's second year as American ambassador to the Court of St. James's embraced many of the same themes as his first year, including steadily working for closer Anglo-American cooperation, making the obligatory speeches and appearances expected of the ambassador, and keeping up with the political homefront. Moreover, Bingham witnessed the continuation of the Geneva Disarmament Conference and the beginning of the London Naval Conference in 1934. That year proved to be the last peaceful respite in Europe before the enveloping war clouds of the mid-thirties.[5]

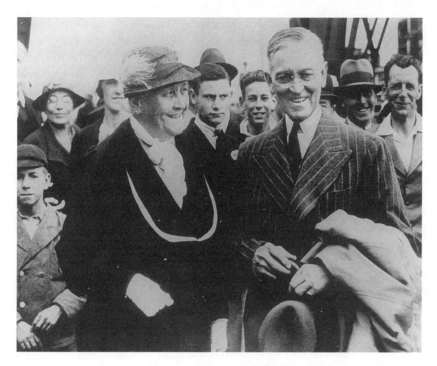

Serving the president as always, Ambassador Bingham greets Sarah Delano Roosevelt on a trip to England in 1934. From the Barry Bingham, Sr., Collection. Reprinted with permission of The Filson Club Historical Society, Louisville, Kentucky.

The ambassador's speeches in early 1934 more fully developed earlier themes. To the American Chamber of Commerce of London in early April, he praised the economic-recovery efforts of the early New Deal. "The first great achievement of the President," Bingham averred, "was the conquest of fear itself." Before a meeting of the Royal Institute of International Affairs a few weeks later, he stressed the political democracy of the English-speaking nations and their desire for peace and understanding in the world. More important, Bingham played a small role in the London Naval Conference, a meeting that proved to be the last chance for arms control in the mid-thirties.[6]

In the spring and summer of 1934, diplomatic maneuvering for reconsideration of earlier naval treaties developed into a test of wills between the major naval powers of the world. Before Bingham returned to London, FDR instructed him to "feel out the British on their attitude towards cooperation with us, in the event a war should break out in Europe or elsewhere" and "to explore the possibilities of united action." Specifically, the president ordered Bingham to relay to the British the American apprehension of giving Japan parity in any new naval arrangement. Bingham later reported that in a meeting with Ramsay MacDonald, the prime minister appeared willing to cooperate in controlling the Japanese desire for more naval tonnage. However, in conversations with other British leaders he detected no determination to stand up against Japan, owing to a more important distraction: the fear of resurgent nationalism and militarism in Germany. The purge of Hitler's stormtroopers, the SA, in Germany in mid-1934 frightened the British into a renewed dread of war and paralyzed improved Anglo-American relations.[7]

When Norman Davis came to London for preliminary negotiations with the British, Bingham kept a wary eye on the Tennessean as the two diplomats sparred over the best ways to approach the British. The ambassador suggested to Davis and Roosevelt that the British appeared so firmly entrenched in their own designs, they would not consider the desires of the United States. He recommended that America for the next several months allow the British to run the course of their present state of mind about armaments and security. "On the whole case, they need us and will need us much worse than we shall need them, and they will come to us in time," he concluded, "if we leave them entirely alone, and make it clear that we have nothing to talk to them about."[8]

Bingham suffered no major illness during his second year in London but continued to have nagging health problems that kept his energy level debilitated. Nevertheless, he fulfilled his duties, which varied in importance. Conferring on world rubber production with the British and presiding at a meeting of the World Wheat Conference were not, of course, as enjoyable as staying in Windsor Castle and having private conversations with King George, who appeared pro-American compared with other members of the government. Probably just as important to Bingham, he could again take up his passion for hunting.[9]

Though often criticized as being an Anglophile by his critics, Bingham took a far more critical view of the British than his detractors perceived. He did not believe that America should bend to the British proposals at the upcoming London Naval Conference. Al-

James Roosevelt greets Ambassador Bingham as he arrives in New York on June 1, 1934, aboard the *Queen Mary*. On the left is Barry Bingham, the ambassador's son. From the Barry Bingham, Sr., Collection. Reprinted with permission of The Filson Club Historical Society, Louisville, Kentucky.

though the anti-American *Evening Standard* claimed that the ambassador had "acquired a remarkably good imitation of an English accent," Bingham himself poked fun at the variety of English accents. Occasionally he criticized the "underlying supercilious attitude" of the English upper classes. Moreover, he echoed the feelings of many of his countrymen when he deplored the lack of British sensitivity about the debt question. To Bingham the attitude of the government of Great Britain needed a complete overhaul. He particularly found its lack of "gratitude" for American aid in World War I to be deplorable. Judging from his correspondence and notations in his diaries, he continually reminded British officials and friends that the majority of Americans felt betrayed by the British course on war debts and the question of stabilization. Notwithstanding, the Louisvillian kept up his pleas on both sides of the Atlantic for Anglo-American cooperation. To Lord Queensborough, a pro-American friend, he explained that "you may be sure that as you love my country next to your own, I love your country next only to my own." The American's greatest fears were that Germany and Japan were about to upset the peace of the world in late 1934.[10]

Bingham's thoughts were often about the uncertainty of events back home. In mid-October 1934 Alice Speed Stoll, the wife of Louisville entrepreneur Berry V. Stoll, disappeared from her Lime Kiln Lane home a short distance from the Binghams' Glenview estate. In the ensuing investigation the police searched the Bingham estate and the surrounding area. To many people this crime appeared to fit a pattern of violence as it coincided with two highly publicized events: the trial of Bruno Richard Hauptmann, the alleged kidnapper of the Lindbergh baby, and the slaying of gunman "Pretty Boy" Floyd.[11]

Bingham reacted quickly to a possible threat to his son Barry, his wife Mary, and their children, fearing that they might be next on the kidnapper's list. He warned Barry to take special precautions, including updating the estate's alarm system, installing lights outside the home, and hiring guards. He also asked that Barry become familiar with firearms. "I am sorry to have to say it to you," the older Bingham implored, "but I think you should carry a short barreled revolver of the type which I always carry when I am at home." Though it was not unusual for even prominent Kentuckians to carry firearms, Barry refused to carry a weapon. The Judge, on the other hand, took pride not only in his ability at hunting with a rifle or shotgun, but also in his skills developed on a pistol range at the Bingham estate. As a sign of his concern for the life of Governor Albert B. Chandler in the mid-thirties, he gave that political figure a revolver. Mrs. Stoll's kidnapper released her after federal agents pursued him into Indiana. After this episode ended, Bingham returned his attention to his somewhat independent role as ambassador.[12]

It was not long until he was embroiled in controversy again, this time because of the content of a speech before the Edinburgh Philosophical Institution on 23 October 1934. In that address he explained that neither Americans nor the English adequately understood the culture, politics, and needs of the other side of the Atlantic, and both should immediately begin to make amends for such misunderstandings. Of course, he stressed the importance of cooperation, emphasizing that the welfare of both nations "is inextricably bound together." He told his British audience that the depression had created worse conditions in the United States than in Great Britain because of the banking crisis of the early thirties, explaining the differences in the problems of each nation. More important, he urged stabilization of the dollar and the pound as necessary moves for improving the economies of both countries.[13]

Adverse reaction came quickly from several antiadministration and anti-Bingham sources. The Hearst and Beaverbrook newspapers immediately attacked the speech. For example, the Manchester *Daily Express* of Beaverbrook branded the speech a "blunder in the eyes of Washington." Before the U.S. Congress, Senator Elmer Thomas of Oklahoma and Representative George Holden Tinkham of Massachusetts scored the ambassador's mention of stabilization. However, Secretary Hull replied to a complaint from Tinkham that Bingham had "repeatedly stated his basis as one of personal opinion" and therefore did not need prior approval from the Department of State for his speeches. Shortly, both Hull and Roosevelt hinted at the same stance in public addresses, and Bingham believed that he had been vindicated for the statement at Edinburgh.[14]

Apparently given his head by the administration, a month later Bingham plunged back into controversy by repeating much of the Edinburgh speech before the Plymouth branch of the English-Speaking Union. He declared that it was time for more than just "lip service" to the idea of cooperation between the United States and Great Britain. This time there developed evidence that the ambassador had gained some support. Lord Mildmay declared the Bingham address "excellent" and the *Plymouth Western Morning News*, which formerly asserted that cooperation with Japan was more important than a move toward the United States, editorialized in bold type about Bingham's "GREAT SPEECH." However, change in English public opinion remained limited and without noticeable momentum.[15]

Bingham's contact with Washington remained strong throughout 1934. Intent on playing a key role in Kentucky political life, he proposed the appointment of either of two friends, Cary Tabb or Stanley Reed, for a federal judgeship in that state. Although he told FDR he disliked "personal political patronage" that allowed senators the privilege of nominating federal judges, he assigned *Courier* Washington chief Ulric Bell the task of lobbying for Tabb or Reed. Shortly afterward the president picked Reed.[16]

Bingham continued to carry out personal assignments for the president, including working for an honorary degree in England for Roosevelt's old Groton schoolmaster Endicott Peabody. There were, of course, more important ways to serve the White House. The ambassador's contact with British officials resulted in the removal of what had developed into a rather embarrassing situation for both governments. After persistent "representations" by Bingham, Sir John Simon of the Foreign Office gave assurances that Lloyd's of London would no longer accept policies for coverage against the possibility that Roosevelt might soon "cease to be President." When FDR traveled to Harrodsburg, Kentucky, in the fall of 1934 to dedicate a pioneer memorial, Bingham assigned Credo Harris, the director of WHAS radio to take care of arrangements. Unfortunately, the ambassador was far away in England and could not personally offer the state's hospitality to Roosevelt, but he could still perform other valuable services for the administration from abroad.[17]

In August, Louis Howe, one of the oldest supporters and staff members of the president, dashed off a telegram to Bingham marked "SE-CRET CODE." Losing his influence in the White House, Howe asked Bingham for money. "Sometime ago you gave a fund in trust for a certain worthy cause. The same cause very urgently needs immediate fund for a particular purpose," Howe advised, "would you be able to get into my hands by September first two thirds of amount previously subscribed." The next day by telegram marked "Personal for Howe from the Ambassador," Bingham wired: "Sending ten [presumably ten thousand dollars] from Louisville tomorrow." No record, other than these two telegrams, has been found. The money could have been used for the pending off-year elections or for one of Howe's increasingly independent projects. Eventually FDR intervened and ordered that Howe separate his business and personal accounting systems. Nevertheless, the appropriation of the money by Bingham proved again his devotion to any cause connected with Roosevelt, even one as muddled as that of Howe's.[18]

As 1934 came to a close, the Binghams made plans to return to the States for a Christmas furlough. In his last interview before departing, the ambassador reiterated his common theme, Anglo-American cooperation. He maintained that, if united, the United States and Great

Britain could bring peace to the world. The *London Observer* applauded the words of Bingham: "Anglo-American solidarity is the one sure thing that can save the world, and their failure to co-operate in time would as surely sink it." In the United States by mid-December, the ambassador conferred with Hull and Roosevelt. The *New York Times* editorialized that it was good to have Ambassadors Dodd and Bingham home for the holidays; it "only hoped that Europe doesn't take advantage of our Ambassadors' absence from their posts and relapse into her worst manners, which can be very bad indeed."[19]

The trip to Louisville offered a change of pace from life in London. When Bingham and his wife arrived in Louisville on Christmas eve, the *Courier-Journal* and *Louisville Times*'s "Newspaper Boys Band" met them at the railway station. A boisterous accompanying crowd of newsboys, twenty-five of whom received a live turkey for adding at least four new subscriptions to their routes, crowded around the train. After playing "My Old Kentucky Home" the band led a parade to the Jefferson County Courthouse and then to the newspapers' offices at Third and Liberty. Signs reading "Fat Fowls" and "Live Turkeys for Live Hustlers" indicated a promotional effort of Barry Bingham's, which apparently succeeded. Relaxation in Glenview and at Pineland Plantation revived the Binghams during the Christmas vacation.[20]

In 1935 the world moved closer to war. The year began ominously with a plebiscite in the Saar Valley overwhelmingly supporting reunion with Germany. At the end of January the U.S. Senate failed to vote for admission to the World Court by seven votes, a decision Bingham blamed on "four foolish and weak-kneed Senators" who changed their votes at the last minute. In the next few months Germany openly rearmed and Herr Hitler announced the beginning of conscription. Meanwhile, Britain and France postured at the Stresa Conference but could not agree on a plan of action as Nazism developed into a more frightening specter in Europe. More important, no one seemed willing to bring up the subject of the fate of Abyssinia (Ethiopia).[21]

The actions of Fascist Italy added to the uneasy sense that war was just around the corner. After the Italian invasion of Ethiopia, the U.S. Congress took a harder look at the developing lawlessness of the world. Nagging suspicions about Japanese intentions in the Pacific complicated American policy toward Europe. "Timid and reserved" reactions of the administration in Washington, according to one diplomatic historian, gave little comfort to a world on the brink of war.[22]

The Roosevelt-Bingham correspondence of mid-1935 offers two examples of the dilemma American policy makers faced during this era, a time in which the general mood of Americans inclined toward isolationism. In late March, Bingham declared "the European atmosphere is surcharged," owing to the growing aggressiveness of Nazism. "I am more than doubtful whether we could keep out of a great European conflagration," the ambassador concluded. The president voiced a more cautious concern: "A very wise old bird tells me that a number of important world forces, including the British, would much like to involve us in some way—any way—in the world's critical problems." Of course, the question would be how much leadership, moral or otherwise, the United States could muster without a public consensus.[23]

Bingham did not return to his diplomatic post until late March 1935, after a complete physical examination by Dr. Young in Baltimore revealed no remaining infection. During his absence the Department of State modernized the communications system of the embassy. In early May an automatic telegraphic typewriter and a new cable link added to the ability of the embassy to communicate more efficiently with Washington.[24]

Bingham kept close touch with affairs in other European nations through his contacts with travelers and other American embassies. He became increasingly alarmed by news from Germany, particularly the word from American and continental visitors who told of increasing Nazi persecution of Jews. By early 1935 the Louisvillian gave up any hope of a more liberal regime coming to power in Germany, predicting war unless European nations put up a united front against Nazism. He also feared the Japanese and privately agreed with an English admiral that joint Anglo-American naval operations in the Pacific might quiet Tokyo's aggressiveness, but then admitted that no such concerted action would be possible until the diplomatic climate improved between Britain and America. To Stanley Baldwin he reported that the United States would stay out of a European war as long as possible. British policy makers, for that matter, appeared unsure of the course their nation should follow. In early April, Bingham sent a lengthy memorandum to Hull on British reaction to German resurgence; in sum, Britain had lost its role of leadership in confronting Nazi aggressiveness.[25]

Anglo-American relations in 1935 remained strained because of the unsettled debt and pound-dollar stabilization questions. Bingham, for his part, continually probed British opinion, not only within White Hall but among the English people as well. His suggestion of tying the value of the dollar and pound together "at the proper time" drew immediate denial from the United States Department of the Treasury. However, Roosevelt said nothing about Bingham's statement. The ambassador reacted by redoubling his efforts to bring about better Anglo-American relations. When the BBC began broadcasting a series, "The American Half-hour" hosted by Alistair Cooke, the ambassador applauded this effort to promote better understanding. Bingham kept close tabs on the program's content, officially complaining about one segment that did not "tend to promote a spirit of friendly understanding." Within a few days Sir John Reith, director of the BBC network, apologized and promised to make amends on the next airing of the program.[26]

Bingham voiced rather strong opinions of the British leaders with whom he had contact in the mid-thirties. He had little respect for the abilities of either Ramsay MacDonald or Neville Chamberlain. During 1935 Bingham kept in close touch with Sir Samuel Hoare, the British foreign secretary whom he believed to be one of the premier political figures in Britain. While the ambassador declared Winston Churchill to be "extremely pleasant" as a dinner companion, he reacted critically to the Englishman's obvious attempt to involve the United States in a naval race with Germany and Japan. Bingham had only good things to say about Anthony Eden, whom he found to be personally charming as well as realistic about the state of Anglo-American relations. The ambassador's views of Stanley Baldwin changed once the Englishman became prime minister. The cordial relationship of 1934, when Baldwin waxed eloquent about a Kentucky country ham that the ambassador had sent, turned sour once Baldwin became prime minister and dismissed Hoare in late 1935. King George, however, continued to express pro-American sentiments and impressed Bingham with his knowledge of world events. In one such personal meeting the king praised Roosevelt and American efforts to end the depression.[27]

In 1935 the invasion of Ethiopia and failure of the London Naval Conference illustrated the accelerating aggressiveness of the totalitarian nations and the inability of anyone to limit naval construction. After two months of border disputes with Ethiopia, Mussolini sent reinforcements into Italian East Africa in February. As American pacifists demonstrated in several large cities, the Nye Committee studied United States entry into the First World War and the alleged role of munition makers and financial communities in that war. Roosevelt soon asked for the largest peacetime defense budget in history and sparred with Congress over proposed neutrality legislation. British and French diplomats tried to work out a peaceful solution knowing that an invasion by the Italian army appeared imminent once the African rainy season ended in September.[28]

Bingham reacted to the Ethiopian crisis by not accepting any speaking engagements, telling his son that the "situation here is too serious and too tense, and I should be a hypocrite if I made any suggestion which could possibly be construed as indicating a possibility that our country would take any hand in their troubles here." However, in late July he returned to the United States for consultation with Roosevelt and Hull on the London Naval Conference, the Italo-Ethiopian crisis, British-American relations, and other matters. While home, Bingham lobbied for the administration's neutrality legislation.[29]

On 31 August 1935 Congress passed the First Neutrality Act, a law, due to expire in one year, forbidding transportation of munitions to warring nations. The law allowed the president no discretionary powers, recalling the policies of William Jennings Bryan more so than those of Woodrow Wilson. Bingham reacted positively to this legislation, except for the latter measure. "I do not mean to claim any great amount of credit for myself, but I have not seen either the President or Mr. Hull since they went into office without bringing this question up [neutrality]," the ambassador explained to his son Barry. The elder Bingham continued: "We surrender only the chance of some traders to make profits. We protect our country from the risks of being involved in war, and, as a peace-loving nation and committed to peace, we put ourselves squarely in support of other nations seeking to maintain the peace of the world." He explained that "the so-called 'freedom of the seas' and 'neutral' rights are mere fictions which can only exist in time of peace." The main thrust of the legislation aimed to keep the United States out of harm's way between warring nations. Bingham predicted that "history may mark this as Mr. Roosevelt's greatest achievement."[30]

Not long after Bingham returned to England, Italy broke off negotiations with the good offices of the British and French and invaded Ethiopia. Of course, the sympathies of most Americans, including the president, were with the kingdom of Haile Selassie against the on-slaught of a modern European army. Although the United States never became privy to the negotiations between the British, French, and Italian governments, Bingham kept close contact with Foreign Secretary Hoare in the Foreign Office. The United States put out feelers intimating that America would support action by the League of Nations. A secret plan by Hoare and Laval to carve up Ethiopia to the advantage of Italy fell through and led to the resignation of Hoare and the fall of the ministry of Pierre Laval in France when word leaked out prematurely. Reaction to these plans ranged from the moral outrage of Roosevelt to the delight of German officials at the embarrassment of the British and French governments. The United States government reacted as only it could legally, implementing the First Neutrality Act and embargoing arms to both Italy and Ethiopia. In the short run, Bingham asserted that the actions of the United States had been both prudent and rational.[31]

On another front, efforts for peace also took another blow as the London Naval Conference completely foundered. Perhaps doomed from the start because of the growing aggression of Germany and Japan, the role of the United States in the proceedings displayed the same tentativeness demonstrated in most other non–Western Hemisphere New Deal foreign-policy positions.[32]

The bad blood between Bingham and Norman Davis intensified when FDR appointed the latter to head an American delegation to the naval conference. Moreover, the ambassador refused to serve as a special delegate at the conference. Throughout his tenure in London, Bingham argued that sending special delegations to Europe, especially headed by dignitaries like Davis, only built up false hopes of American participation among Western nations. In the long run, when America did not assert itself, European heads of state became even more cynical about the intentions of the United States. On at least one occasion in early 1935, Roosevelt told Colonel House that he agreed with Bingham "about having no special missions abroad this summer," accepting the reasoning that it might be better to function through regular diplomatic missions for a while.[33]

British fears of German-Japanese militarism intensified in early 1935. Bingham kept before the British government an American proposal that the Japanese not be given naval parity under any threats or circumstances. The president encouraged Bingham and other diplomats to walk a diplomatic tightrope on the naval armaments question. Nothing dramatic should be expected from the meetings, but no one should believe that the United States was "taking this naval conference casually." Bilateral talks between Britain and Germany brought a response from Hull, who urged Bingham to tell the British that the United States hoped for a permanent Anglo-German agreement on naval tonnage ratios.[34]

The Davis-Bingham relationship deteriorated the longer the Tennessean stayed in London. Bingham interpreted Davis's actions in London as a political game that had nothing whatsoever to do with good diplomacy. He suggested Davis be recalled before any more damage could be done. At first the president appeared to agree with Bingham, but then reversed his tack and sent Davis anyway. Bingham asserted he did not receive adequate explanation for this decision by the White House.[35]

Apparently, Davis exceeded instructions from the beginning of his negotiations with the British. Roosevelt finally dashed off an urgent note asking Hull to "keep me in daily touch with what Davis is doing—I hear several dispatches have come from him showing that Davis is talking debts and economics. That is not his job!" Later in November 1935, in nearly identical letters, Hull and Roosevelt apologized to Bingham for the behavior of Davis and for their decison to send him to the London Naval Conference. Both extolled Bingham as occupying the "premier position of all the notable Americans" serving in diplomatic posts. Bingham could hardly contain his elation at being vindicated in his judgment of Davis. In early 1936 the conference sank into impotency after the Japanese walked out, and apparently another chance had been lost to keep the peace in the world. But events as well as the efforts of Bingham and others began easing Anglo-American tensions of the early thirties, and both nations moved ever so slowly toward cooperation.[36]

Though dedicated to his ambassadorial duties, family, business, and the current condition of local, state, and national politics were always on Bingham's mind. When he accepted the diplomatic post, he pushed his youngest son, Barry, then only twenty-seven years of age, into the publisher's chair. Robert Worth, Jr., who could never "take hold" of the newspaper business because of his alcoholism, worked for Carters Merchants, a wholesale grocery firm in London, but still depended on his father for an allowance. Henrietta spent a good deal of the thirties in Europe as the companion of world-class tennis player Helen Jacobs. Unfortunately, her bouts with alcoholism continued, as on one occasion when Jacobs reported to the ambassador that Henrietta had lapsed into a state of depression, being "in one of her martyr moods." These circumstances thrust Barry into a position of family leadership because both older siblings showed neither the inclination nor the ability to take on any of Robert Worth Bingham's enterprises.[37]

During his tenure as ambassador, Bingham kept in close contact with his Louisville papers. Although Barry stepped into the position of publisher, Emanuel Levi, Harrison Robertson, and Tom Wallace continued to hold sway over *Courier* and *Times* business and editorial policies. Before leaving Louisville, the ambassador announced that Barry would handle policy as president and copublisher of the companies. His long-term plans included finding a "first-rate man with a southern background, to begin with, but who has been to one of the Eastern colleges, and who is primarily a gentleman" to take over the day-to-day operations of the papers. The search began for such a person. If Barry lacked credibility with the older staff members because of his inexperience, he determined to assert his prerogatives as publisher, and would be soon tested by Levi, Robertson, and Wallace.[38]

During Bingham's second year away from Louisville, the newspaper business in that city reached a critical point. The fall of Banco-Kentucky in the early thirties caused the eventual sale of James B. Brown's *Herald-Post*. From London, Bingham suggested to Levi that when the opportunity presented itself, the plant of these competing papers should be bought up and shipped out of the city for "junk." "As long as that plant is free," he maintained, "it is an invitation to adventurers, who may be only temporarily troublesome." Nevertheless, only the physical dismissal of the *Herald-Post* would suit the designs of Bingham to control completely the daily print media of Louisville. Although in its death throes, the *Herald-Post* struggled on for a few more months.[39]

At the *Courier* and *Times* offices, momentum carried the papers for a while. Levi, Robertson, and Wallace dominated their respective roles on the staff. Herbert S. Agar, who served stints with the *Courier* as editorial-page editor from 1929 to 1934 and 1940 to 1942, became the elder Bingham's first candidate to serve at the right hand of his son. Agar presented some outstanding credentials, having just won a Pulitzer prize in 1933 for *The People's Choice: From Washington to Harding;*

A Study in Democracy, an ardently pro–Democratic-party work. However, in 1934 Agar traveled extensively on the continent and became more detached from the Louisville papers. Apparently Barry and Agar could not work out a satisfactory arrangement over time off for lecturing, and the latter left the papers later that year.[40]

The irascible Robertson occasionally printed an anti–New Deal or anti-Roosevelt editorial or article without first clearing them with Barry, the titular head of the papers. The Judge usually reacted quickly when he received word of these indiscretions. "I am in real distress of mind over the attitude of the editorial page towards the President and the administration in some important phases," the elder Bingham once wrote Robertson. Although the old editor soon replied that "it is my misfortune, to my sorrow, to have displeased you," he soon returned to sniping at the administration.[41]

In November 1935 Robertson contributed to one of the most embarrassing incidents in Bingham's long connection with the papers. The *Courier* published a letter in the "Point of View" column asserting that Patrick Henry Callahan, a well-known Louisville industrialist and dry Catholic, had accepted delivery of liquor to his home. In fact, his daughter Edith had placed the order for a party, one to which Barry and Mary Bingham were invited. Barry later confessed the whole disconcerting business to his father. He explained that Robertson printed the letter because he did not believe that Callahan could possibly have been legitimate in his prohibitionist sentiments. Barry stopped the story after the first edition reached the streets, but the damage had already been done. He made a personal trip to apologize to a badly shaken Callahan.[42]

Bingham and his son soon began working on a strategy to take primary responsibility for the *Courier* away from Robertson. Barry tried to persuade the elderly editor to take on the task of writing a history of the papers, a job that would absorb all of Robertson's writing. He did not succeed, and Robertson continued to be a thorn in the young copublisher's side.[43]

Otherwise, the papers appeared well-off through 1935. Popular cartoonists Paul Plaschke in the *Times* and Grover Page in the *Courier* turned out award-winning cartoons. Under the financial and circulation leadership of Emanuel Levi and Howard Stodghill, the papers prospered and returned bigger profits than ever before during the ownership of Bingham. When Levi pushed for a partial ownership of the papers in reward for his years of service to Bingham, the ambassador instead allowed Levi and Stodghill to organize an insurance company and use a circulation promotion that enticed new subscribers by selling to them an inexpensive accident-insurance policy. In the mid-thirties Levi increased the investments of the papers in such areas as telephoto service and magazine features. Although Bingham urged his son to assert himself in his dealings with Levi, he displayed the utmost confidence in both Levi and Stodghill. Levi, he found, had "an extraordinary grasp of the financial end" of the papers. Stodghill he believed was "the best all-around newspaper man in the country."[44]

Concern for the political welfare of his adopted state was never far from the mind of Ambassador Bingham. For most of his life he remained independent on the local and state political scene, and through the early thirties he continued to fight the remnants of the old bipartisan combine. In the 1931 gubernatorial race, for example, he and his papers gave lukewarm support to Republican William B. Harrison, former mayor of Louisville, in his race against Democrat Ruby Laffoon. From 1932 on, however, Bingham understood that supporting a Republican in local or state races reflected on the White House. He determined to stay, if at all possible, with the Democratic party in Kentucky politicism and became even more concerned about nominating a Democratic gubernatorial candidate in 1935 who would not be tainted by contact with the combine or other special interests. The services of old political warhorse Percy Haly became more important as Barry depended almost entirely on the sagacity of the old general in his father's absence. Ironically, the Binghams willingly worked with Louisville Democratic bosses Mrs. Lennie McLaughlin and Mike Brennan, who "worked the precincts" and turned out the vote with regularity. Bingham, however, never lost his visceral disdain for professional Irish-American politicos and hoped that Haly could influence the more "substantive" matters in the Louisville Democracy.[45]

Throughout the early thirties Bingham kept his pledge to rid the state of the influence of the "bipartisan gang" and Governor Laffoon, whom he labeled "a fool and a tool" of the old crowd. Bingham displayed every intention of using his papers and his fortune in changing this political climate. Either directly to the president or Louis Howe or through presidential secretary Marvin McIntyre, a native Kentuckian who early in his career had worked at the *Times,* Bingham kept the

White House informed of his efforts to cleanse the Commonwealth of Kentucky of the remnants of the old bipartisan combine.[46]

Part of that plan included a challenge to the usual political appointments in Kentucky. Bingham first tried to obtain for Haly a federal appointment as internal revenue director for Kentucky, but the administration gave Seldon Glenn that position. The ambassador declared Glenn to be the antithesis of good government, one who constantly sought ways to line his pockets with public funds. The administration apparently listened to the Democratic old guard rather than to Bingham. With the upcoming gubernatorial campaign of 1935 Bingham searched for a candidate who would make "one able, upright Governor." John Young Brown, a young lawyer noted for his oratorical skills, who had suffered defeat in reelection to the U.S. House of Representatives in 1934, first caught the publisher's eye. Most important, Bingham feared that the "present bipartisan regime" of Democrat Billy Klair and Republican Maurice Galvin would control the election.[47]

Political events of 1935 in Kentucky proved to be among the most interesting and colorful in the history of the commonwealth. The ambassador and his papers played a crucial role in one of the most controversial gubernatorial elections in Kentucky history. Bingham resolved to defeat the old guard conservatives in the Democratic party, that is, those forces that had put Ruby Laffoon in office in 1931 and often cooperated with their Republican cohorts in the guise of the bipartisan combine. Long before the gubernatorial election of 1935 Bingham began to muster his own forces against the Democratic machine in Frankfort. He used a network of personal friends, political allies, and business associates to look for an opponent for Thomas S. Rhea, the choice of Laffoon. Ulric Bell in Washington and Percy Haly in Louisville worked diligently to find a reform-minded candidate who would be receptive to the idea of opposing Rhea and who would also receive the wholehearted support of the Roosevelt administration.[48]

"The election of a Republican governor in November would be a blow to the national administration," Bingham explained to an old political ally, "and it should be prevented, if possible." He predicted that if no reform-minded candidate could be found, "this bi-partisan gang of unprincipled robbers will follow Huey Long's methods with [the next] Governor and servile legislature."[49]

As Bingham searched about for a candidate, he considered: John Y. Brown; Neville Miller, mayor of Louisville; and old Democratic party warhorse J. C. W. Beckham. At first Bingham paid little attention to the rising young star among Kentucky Democrats, Lieutenant-Governor Albert B. "Happy" Chandler. The White House took an increasing interest in the upcoming gubernatorial race. Colonel House personally assured Bingham that the administration wanted to keep Democratic control of the governor's seat in Kentucky, but not if it meant electing a machine politician. Bingham wanted Beckham to run. A longtime political ally of Haly and Bingham, Beckham epitomized progressivism to some Kentuckians; to others he represented only weak leadership that ascended to power in the wake of the assassination of Governor William Goebel in 1900.[50]

In early 1935, before returning to his European post, Bingham conferred with Roosevelt in Washington about the "Kentucky situation." Apparently, the White House agreed with the ambassador's plans of stopping Rhea at all costs by supporting Beckham. Bingham and some others in the state visualized the election as an important test of grassroots support for Roosevelt, one that would have great impact on the presidential election of 1936 a year later. Several problems militated against the candidacy of Beckham in 1935. First, the recent tragic death of his son, Crepps, broke the hearts of both mother and father. Second, Mrs. Beckham's mental health deteriorated to the point that her husband feared a possible suicide attempt.[51]

However, Bingham persuaded Roosevelt to urge Beckham personally to run for governor. The Louisvillian did his part, donating at least twenty-five thousand dollars for Beckham's campaign. Beckham, sixty-five years old at the time, also needed money for his own personal finances. As the Talbott-Johnson and Laffoon-Rhea factions in the Democratic party jockeyed for position in the upcoming August primary, Beckham decided not to run for governor in late April, citing age, health, and family problems as the causes. As a parting tribute, Bingham immediately set about the task of having Beckham appointed to a federal position.[52]

Meanwhile, Lieutenant-Governor Chandler and Governor Laffoon became locked in a titanic political struggle. Chandler, who had had designs on the governor's seat since he had entered politics, supported the primary over the convention nominating process and opposed

Laffoon's sales-tax proposal from his position as presiding officer of the state senate. Called to Washington to explain the inability of Kentucky to comply with New Deal policies, Laffoon had barely cleared the state when Chandler, who technically became governor at that point, called a special session of the Kentucky General Assembly. After several court decisions and political compromising, the general assembly adopted a dual, or "double-barrel," primary system with a runoff provision in the event that a candidate did not win a majority in the first primary.[53]

After Beckham declined to run for governor, Bingham had little choice but to support Chandler. "As soon as Gov. Beckham refused to become a candidate for the nomination," Bingham explained to Ulric Bell, "I made up my mind that Chandler was the best bet." Although Bingham wanted Chandler to win the nomination and subsequent election to the governorship, he did not rule out the possibility of supporting the Republican nominee, Judge King Swope, if Rhea were nominated. In early June, Barry Bingham and Chandler met and discussed the needs of the state. Based on Barry's recommendation, the Judge backed Chandler.[54]

Once committed, Bingham and his papers pushed the candidacy of Chandler with vigor; he also added a much-needed ten thousand dollars to the campaign coffers of the candidate. After a summer of hard campaigning Chandler ran second to Rhea in the first primary. In the runoff primary several weeks later in September the lieutenant governor carried a majority to become the Democratic-party candidate against Republican Swope.[55]

As the 1935 fall general election heated up, Bingham offered some practical, if unethical, advice for the upcoming campaign to Marvin McIntyre in the White House. "The contracts let by the WPA should be handled in such a way that they are not hurtful in any way to our cause," he suggested. Whether McIntyre passed along this advice is unknown, but the payrolls of the Kentucky WPA in the fall of 1935 more than doubled in the weeks before the general election. Swope cried dirty politics, but to no avail. Barry reported to his father that Chandler appeared willing to accept the good counsel of Beckham, Dan Talbott, and General Haly in the coming months. While the younger Bingham did not find Chandler's rough campaign style to his liking, he declared that the candidate has "a most ingratiating way of presenting his case, and I can see why he has been such a success as a stump speaker." Barry and Chandler began to work together in the coming weeks. Chandler praised the friendship of "your fine son, Barry Bingham" and the warm support of Beckham in a letter to Robert Worth Bingham.[56]

Although Laffoon and Rhea did not support Chandler in the general election, the latter swept into office by a large majority in what many political observers interpreted as a successful referendum for the New Deal. Chandler carried Louisville by over seventeen thousand votes, no doubt due to the cooperation of Mayor Miller, Democratic-machine politicians Mickey Brennan and Mrs. Lennie McLaughlin, and the editorial support of the *Courier* and *Times*. That margin offset the strong race that Swope ran in other parts of the state.[57]

Bingham had the greatest faith that Chandler would fulfill his promises to run a clean, efficient administration. "I believe he is honest, sincere and intelligent, and that he will go into office with a firm purpose to make good," the ambassador told a close Louisville friend. He also ordered the *Courier* and *Times* editors to support the new governor fully in the upcoming session of the Kentucky General Assembly scheduled to meet in early January 1936. "We should give Chandler a real chance," the Judge told his son, "and avoid any form of carping, nagging criticism." To another Louisville associate, Bingham expressed his hope for the future of the state: "the great thing, though, is that at last we are on our way" toward cleaning up the state. Over the next two years Bingham attempted to influence heavily, if not to dominate, the Chandler administration.[58]

In the remaining months of 1935 Bingham became increasingly concerned about deteriorating peace in Europe. The Johnson Debt Default Act of 1934, prohibiting private loans to any government that had not paid its war debts, complicated Anglo-American relations throughout 1935. British stubbornness about making even token debt payments exasperated the normally mild-mannered Bingham. Nevertheless, in his final speech of 1935, on Thanksgiving Day, he connected the destinies of "the two great Democracies, the British Commonwealth of Nations and the United States." "Neither has any hostility towards any other nation; any designs upon the territory of anyone else, and any purpose except that by promoting the prosperity and welfare of their own peoples, and by exerting their great weight throughout the world on behalf of peace," Bingham explained, "they will, after first caring for their own countries, contribute to the welfare of the whole world."[59]

In a more realistic sense, however, Bingham found little cause for optimism in late 1935. During the Christmas season he explained not only his own fears but those of the British in a letter to Roosevelt. The British were, above all, afraid of playing "into Germany's hands." Ominously, there appeared to be no united front against Nazism in Britain. "The better informed people here regard Germany as the real menace but there is much pro-German sentiment in the country and widespread criticism of France, and some actual feeling of antagonism and hostility," Bingham warned the president. The ambassador had little respect for the Prince of Wales, the heir to the throne, whom he declared to be little more than a "German protagonist." He had no hope for action by the League of Nations or collaboration of the European powers against the growing militarism of either Germany or Italy, but hinted that a change of government at White Hall might bring a fresh approach to settling the problems of Europe.[60]

chapter ten

Turning Points

DURING 1936 BINGHAM DEMONSTRATED a growing confidence in his ability to influence events as publisher and as ambassador. He continued his role as chief advocate of the Roosevelt administration in the United Kingdom. Never relenting in his belief that closer ties between the English-speaking nations offered the only hope for world security, he became even more aggressive in his attempts to influence British opinion. He wisely understood that events would perhaps dictate the future of Anglo-American relations, and he, more than his critics knew, did not want the United States to become subservient to British policy.

In 1936 the Bingham papers went through great turmoil. Barry Bingham asserted his position as copublisher, assuming more responsibilities for the papers. In state politics the elder Bingham sustained his role as tormentor of old-guard Democratic-party politicos as he gave wholehearted support to the administration of upstart governor Albert B. Chandler. On the national scene he persisted in his support of FDR, whom he regarded as the greatest political figure of his lifetime.

During Bingham's diplomatic career he operated within a well-defined milieu. In American government, and more particularly in the administration of foreign affairs of the thirties, an "old boy" network operated within the Roosevelt administration. Moreover, Bingham participated in a coterie of diplomats with a decided southern flair, including Bingham in Great Britain, Josephus Daniels in Mexico, W. E. Dodd in Germany, and Breckinridge Long in Italy. Even native Hoosier Claude Bower's prosouthern interpretation of history qualified him for the group as ambassador to Spain. All, of course, were among the first to support the presidential bid of Franklin D. Roosevelt. Most followed the internationalist zeal of Woodrow Wilson and the latter-day advice of Colonel Edward House. With Kentuckian Marvin McIntyre as secretary to the president, Bingham had little difficulty gaining the attention of the Oval Office. His circle also included both American and English connections in the Masonic order and other fraternal organizations.[1]

Poor health plagued Bingham's tenure as chief American diplomat to the Court of St. James's. Never entirely free from occasional pain and weakness, he submitted to complete medical examinations in England in December 1935, and at the Brady Institute in Baltimore in March 1936. When neither examination diagnosed any cause for Bingham's recurring health problems, he stoically blamed his suffering on the ravages of advancing age. Particularly noticeable to Barry, the Judge began to develop "a bit of a stomach," which appeared unusual owing to his spare diet and fastidious concern about his health and appearance.[2]

Other sources made his life uncomfortable as well. Throughout his time in Britain, Bingham received censure from critics who most often cited his allegedly pro-British stance. For example, one anonymous correspondent, who signed the letter "An American for America Only" railed: "Honored Sir; Be damn careful with secretive agreements and diplomatic pitfalls with the wily hipricritical [*sic*] English, lest you emulate the disgraceful pro-English record of Walter Hines Page." He also continued to receive periodic broadsides because he appeared to be anti-Irish. And then there was always William C. Bullitt, whom Bingham argued worked against him within the State Department. After weathering these verbal storms for nearly four years, Bingham seriously considered retiring from his post in 1936. Discussions with Hull, House, and Roosevelt brought an agreement that Bingham should remain on the job until January 1938.[3]

In a critique of the early years of New Deal diplomacy, Howard Jablon has postulated that the single-minded, domineering leadership of Secretary of State Cordell Hull blunted any hope for creative policy from 1933 through 1937. Hull, in short, was obsessed with free

trade and reciprocal trade agreements to the exclusion of more substantive foreign policy. In several ways Bingham played a part in this
"devotion to the reciprocal trade program." First, the secretary of state
and House headed a powerful interest group within the administration, and the Judge followed their lead. Second, southern congressmen and southerners historically had accepted the ideal of world peace
through better trade relations. Perhaps most important of all, the
American people and the administration in Washington indicated no
consensus on any policy save that on domestic issues in the early New
Deal years. Bingham's early suggestion that the United States should
"stay on our side and let them come to us" suited the times. No one
agreed more than President Franklin D. Roosevelt.[4]

If the United States still lacked a coherent foreign policy in 1936,
Bingham went about his task from another perspective. His raison
d'être to bring about closer relations between the United States and
Great Britain finally began to bear fruit as British attitudes began to
shift. While the British government hesitated to talk about a reciprocal trade agreement early in 1936 because of the uncertainty of the
reelection of FDR, the English people moved ever so slowly toward a
consensus that allowed them to produce a coherent defense and rearmament policy.[5]

War clouds gathered more intensity over Europe and the world in
1936. Bingham relayed to Roosevelt his feeling that Germany would
go to war "if they feel they can get away with it, and it may happen
through some untoward event which we cannot immediately foresee."
To an English friend he declared that "there is grave reason to suspect
that Hitler and Mussolini are beginning to work together on the basis
of dividing up the world between them." Unfortunately, he also found
a strong pro-German sentiment among a minority in Britain and
people "more anxious and apprehensive than I have ever seen them
before."[6]

If there was growing concern in England about the threat of aggression, the same held true in the United States. Japanese aggressiveness caused apprehension as that island nation continued its military
expansion in Asia. Bingham's contacts with Japanese diplomats in
London led him to some rather strong conclusions. When a new Japanese ambassador came to London, the Louisvillian found him to be
"very suave and able and determined to convince both the British and
ourselves that the Liberal element in Japan again has the upper hand;

that excesses of the army clique are being restrained, and, on the whole, that the Japanese are peace-minded, and really good fellows indeed." However, Bingham asserted to his government and his English friends that the only hope of restraining Japan lay in complete Anglo-American cooperation in the Pacific. "I do not think the Japanese will ever respond to any argument but force," he averred.[7]

The European scene, of course, remained the primary focus of most Americans. The advance of German soldiers into the Rhineland on 7 March 1936 shocked the world. "The timing of the maneuver caught everyone off guard, even the wary French," according to diplomatic historian Arnold A. Offner. One week later FDR signed a congressional resolution that extended the 1935 Neutrality Act through May 1937. In London, Bingham reacted with alarm, declaring that German diplomats were "trying to ingratiate themselves not only with the British, but with us" in a ploy to gain support for their aggression. When German ambassador Von Hirsch died suddenly, Bingham reported that he thought the poor diplomat had either been murdered or forced into suicide. In contrast to Joseph P. Kennedy, who succeeded the Louisvillian at the Court of St. James's and initially "supported German economic expansion and closer Anglo-German relations," Bingham opposed any such appeasement. But he also agreed with American Ambassador William E. Dodd, who saw little hope of forestalling the Hitler war machine in the mid-thirties. In 1936, as Germany grew stronger the Louisvillian intensified his pleas to Hull and Roosevelt for closer ties with the United Kingdom.[8]

Throughout 1936 Bingham kept up a steady barrage of pro-cooperationist speeches and press releases. Before the Association of British Chambers of Commerce he praised the benefits of Wilsonian internationalism and Hull's proposal for reduced tariffs. "The surest method of preventing war," he argued, "lies in the restoration of normal international trade, bringing with it the promise to the peoples of the world of a better standard of living and the hope of a fuller life." More specifically, he declared his belief that both the United States and Great Britain were at last ready to arm against aggression.[9]

After a brief trip to America in June to welcome FDR at the dedication of the Lincoln Memorial near Hodgenville, Kentucky, and discussions with the president about "matters political," Bingham rushed back to his diplomatic post. On the Fourth of July, in a short speech to the American Society in London, broadcast to the United States on

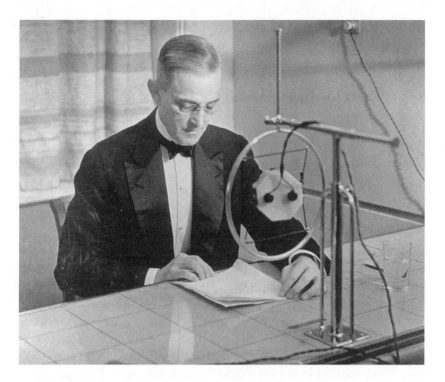

Always interested in communications, Bingham used radio transmissions to America. He warned of imminent war during this July 4, 1936, broadcast. From the Barry Bingham, Sr., Collection. Reprinted with permission of The Filson Club Historical Society, Louisville, Kentucky.

the CBS network, he expounded on the same themes he had been preaching for nearly four years. The English speaking and "other free peoples in the world" must cooperate to confront the forces of "tyranny." "In a world armed and arming, we must and will be fully prepared, gun for gun, ship for ship, plane for plane, man for man, to protect our homes and our country," Bingham challenged. Dramatically, he ended his address exclaiming: "I say again that ours is the supreme heritage among men, to be cherished, to be loved, to serve, to live and, if need be, to die for!"[10]

It did not take long for an isolationist reaction to set in. Bingham "should be recalled," demanded one Irish-American lawyer in Philadelphia of FDR. Another critic told Hull that the American ambassador's remarks would lose votes in the upcoming presidential race. Bingham did not relent. Not long after the revolt of General Franco and the beginning of the Spanish Civil War, the Louisvillian spoke before an English-Speaking Union garden party at Capesthorne in Cheshire. Although in the early part of his speech he appeared to back off slightly from his previous call for Anglo-American cooperation, he continued to stress the common culture, language, and ethnic background of the two countries. The United States did not desire an alliance with any nation; however, Bingham explained, "there are many ties which draw the English-speaking nations together." "We are the great free peoples of this earth," he exclaimed.[11]

In 1936 momentous changes came at the Bingham papers in Louisville. Some of the old problems continued. Robertson wrote occasional irritating editorials that slipped by Barry, but the old editor slowly began to give up his control over the *Courier* editorial page. The *Herald-Post* tottered on the brink of bankruptcy under the ownership of Louisville industrialist Walter Girdler, Sr. Earlier in August 1935, *Courier* and *Times* vice-president Emanuel Levi came up with a scheme "for taking over" the *Herald-Post* by forming a partnership of Bingham and Girdler. Bingham would hold the majority of stock in the subsequent holding company; Levi, Stodghill, and Girdler, smaller amounts. Bingham reported in his diary that "it was, of course, disappointing that he [Levi] should even suggest such a proposition to me, but I had great difficulty in making him understand it was impossible, from my point of view." The ambassador became more and more uneasy about the work of Levi and Stodghill, suspecting that they had not been as loyal to his companies as he had earlier believed.[12]

As copublishers the Binghams sought solutions to some problems at the papers in 1936. Moreover, the Judge not only thought about leaving his ambassadorial post, but also contemplated the time when he would no longer be actively engaged in running the papers. Wilson Wyatt, a junior partner in the firm of Peter, Heyburn, and Marshall began handling most of the Bingham properties' legal affairs. He became close friends with the younger Bingham and a trusted adviser and business associate for many years to come.[13]

More important, the ambassador and his son persisted in their attempt to find a southerner to take over the managerial duties at the papers. In early March 1936 Barry initiated talks with Mark Ethridge, editor of the *Richmond Times-Dispatch* and a native Mississippean. Within a matter of days the Binghams presented an offer to Ethridge in which they made it plain that he would never be allowed to own stock in the Louisville papers. The Judge offered a two-thousand-dollar-per-month salary for a position as general manager, plus the promise of a substantial loan in a few years if Ethridge decided to leave Louisville and purchase an interest in another paper. After talking to Ethridge personally during the trip home in early March, the Judge declared that "the more I talked to him, the more eager I became to have him come to the C-J." In early April, Ethridge accepted the Binghams' offer. Barry soon wrote his father: "I don't believe there is any limit to the amount of good he [Ethridge] can do us after he gets into action."[14]

Even as negotiations proceeded with Ethridge, the Binghams worked to sever the connection of Levi and Stodghill with their enterprises. Not long after allowing Levi and Stodghill to organize the insurance-subscription promotional scheme for the papers, the Judge doubted the wisdom of his decision. Moreover, he and Barry uncovered evidence that Levi had not been completely honest with them over the years. Levi, in particular, appeared to resent the younger Bingham's assertion of his prerogative as copublisher of the papers. In the middle of February a meeting between the Judge and Levi left the publisher with the impression that Levi had a "power mania." The Binghams collected a rather strong indictment against Levi. They believed that he had abused several longtime advertisers and misused funds lent for the formation of the insurance company. Moreover, the Judge could not abide Levi's push to purchase control of the *Herald-Post*. After conferring with his father, Barry fired Levi and Stodghill. At the suggestion of Percy Haly he hired Lisle Baker, Jr., a Frankfort banker, who immediately replaced Levi as the chief financial officer of the Bingham enterprises.[15]

With the coming of Ethridge and Baker the environment at the papers began to change. First, Herbert Agar wrote only occasional pieces for the papers, and Robertson loosened his control over the editorial page. Second, after the tough times at the beginning of the Great Depression, the papers began to turn substantial and consistent profits. Easing out of the insurance business became the number-one priority of the papers. When the papers stopped soliciting insurance policies, all expected a drop in circulation. After a few months, however, Ethridge reported to Bingham that publication expenses had been reduced by forty thousand dollars a year while circulation increased for both papers with the *Courier* up to nearly 230,000 daily, making it one of the leading regional papers in circulation in the nation. Remodeling changed the appearance of the old building. By October the Judge declared that Barry, Ethridge, and Baker were running the papers "for the first time, as I have always wanted them run." The ambassador vowed that he wanted nothing less than making the *Courier* "the outstanding liberal paper in the United States." Barry could report that he, Baker, and Ethridge were entirely compatible in their working relationship, forming a "close triumvirate." The bottom line for 1936 was that the papers cleared over $190,000 after taxes and dividends.[16]

The problems caused by Levi and the *Herald-Post* came to a head in late 1936. Levi went to work for Hearst in Chicago at the *Herald,* but left behind the legacy of the Independence Insurance Company. "If we can just get this damned insurance thing out of the way," Barry declared, "I feel like we will have a clear track ahead and we ought to make grand progress." Although the Judge charged that Levi and Stodghill had taken more than eighty thousand dollars for their insurance company from the *Courier* and *Times* without his knowledge, he allowed the matter to rest. The *Herald-Post* made its last gasp in late 1936 as it passed into receivership in early November. The Bingham papers, in order to have "insurance," subscribed to several features that had been carried in the *Herald-Post,* including "that God-awful Popeye," Barry reported to his father. One final difficulty could not be so easily resolved. Harrison Robertson refused to resign, retire, or take time off to write a history of the papers and continued to write an occasional annoying piece. The Judge urged Barry and Ethridge to "be patient with him and with me. He is an old man, a fine character, and has given his best to you and to me." Otherwise, in late 1936 the papers appeared to be in their best shape ever.[17]

Nineteen thirty-six brought not only the first year of the Chandler administration, but also an important Kentucky senatorial race coinciding with the reelection bid of Franklin D. Roosevelt. Bingham kept up his interest in the affairs of Kentucky, intending to press his advantage to obtain action from Chandler on issues that had concerned him for some time. He hoped that Haly and Beckham would become the closest advisers of the young governor. Chandler, however, did not rely solely on Bingham and his clique for counsel, but also sought out J. Dan Talbott and a few others.[18]

Both Binghams insisted on Chandler's ear because of their all-out support in the 1935 gubernatorial race. For example, returning from a trip to Washington, D.C., in late 1936, Chandler, Barry, and Haly rode the train together from Richmond, Virginia, to Kentucky. As soon as circumstances permitted, Barry reported: "I cleared out and let the General [Haly] get a chance at him. He talked to him for three hours, and I believe got over some excellent advice. He needs it, and if he will only take it from the General he will avoid the mistakes that have been threatening him." Chandler, for the most part, satisfied the Binghams with his running of the state during the first two years of his administration.[19]

In those years the Judge used his political alter ego, Haly, as his political point man in Kentucky. By letter, telegram, or telephone from London, or personally whenever he came to the commonwealth, he made known his ideas about governing the state. He suggested appointments, urging Chandler to work closely with Louisville mayor Neville Miller. Characteristic of Bingham's old progressive predilections, he warned the young politician to beware of "the forces of evil" in the state, which "have always existed and always will exist." "Step by step you are producing for Kentucky what I have worked for and hoped for these many years," the publisher explained to Chandler. When the governor hired Thomas H. Cutler, a nationally known highway administrator, as chief engineer of the Kentucky Highway Department, Bingham personally supplemented the engineer's salary with a monthly check for $583.33 from a special account he used for such purposes. In this case Bingham fulfilled his old claim from the anti-bond-issue days of a decade before that he desired a highway system in Kentucky that was not only well planned but honestly administered as well. Paying the extra stipend enticed Cutler to come to Kentucky from Virginia and avoided the five-thousand-dollar constitutional salary limit for state officials.[20]

With his influence in the state capital at an all-time high—thanks to his support of Chandler in the 1935 gubernatorial election—Bingham pushed the election of his old political ally, J. C. W. Beckham, to the U.S. Senate in 1936. The ambassador urged his old friend into a race for which Beckham only halfheartedly campaigned. In the August primary Beckham, with the support of Chandler and Bingham, ran against incumbent M. M. Logan and John Y. Brown. The candidacy of Brown infuriated the Judge because he realized that the former U.S. congressman would take votes away from Beckham. Bingham gave unstintingly of his money to the Beckham campaign, and the Louisville papers editorialized in favor of the old governor.[21]

On primary election day Logan won by nearly three thousand votes, with Beckham finishing in second place, and Brown polling about half as many votes as the former governor. Owing to the influence of the Bingham papers, Beckham carried Jefferson County but lost in northern and central Kentucky. Barry reported to his father that Beckham did not run a very energetic race, even suffering from over-confidence. The ambassador, however, placed the entire blame on the candidacy of John Y. Brown, whose "base conduct," he declared, "deserves nothing more from any one who is decent." Moreover, the scars of the old bipartisan-combine days returned to haunt the candidacy of Beckham, perhaps for the last time in Kentucky political history.[22]

After "Happy" Chandler settled into the governor's chair, he followed a more independent path than that preferred by Barry and his father. True to his word, the young governor saw to overturning the hated sales tax; he then pushed the general assembly into passage of new separate excises on such items as cigarettes and liquor. Chandler proved to be a fiscal conservative who took most of his cues from his mentor, Senator Harry Flood Byrd of Virginia. He bickered with New Deal administrators and often aroused the ire of WPA head Harry Hopkins. Moreover, the little political engine that drove the governor into the statehouse also pushed his ambitions toward other offices. He desired a seat in the U.S. Senate and seriously considered one day running for the White House.[23]

The 1936 presidential election presented the Binghams with another opportunity to serve FDR and the administration. Early that spring Louis Howe, the president's oldest staff member, imposed again on Bingham's support of the president by asking for and receiving a contribution of ten thousand dollars for a hazy "educational campaign." Howe's plans presumably included organizing a publishing company to print proadministration material. After Bingham asked for clarification from Roosevelt, Jim Farley investigated and found that Howe had been using the money for personal reasons. FDR stopped this practice and the accelerating "embarrassment" that Howe had brought to him. Within weeks Howe died.[24]

Several months before the Democratic National Convention, Chandler suggested that Bingham head the Kentucky delegation at the

Governor A. B. "Happy" Chandler and Ambassador Bingham greet each other at the 1936 Democratic convention. From the Barry Bingham, Sr., Collection. Reprinted with permission of The Filson Club Historical Society, Louisville, Kentucky.

Philadelphia meeting. The ambassador declined, maintaining that such a move would make him too much of a "partisan." However, he fully intended to play some role in the upcoming election. As much as Bingham wanted to get back to the States, he suggested, owing to the turbulent political climate in Europe, that neither he nor other American diplomats stray from their posts for long. Roosevelt insisted, however, that the Louisvillian come home briefly to work on press relations, specifically "to lay a lot of ground work in the Associated Press organization looking toward complete fairness by them." Bingham acceded to the president's wishes that he should "be on hand to watch every move by the Associated Press control, and to do anything else which you may think desirable," a duty that also included working with the radio networks.[25]

In late May, Bingham boarded the SS *Queen Mary* on its maiden voyage to the United States. While on board he broadcast several short messages describing the ship. As the vessel reached New York harbor, he reiterated his long-held belief that such a "supreme achievement in marine architecture . . . should serve to play an important part in bringing nearer together in friendship and understanding the two great English-speaking peoples." Bingham traveled from New York City to Washington, D.C., and then to Louisville for a brief rest before again going to the nation's capital. Along with Barry and his wife, Mary, Governor Beckham, and General Haly, he journeyed to the Philadelphia convention a few days later. Bingham effusively praised the president's address in which, at an outdoor stadium, the New Yorker declared that "this generation of Americans has a rendezvous with destiny." "Your acceptance address has affected me more deeply than any other utterance I have heard, or read," the ambassador explained. "I am convinced it stands supreme over all public utterances by our Presidents except Lincoln's at Gettysburg, and that the two stand together and alone."[26]

Republicans counted on an antiadministration coalition uniting the followers of Father Charles E. Coughlin, Francis E. Townsend, Huey Long, and the Liberty League to defeat FDR in 1936. Governor Alf Landon, himself more liberal than most of his supporters, fought an uphill battle against the incumbent. After nearly four years in office Roosevelt's coalition of farmers, blue-collar workers, and ethnic groups proved formidable. A good many individuals in the business community had built up such an intense hatred of the president that they could do little more than obliquely refer to him as "that man in the White House." Bingham reported that one of their number demonstrated the shortsightedness of many an unthinking businessman. When the man told the ambassador that he would put all of his wealth in cash and move to Great Britain if FDR won in 1936, Bingham replied that Roosevelt's election "was a certainty." Moreover, he suggested that if the man moved to England, he should "secure a deep cave for himself . . . and also provide himself with a gas mask and a gas proof chamber. . . . It is amazing that an intelligent man with a very large and successful business should be as mad as he is, and there are numerous others in New York who are just as bad."[27]

After the nomination of Roosevelt and the lull in election-year campaigning before the usual post–Labor Day push, Bingham returned to his post in London. Tensions in Europe continued to concern the ambassador, and although he would have liked nothing better than to participate directly in the election back home, he remained in Britain. FDR reported to Bingham in mid-September that "THINGS HERE ARE GOING ALL RIGHT." To make sure that all went smoothly, the ambassador assigned Ulric Bell, the *Courier* Washington bureau chief, and Herbert Agar to write special articles and editorials in support of the president. Bell kept close contact with the White House and "Fairfax," a code name for FDR in the Bingham-Bell correspondence. Bingham charged Bell with the special task of keeping "a close watch on the A.P."[28]

The relationship of Bell and the *Courier* with the president and the administration indicated a less than objective reportorial position. *Courier* coverage of the campaign also did not give the Republican candidate an unbiased press. Although the ambassador played only an indirect role in the reelection campaign of Roosevelt, he did his part. For example, the Louisvillian discouraged a proposed trip to America by deposed Ethiopian emperor Haile Selassie, a journey that he believed "would be embarrassing for our State Department." FDR took for granted that he would receive wholehearted support in the Bingham papers, and he was kept informed of their efforts. In response to a page proof of a *Courier* editorial, Roosevelt reacted succinctly: "Grand." Percy Haly worked among the political elite in Kentucky and played his usual quiet role as the behind-the-scene's power broker. As usual, Bingham also made substantial contributions to the Democratic party's campaign chests.[29]

The *Literary Digest* public-opinion poll to the contrary, a "Landon-slide" did not materialize in the fall of 1936. With nationwide voter participation at its highest since 1916, Roosevelt won over 60 percent of the poll, winning every state except Maine and Vermont. Ulric Bell's lead article in the *Courier* the day after the election claimed the election endorsed liberalism and the New Deal and scolded Al Smith,

Coughlin, Lemke, Townsend, and "all the other motley Republicans" for their folly in opposing the president. Bingham could not contain his elation in a telegram to FDR: "I have no doubt yours is the supreme achievement since the union of states was formed."[30]

Bingham immediately made the obligatory resignation from his post, but, as expected, Roosevelt asked him to stay on as the chief American diplomat to His Majesty's Government. A few days after the election Bingham explained the reaction of the British to the president. Although the average English person "warmly" appreciated FDR's victory, Bingham declared that the "British press service is so bad and so insufficient," they reported that Landon stood a good chance of winning. Unfortunately, British government officials did not believe Bingham's disclaimers about a Landon victory and correspondingly temporized their policies toward the United States for several months prior to the election.[31]

Nevertheless, in the latter months of 1936 Bingham noticed a discernible turning point in relations between the United States and Great Britain. A combination of factors led to this trend. First, the overwhelming reelection of Roosevelt finally convinced the British government that the president had a majority of the American people behind him. Second, war appeared more ominously on the horizon than ever in late 1936, and Bingham's letters and dispatches often relayed that feeling to Washington. Third, the British experienced difficulty rebuilding their defenses, particularly having trouble in their aircraft construction program. Combined with the aggressiveness of Germany, Italy, and Japan, this led to a developing British consensus that the United States could again be their best ally in case of war in Europe.[32]

In his meetings with British leaders, particularly with Foreign Secretary Anthony Eden, Bingham stressed the necessity for Anglo-American trade agreements as a beginning for closer general ties between the two nations. The Imperial Policy Group, made up of fifty-five members of Parliament, offered some hope when it urged that the British government seek monetary and trade agreements with the United States. One prominent member of the group reported to Bingham in early October that after an extensive tour of European capitals, his entourage concluded that "quite clearly our path must lie alongside the United States, and as far away from Europe as possible." Although Roosevelt agreed with his ambassador to Britain that such moves were welcome, he refused to recognize "unofficial foreign missions of any kind," such as that of the Imperial Policy Group, fearing adverse re-action in the press.[33]

Bingham was perceptive enough to discern that although there was "a wide-spread, persistent, increasing feeling here that it is to their interest to cultivate better relations with the United States," the British government lacked the will to move in late 1936. In the British effort to cultivate relations with America, several members of the House of Commons informed Bingham that they were at work on forming an organization to promote better understanding with the United States. As part of this obvious change, Commons gave a dinner in honor of Bingham in mid-December. In his remarks the ambassador suggested that when the English visited the States, they would be well served to explore areas other than the eastern United States in order to find a true understanding of his country. Two days later the *London Spectator* praised such meetings as valuable and editorialized that Great Britain should never have suspended "token payments" of its war debt to the United States. This admission represented fulfillment of Bingham's prediction that the United States should bide its time and allow the British "to come to us."[34]

chapter eleven

"A Good Friend Lost"

EVEN AS THE AGGRESSIVENESS OF Germany, Italy, and Japan increased, events in Britain, for one brief moment, took on an appearance of more style than substance in late 1936 and early 1937. A constitutional crisis developed when Edward VIII, who had followed his father, George V, to the throne, never having been coronated, ran afoul of the court and tradition by romancing an American divorcée, Mrs. Wallis Warfield Simpson.[1]

The publicity of the media and general rumormongering of the British people about the affair between the king and Mrs. Simpson created a swirl of activity by late 1936. Several options were discussed in the press, including the possibility of a morganatic marriage, in which neither Mrs. Simpson nor her children from the marriage would have any claim to the royal throne and property. Bingham became deeply disturbed by what he heard about this romance. Rumors were rife. One story circulated that the king had been observed staying at Simpson's apartment through most of one night. By late October word leaked out that the Archbishops of Canterbury and York vehemently protested the king's behavior. Moreover, these prelates refused to attend a "function at the Palace at which she was to be present." Mrs. Simpson soon fled to the Continent to avoid publicity hounds.[2]

When Edward hinted at his desire to marry Mrs. Simpson and make her queen, Ambassador Bingham reported to Washington that he found no support anywhere among the British people or government for the nuptials. As that avenue of action closed to the king, and his imminent abdication appeared certain in early December 1936, Bingham observed a sense of gloom in the British government. The Louisvillian witnessed the parliamentary system at work in the House of Commons on 10 December 1936, when that body officially declared what most people had known for days: Edward VIII would abdicate, and the crown would pass to his younger brother, the Duke of Kent. Although a Communist member of Commons demurred, that body "heaped" praise on the departing Edward. In two days came a proclamation announcing the accession of George VI to the throne.[3]

As one who greatly respected Britain and feared for its safety, Bingham rejoiced that the "crisis" had "successfully and triumphantly" concluded. He found the new king to be the better of the royal brothers. "The Duke of Windsor [Edward VIII] was surrounded by a pro-German cabal and many people here suspected that Mrs. Simpson was actually in German pay," the ambassador told Roosevelt. Although Bingham did not believe she worked for the Nazis, he felt relieved that "the whole crowd has been cleared out. The Court has become respectable again, and the situation from the dynastic end is immeasurably improved." The latter reference came in response to the rumor that Edward could never have children.[4]

Bingham's diplomatic duties continued unimpeded in early 1937. Through early spring he fought a valiant rear-guard action in his attempt to keep from having to wear the detested knee breeches at the upcoming coronation of the new king. The court made one concession when they allowed that the American ambassador could wear breeches made of the same material as his coat rather than of silk. Mild protestations by Bingham to Roosevelt brought the following response from the Oval Office:

> Having a sense of humor I have been delighted with your letter in regard to the famous case of Trousers vs. Breeches. My ruling is: that Ambassadors should wear trousers unless the Sovereign of the State to which he is accredited makes a personal demand for knee breeches. I am fortified in this ruling by the pictures I have seen of Comrade Litvinoff in the aforesaid short pants. If Soviet Russia can stand it I guess we can too.

The ambassador replied in the same spirit. "It seemed a pity to take up your time with matters of this sort," Bingham explained, "but at any rate I am happy you got a laugh out of it." The new king was crowned on 12 May 1937.[5]

As the British constitutional crisis resolved itself, other events in 1937 only reinforced Bingham's forebodings of war. Early that year Roosevelt signed into law a new neutrality resolution in response to the continuation of the Spanish Civil War. Bingham's advice to retain a "wide measure of discretion" had, by that time, become the consensus of many Americans, who feared complete neutrality to be both impossible and unwise. Although Adolf Hitler partook only in verbal saber rattling for the remainder of the year, the Japanese moved one step closer to all-out war in Asia in early July by storming across the Marco Polo Bridge into China.[6]

While the United States and Great Britain could not agree on any form of action to impede the Japanese in 1937, they moved closer toward cooperation that year. The trend that Bingham sensed in 1936 continued into the new year. Undoubtedly, the reelection of Roosevelt finally convinced the British government that the New Yorker was there to stay, at least for four more years. In early January 1937 Bingham reported an obvious British "drive" under way to gain American support, reinforcing "my thesis that events must eventually force the British to come to us." Hull's determination to gain an Anglo-American trade agreement apparently now had the blessing of several leaders in the British cabinet, particularly Foreign Secretary Anthony Eden, but also Neville Chamberlain after he replaced Stanley Baldwin as prime minister in midyear. One M.P. assured Bingham that "effective economic co-operation between Great Britain and the United States is the only ultimate hope of saving what is left of civilization." Whether from government official or private citizen, in public or in private, the British disposition toward the United States had obviously changed by mid-1937.[7]

For his efforts toward this new direction in Anglo-American relations, Bingham received the usual round of censure from his own countrymen and heard revived rumors of his imminent dismissal. Whenever he took umbrage at misrepresentation in the British press, he immediately asked for retraction and usually got it. However, it was much more difficult to answer charges from isolationist Americans. One such critic asked Cordell Hull: "Why must we have such sycophants as Democratic Administrations appoint as Ambassadors to Great Britain? I mean Page and Bingham. Why should we send a boot-lick to a nation of dishonest and ungrateful welchers, whiners, repudiators and cads, instead of an upstanding American?" Another critic addressed a vitriolic letter to "Robert Worth Bingham, Wilsonian Ambassador of War to England." Notwithstanding, for all the rumors and criticisms Bingham continued to please the president with his role as his foreign-policy point man in Britain. "You are doing a grand job," FDR exclaimed in mid-1937.[8]

Robert Worth Bingham never slackened in his support of FDR. Like many administration loyalists, he let his better judgment become clouded during the court-packing episode that year, not realizing the divisive nature of this controversy within the Democratic party and the country at large. He scored the "six blind usurpers" as doing the "greatest wrong" since the Dred Scott decision in overturning the Agricultural Adjustment Act. In the long run this controversy contributed heavily to weakening the Roosevelt coalition in the Democratic party. However, Bingham, the consummate supporter of Roosevelt, could only proclaim: "I think you may have lost a battle in connection with the Supreme Court, but I feel you won the war, and that this will mean unlimited benefit to our country." Roosevelt thanked Bingham for his support during the crisis but admitted to "laying low" for the time being.[9]

The ambassador found other ways to continue serving FDR. Bingham's support for the chief executive extended into a campaign from London to fight against southern defection from the administration. To one fellow southerner, for example, he explained, "Mr. Roosevelt saved the capitalist system in the United States, which was in its last throes." Bingham provided one final service to his political mentor in the fall of 1937. When he got wind of a proposed Associated Press political "gossip column" he never hesitated writing Kent Cooper, director of that press group. In letters to Cooper the publisher explained that his papers paid over one hundred thousand dollars per year for the services of the AP and demanded that the press service remain completely "non-partisan" in its coverage. Bingham explained to Roosevelt that he would write the entire AP membership if he did not get satisfaction. "I think it is a plot to start an anti-administration sewer and I intend to break it up," he exclaimed to the president. The Louisville publisher won the day as the AP gave up its plans to initiate the new column.[10]

In 1937 Bingham also kept up his running battle with Norman Davis and attempted to shield the president from the influence of the Tennessean, whom he believed "was working in connection with Baruch" to discredit Hull. Throughout his career in London, Bingham insisted that only he should represent American foreign policy in that capital. When Davis apparently spoke to Chamberlain and Eden without his knowledge, he bitterly complained to Davis and FDR. Within days Roosevelt straightened out the matter by asking that Hull keep Bingham fully advised of any such conversations in the future. To Bingham the president explained that "there was no intention of withholding from you anything that was said about proposed visits by British officials. There has obviously been a misunderstanding with respect to the whole matter." Bingham appeared satisfied with this explanation.[11]

In January 1937 one of the worst natural disasters in history struck the Ohio River watershed. After steady rain for several days the river rose into its traditional floodplain and beyond. All along the Ohio Valley from Pittsburgh to Cairo, Illinois, more than nine hundred miles of river swept over its banks. In the end five hundred people died and property damages reached $400 million in the valley. Louisville became the largest city to feel the full brunt of the flood waters as water breached the old riverbanks and then backed up through the sewer system covering the streets beyond Broadway in midcity.[12]

Within days nearly two-thirds of the population had been evacuated as 70 percent of the city suffered water damage. Thousands of Louisvillians were moved by train to outlying Kentucky towns. When exhausted policemen could no longer cope with the problems of maintaining peace, law-enforcement officers from as far away as Philadelphia and Boston came to their aid. Boats supplied trapped families and individuals. Mayor Neville Miller called for more outside help, and military personnel came from surrounding areas to control looting. General Percy Haly worked night and day to help coordinate disaster relief in support of Miller. To make matters worse, the weather turned cold and snow fell on the flooded city.[13]

As the flood tide moved into the city, creating the "flood of record," the Bingham papers retreated to the upper floors. With the press rooms covered by water, weekly newspapers in nearby Shelbyville, and later the *Lexington Leader*, printed the *Courier*, which missed only one issue. WHAS radio proved to be invaluable during the crisis and stayed on the air for over 187.5 straight hours by using a telephone wire, transmitting through WSM in Nashville. Other communication sources had been cut by the flood. The threat of fire became a constant danger, as marooned buildings could not be reached by fire equipment. A disastrous fire at Patrick Henry Callahan's Louisville Varnish Company destroyed the warehouse facilities of that industry.[14]

In London the ambassador kept in constant touch with Barry and the papers by telegraph and telephone. As soon as he understood the extent of the flood, Bingham sought permission to return to Louisville. "I do not want to cause any inconvenience but I really am very, very anxious about that affair," he explained to Hull. Returning to the States on the first available ship, Bingham lobbied with the president and Harry Hopkins for flood relief.[15]

Among the many tragedies of the flood came the death of General Haly, who, at the age of sixty-two, died of pneumonia on February 16. Most people attributed his death to overwork and the cold weather of the flood days. Haly represented a link with the old progressivism of the Goebel era; his political activity connected old and new generations in Kentucky politics. For two generations he actively participated in politics knowing that his Catholic religion barred him from elected office. Yet he continually sought out fresh political talent. "You don't know how much I miss the General," Ulric Bell exclaimed. "His loss is irreparable to our country and our state," Bingham lamented, "and to his friends."[16]

Before returning to England, Bingham participated in a community rally at the Louisville Armory, not long after the floodwaters receded with the cleanup process in full swing. Along with other speakers he praised the courage and work of Louisvillians in facing the flood, in hopes of bolstering them for the massive job ahead. Over fifteen thousand crowded into the arena for the speeches and free entertainment, including one of the most popular comedy acts of the day, Baron Munchausen and his friend Scharlie.[17]

After returning to its offices, the Bingham papers prospered through the remainder of 1937. Although Harrison Robertson's name remained on the masthead of the *Courier*, Barry, Lisle Baker, and Mark Ethridge now controlled both the business and editorial sides of the paper. Tom Wallace at the *Louisville Times* occasionally needed to be reined in because of his editorial independence, but otherwise the papers thrived under the new leadership. Although Bingham supported the prounionism of the New Deal, it was another matter if his own newspapers were involved. When a few employees tried to organize a local of the American Newspaper Guild, the effort failed, owing to lack of support by the editorial staff and opposition by management. Heywood Broun, national president of the guild, charged that two employees of the papers had been fired because of their support of the application for guild membership. The ambassador immediately wired Broun that "YOU HAVE BEEN WHOLLY MISINFORMED." Actually, two employees of the editorial staffs of the papers had been dismissed, although Bingham claimed that their firings "had no connection with Guild activities." In the end guild organization failed in Louisville.[18]

The toilsome years in London coupled with recurring illness forced Bingham to reconsider plans for his estate in 1937. Now in his sixty-fifth year, he sensed his own mortality. With the advice of Lisle Baker and Judge Arthur Peter in Louisville and a New York estate-planning firm, he looked for ways to smooth transition of the papers to Barry; to provide for Robert, Jr., and Henrietta; and to leave the remainder of his affairs in order.[19]

By mid-1937 the Louisville publisher had in force $850,000 in life insurance as a method of producing cash for settlement of his estate. Recapitalization and reorganization of the parent *Louisville Times* Company led to a declaration in his will that majority interest would go to Barry, who would serve as trustee for Robert, Jr., and Henrietta. Barry already understood the sensibilities of his siblings on this matter, having earlier rebelled against writing checks for his brother. Ethridge, Robertson, and Baker held five shares each of *Times* stock in order to sit on the board of directors. Judge Peter estimated that estate taxes would be paid on an amount over $4.5 million.[20]

Upon his return to England, Bingham reentered his post with a flurry of activity. Rapport with Foreign Secretary Anthony Eden gave him an entrée into the inner circle of British policy makers that he had not had in his first months in Great Britain. Talk about an upcoming trip of British leaders to America, and American participation in an international conference, proved to be just that, as nothing substantive came from Bingham's efforts. Notwithstanding, he believed that the British in 1937 moved toward a foreign-policy consensus.[21]

The Spanish Civil War increasingly confounded both British and American diplomats in mid-1937. Bingham relayed Eden's belief that "a Franco victory would not jeopardize British interests in the Iberian peninsula," but that an American embargo would "complicate his task" in working toward a peaceful solution there. The Louisvillian accepted Eden's conclusion that anything other than "strict neutrality" by the United States in that conflict "would be regarded by Europe as a gratuitous interference in continental affairs." British policy followed strict neutrality to the point of allowing the warring "parties in Spain" full "belligerent rights at sea." British rearmament and public-relations efforts to win American approval to the contrary, Hull told FDR that "the British tories are still tories and in spite of Eden's denial, want peace at any price." Bingham sensed that the continuation of the Spanish crisis generally deepened suspicions among the major nations of Europe.[22]

Bingham maintained a spirited censure of Germany and its allies. At the annual Pilgrim's Dinner in mid-May he praised Anglo-American efforts for world peace and scored the militarization of the Axis powers. "They rearmed and for what—for aggression," the ambassador charged. "No nation needs bombing airplanes, big tanks and heavy artillery unless it intends to plunder its neighbors."[23]

However, these remarks were mild compared with those made a few weeks later at the American Society's annual Fourth of July festivities celebrated at the embassy in London. After a crowd of over three hundred heard Columbia University president Nicholas Murray Butler give an appropriate patriotic speech, Bingham's brief remarks left no doubt about his views of Germany, Italy, and Japan. "Let us admit for the moment that the dictatorships are better prepared for war," he explained, "but if the dictatorships are better prepared to begin war certainly the democracies are better able to finish it." Now the British and Americans were rearming, he said. Although Bingham refused to be totally pessimistic about world peace, he faced up to the threat to democracy. In the strongest possible terms he proposed:

> If we must deal with people who cannot and will not listen to reason, if we must deal with despotism and people who regard war as a cult and blood and honour as something to teach little children, and who only listen to the argument of force, then we must fall back on that. But my hope is that there must be in these despotisms at least some remnant of reasoning power and of sanity.[24]

Negative reactions to Bingham's remarks came within hours. From Ambassador William E. Dodd in Berlin, Hull received word about strong Nazi press reaction. A Berlin newspaper scolded the American for an "inbred Anglo-Saxon habit of playing the schoolmaster." One paper charged that Bingham's speech "incited the so-called democracies against the so-called dictatorships in almost unbelievable fashion." Another asked: "Should an American ambassador accredited in a European capital make agitative speeches against other European peoples?"[25]

The speech also caught the eye of critics in the United States. The *Chicago Daily Tribune,* an old Bingham foe, replied with a front-page cartoon that depicted Uncle Sam remonstrating, "I don't remember ever authorizing him to enter into a military alliance with Great Britain" as a prim Bingham spoke to a circle of English friends in the background. An editorial on the inside lumped together Bingham and former envoy Walter Hines Page as Anglophiles, charging that the present ambassador had violated his nation's own neutrality laws. Others kept up the attack through personal correspondence. Writing to "R. Worthless Bingham," one American critic addressed Bingham as "You Bumbling British So-&-So," while another predicted "President Roosevelt will hand you out a good stiff kick in the pants." What the United States needed was "an American Ambassador not a British stooge," another declared. "If you are correctly reported in the enclosed you are just another damned ass who should be recalled and disgraced," a Chicagoan insisted. "An American Tourist" applauded the rumor of U.S. Steel executive Myron Taylor's imminent appointment as Bingham's replacement.[26]

Not only did Nazi newspapers and Bingham's American critics score the 4 July speech, the Department of State criticized the ambassador's remarks as well. Undersecretary of State Sumner Welles submitted a circular letter to FDR, asking that hereafter ambassadors submit all speeches to the department before being delivered. The president replied by requesting more information as well as a copy of Bingham's speech. The latter proved impossible. Bingham either had no copy of his speech, being spontaneous and made off the cuff, or he had destroyed any notes or script. Only newspaper accounts are extant today. Attempts by Welles to find a copy elsewhere or to obtain one from the embassy failed. Bingham chose to ignore Welles's entreaty. More important, FDR supported Bingham. A couple of weeks later the president had no criticism for the Louisvillian's diatribe against totalitarianism, declaring: "You are doing a grand job." In a few weeks the incident was nearly forgotten, but Bingham refrained from making such public statements for a while.[27]

Bingham's correspondence after the 4 July remarks revealed an increasing mood of pessimism. He explained his diplomatically intemperate talk by telling friends that he had lost patience with the world crisis. "I thought it was high time that those of us who believe in liberty, justice and democratic institutions should have a word to say to these bloody dictators who repeatedly broadcast their contempt for democracy, which they describe as being rotten, inefficient, and decadent," Bingham told one colleague. He denied having called for a military alliance between the United States and Great Britain, although he believed "in a decent and reasonable mutual and beneficial cooperation among the English-speaking peoples." Unfortunately, the "only language the Japanese and the Germans understand is guns, and neither Britain nor the United States is prepared to go to war." Moreover, he believed "the Germans intend to attack as soon as they think they are ready."[28]

At the dedication of a chapel at the American Military Cemetery in Brookwood, Surrey, on 15 August, Bingham continued his warnings. In this short speech the ambassador praised the British and French democracies. The tenuous nature of peace still played on his mind, and he could not help but return to the theme of his Independence Day address. "Upon us rests, unless we basely betray our dead, the inescapable duty to preserve and maintain for those who shall come after us, the freedom, the justice, and the democratic institutions for which they died."[29]

Bingham's outburst at the Fourth of July festivities coincided with deteriorating health. Indeed, physical pain may well have contributed to his blunt remarks. He complained of a lack of energy, suffering from unexplained pain throughout his body. Nothing seemed to ease the discomfort, and, being unable to carry out his diplomatic tasks, he applied for leave from his diplomatic post in late August. On the twenty-third of that month he boarded ship for home amid the usual rumors of his impending dismissal. Upon reaching New York, Bingham checked into Johns Hopkins in Baltimore for a thorough examination by old friend Hugh Young. However, no cause could be found for his deteriorating health. After a brief convalescence in the hospital, he talked with Secretary Hull in Washington for an hour about world affairs and then traveled on to Hyde Park for a brief conference with FDR. At both locations he denied to the press that either leader sought his resignation.[30]

After spending a few days with Barry and his family at White Sulphur Springs and in Louisville, Bingham again visited the president with the intention of returning to England in late September. Continuing weakness forced him back to Louisville for rest. A painful tooth extraction in mid-October, which Bingham admitted "has knocked me out rather badly," compounded his problems. After several days of recuperation and a third trip to visit the White House, Bingham returned to Britain in late October, having stretched his leave to six weeks.[31]

During Bingham's stay in the United States, FDR made his Quarantine Speech in Chicago on 5 October. Reversing an isolationist-tinged address of over a year before, the president declared: "The peace, the freedom, and the security of 90 percent of the population of the world is being jeopardized by the remaining 10 percent, who are threatening a breakdown of all international order and law." Something must be done; he suggested a "quarantine of the patients," implying that the United States was now ready to move toward collective security.[32]

From his sickbed in the Johns Hopkins Hospital, Bingham lauded the president's speech. He must have felt some vindication for the strong words he had spoken at the Independence Day address and for the general tenor of his pronouncements since early 1933. In a telegram to Roosevelt he declared: "YOUR CHICAGO SPEECH UNDOUBTEDLY ENCOURAGING AND HELPFUL TO ALL DECENT PEOPLE THROUGHOUT THE WORLD AND MAY WELL LAY FOUNDATION FOR THEIR SALVATION FROM THE MURDEROUS BRIGANDS INFESTING THE WORLD." Isolationists like the Hearst press cried foul, but an increasing number of Americans agreed with the White House and Bingham. However, this "uncertain feeler," as described by diplomatic historian H. G. Nicholas, failed to bring about immediate change. FDR soon backed off from implementing any initiatives in American policy abroad.[33]

On the return passage to Great Britain, Bingham suffered a "chill," as reported in the press. He was not too ill, however, to miss a chance to lash out at Wall Street speculators, whom he scored for causing a current economic downturn in the United States. Less than two weeks later Bingham's condition worsened, and he requested leave to come home. In a telephone conversation with Hull he pleaded for relief from his duties: "I've had a hard time. If I can get a rest—a little rest—I feel I will be all right. . . . I believe some treatments at Johns Hopkins will help me and will knock out the trouble all right." Already communicating with the president about a replacement, Bingham supported the appointment of Thomas J. Watson, an official with the International Chamber of Commerce.[34]

On 20 November 1937 the Louisvillian set sail for home on the SS *Manhattan* as the press announced that he suffered from a "recurrence of malaria." As he arrived in New York, Mrs. Bingham took his place at a Thanksgiving Day celebration in London. After checking into the Johns Hopkins Hospital, Bingham's fever abated slightly, and for a few days he permitted meetings with reporters wherein he answered queries about world problems. In these conversations he left no doubt of his obsessive fear of Germany.[35]

His health did not improve. On 8 December, Bingham officially resigned his post and thanked FDR for the honor of having the opportunity to serve as ambassador to Great Britain. He predicted that doctors would eventually be able to find the cause for his "peculiar recurrent periodic form of fever." Although Barry reported to Roosevelt that his father was "making slow progress," by 11 December the press reported that FDR had already chosen a replacement, Joseph P. Kennedy, who vigorously sought the ambassadorship.[36]

Meanwhile, Hugh Young convinced Bingham and his family that exploratory surgery was needed for an inflamed abdomen. On 14 December, Young and his team of surgeons discovered that Bingham suffered from abdominal Hodgkin's disease, a form of cancer that attacks the lymph nodes and other lymphoid tissues, especially the spleen. Young immediately understood there would be no hope of saving his old friend's life. After briefly regaining consciousness, Bingham lapsed into a coma. He died on the third day after the operation at the age of sixty-six, having reached that age on 8 November.[37]

Roosevelt issued the following statement: "I feel the loss of Ambassador Bingham keenly. He was not only an old personal friend but, as one of the foremost citizens of Kentucky and of the nation, he exercised an active and consistent influence in the cause of decent government and of high ideals in politics. As the Ambassador of the United

States to Great Britain he truly represented the best interests of his country. All of us have suffered a heavy loss." In the end he had taken no official action on Bingham's resignation and wrote a note of tribute to Barry with the explanation that his father "died on December eighteenth—still American Ambassador to Great Britain."[38]

Condolences poured in from numerous sources. The royal family, Prime Minister Neville Chamberlain, and Foreign Secretary Anthony Eden made prominent comment about Bingham. As a tribute to Bingham, memorial services in Westminster Abbey included the rare occurrence of the playing of the U.S. national anthem. Lord Darby, chairman of the Pilgrims, praised the American's efforts on behalf of better Anglo-American relations. Several English newspapers added their own compliments. The *Daily Telegraph and Morning Post* described Bingham as "A Good Friend Lost." The *Manchester Daily Telegraph* ran the headline: "Britain Loses a Friend by Death of Ambassador." In a long obituary the *Times* found that Bingham had an unusual "understanding of British life" and "had all the grave, old-fashioned easy grace that is usually associated with a southern gentleman of the old school," while "Atticus," a columnist, declared that "many of us feel that we have lost a personal friend." Secretary Hull identified the ambassador as "a faithful interpreter of all that we stood for, and, by his loyalty and sense of fair play, he won the respect, confidence and friendship of the people and government to which he was accredited. His passing will leave a sense of genuine grief in both countries."[39]

At the Bingham funeral in Louisville about fifty friends, family members, and government representatives paid their last respects. Kentuckian Marvin McIntyre represented the president. Sir Ronald Lindsay, British ambassador to the United States, acted as official envoy of the king. The ceremony concluded with a formal Episcopalian service led by Bishop Emeritus Charles E. Woodcock. Eight servicemen from Fort Knox placed Robert Worth Bingham to rest beside his first wife, Eleanor Miller Bingham.[40]

Several days after the funeral Barry wrote FDR that his father "regarded you with the warmest feelings of friendship, as well as admiration for your great achievements." The younger Bingham also declared his "devotion to the cause of true and enlightened liberalism, which you exemplify in the world today. I treasure the ambition of carrying on our papers in this tradition, and keeping them in the very forefront of the battle." The president shortly replied: "I hope you know of the deep pride he had in you and his great hopes for you in the future. . . . You know of the deep affection I had for him and of my appreciation for the splendidly loyal service he rendered."[41]

The will of Robert Worth Bingham was probated in Jefferson Circuit Court a few days after the funeral. The will passed the papers and the bulk of the Bingham holdings to Barry "as a public trust . . . to render the greatest public service possible, rather than as commercial ventures." More important, he assumed control of a powerful left-of-center voice in American political life. The will also provided for a payment of seven hundred thousand dollars to Aleen M. Bingham in a series of notes, as completion of the million-dollar marriage agreement. Barry Bingham served as overseer of trusts based on *Louisville Times* Company stock established for both Robert, Jr., and Henrietta. Each trust consisted of preferred stock of the papers. In addition, Henrietta received titles to farms at Harmony Landing and Pineland. To his longtime devoted secretary, Emily Overman, the Judge bequeathed a pension of three hundred dollars a month for life. No gifts were bestowed to charities or to other relatives, as they had been provided for in earlier grants. Robert Worth Bingham's personal and real estate was valued at over $4.8 million, including the newspapers' stock, valued at $3.7 million for tax purposes and settlement. After deduction for debts, state inheritance taxes amounted to over $14,000 and federal estate taxes to just over $938,000.[42]

Commemorations and memorials to Robert Worth Bingham came in later years in several forms. The dedication of a tree on the lawn of the Louisville Free Public Library and the Robert Worth Bingham memorial state conservation camp in Washington County were completed before the beginning of World War II. During that war the United States government launched the SS *Robert W. Bingham,* a liberty ship, at the Delta shipbuilding yards in New Orleans. In later years Barry Bingham, Sr., presented to France over five hundred volumes from his father's collection of Joan of Arc books, in honor of the ambassador and in recognition of his own service as director of the Marshall Plan in that country from 1949 to 1950. A dormitory at Berea College and donation of books and a poetry room to the University of Louisville were memorials to Robert Worth Bingham completed in the mid-sixties.[43]

chapter twelve

From the Old South to the New South and Beyond

SERVICE AS A NEW DEAL DIPLOMAT crowned the significant career of Robert Worth Bingham. A wealthy southern Democrat in the twenties and thirties, he used his media holdings to support the causes in which he took an active role. His efforts on behalf of cooperative marketing and in opposition to Governor Fields's road-bond funding plans were logical attempts, from his perspective, to develop businesslike accountability and self-sufficiency for American farmers and Kentucky taxpayers. He relished using his wealth and newspapers for what he considered the public interest. The money and the power, however, never brought complete social acceptance in Louisville or his adopted state; he was always the outsider. Money and power set him apart from the average Kentuckian; his political independence distanced him from the typical Kentucky politician.

The old gossip about Bingham's complicity in the death of Mary Lily was whispered behind his back for two decades, becoming public only on occasions such as the confirmation hearing on the ambassadorship in 1933. In later years such charges would rarely surface, except in Michael Lesy's 1976 *Real Life: Louisville in the Twenties,* until the onslaught of anti-Bingham books beginning with David Leon Chandler in 1987.[1]

All of the foregoing raises questions. Who was Robert Worth Bingham? What kind of "southerner" was he? Did he indeed have something to do with the death of Mary Lily Kenan Flagler Bingham?

Was his crusading in Kentucky politics only for his own political gain? Was he a real progressive? What role did he play in early New Deal diplomacy? Was he merely a cipher doing the will of President Franklin Roosevelt? Finally, what kind of father was he, and what did he bequeath to his children?

For Robert Worth Bingham the Old South / New South legacies remained strong throughout his life. To the end of his days, service to FDR notwithstanding, he displayed a distrust of "Yankees," particularly of the Wall Street variety. His high praise of Margaret Mitchell's *Gone with the Wind* in early 1937 proved that his Old South / New South heritage had lost none of its intensity since his early days in North Carolina. Like many southerners, he mythicized the Old South / New South mystique into a historical view that influenced a lifetime of public activity. In the last months of his life he pronounced a final tribute to his father, Colonel Robert. "The South owes most of what it is to his generation, the survivors who came back to ruined homes and a shattered civilization to rebuild for those who were to come after them," the son eulogized his father. Robert Worth was not the same type of racist as his father, and advanced slightly left of the southern racial mores of his time. For example, while opposing the resurgent Ku Klux Klan of the 1920s and supporting African-American educational institutions, he continued to allow his papers to print racist cartoons and stories.[2]

Most of his reactions to racial matters were reflexive, and he wore his southernness on his sleeve. In the mid-thirties his response to an Englishwoman's query about when southerners would "stop your hideous, horrible lynching of negroes [*sic*]" illustrated the hold of southern folkways on the ambassador. "This was a little too much for me to stand and I told her that we would probably stop it when negroes [*sic*] stopped raping white women and girls," he retorted. These racial mores also influenced his views of the world in the thirties. His distrust of Japan extended along racial lines to Japanese-Americans who lived in Hawaii, and for that reason he encouraged FDR to stoutly oppose the admission of these Pacific Islands to the union as a state. Beneath his impeccable cosmopolitan exterior beat the heart of a much unreconstructed southerner. Perhaps Wilson Wyatt, Sr., best described him as a "southern patrician gentleman," who made slight adjustments to the twentieth century. Upon his death, for example, a black Louisvillian credited the publisher for teaching Negroes of that city to be politically independent.[3]

From the beginning of his law career Bingham appeared always to be in the thick of one political battle or another. His efforts as interim mayor of Louisville in 1907 suggested the type of urban progressivism displayed in many American cities during the early years of this century and hinted of his independence. Throughout the progressive era he maintained the same standards. His progressive ideals remained alive well past the post–World War I period.

After receiving his bequest from the Flagler fortune and subsequent purchase of the Louisville newspapers, he had both the will and the power to bring about change in his adopted state. His "progressive" agenda included reforming what he saw as the backwardness and corruption of the Kentucky body politic. Here he clashed with the fabled "bipartisan combine" and factions in the Democratic party he deemed antiprogressive. Bingham's political connection with General Percy Haly and former governor J. C. W. Beckham in the 1920s radiated those ideals. Normally viewing life in shades of light and darkness, he invariably viewed his enemies as practitioners of the political black arts. To his death he followed what he perceived to be Wilsonian progressivism, which, after all, was southern to the core.

His efforts on behalf of cooperative agriculture in the 1920s offered an example of business progressivism. During a critical time in the life of his newspapers, Bingham gave unstintingly of his time and wealth to support the cooperative effort, not only in Kentucky but in the nation as well. The effort failed for many reasons, as developed in chapter 5. However, during the New Deal, ten years later, governmental support of farm cooperation proved workable. The 1920s had simply not been the right time for development of cooperatives on the grand scale that Aaron Sapiro and Bingham proposed. Only Bingham's timing was wrong.

When the Great Crash and the Great Depression broke the back of the Republican ascendancy, Bingham quickly fell behind the presidential candidacy of Franklin Delano Roosevelt. The Louisvillian's total support of FDR and the New Deal confirmed the consistency of a lifetime of political involvement as a progressive Democrat.

Bingham proved to be a perceptive diplomat as Franklin D. Roosevelt's representative at the Court of St. James's and not the Anglophile his critics charged. He was not just a conduit of information and observer as diplomat, but worked incessantly for better Anglo-American relations. His warnings about the dangers of fascism and German militarism and the necessity of a united front by the western democracies against totalitarianism proved prescient. He hated fascism in all its forms.

If he was used by Roosevelt as a diplomatic stalking-horse, he complied willingly, because he implicitly trusted the leadership of the New Yorker. He found no alternative to unquestioning support of New Deal foreign policy, pushing FDR toward closer ties with Britain. Moreover, he never doubted that Roosevelt saved the United States from economic destruction during the Great Depression.

The ambassadorship not only represented the highlight of Bingham's career but also symbolized the acceptance of Bingham and his region into the American mainstream. If never completely reconciled to the East Coast intelligentsia or business elite, Bingham nonetheless believed that his identity as an American transcended regionalism. Perhaps Reconstruction ended for him, at least partially, when he became ambassador in 1933.

The recent furor over publication of several books about the Binghams has revived once again old charges and innuendos that the Judge murdered or, at minimum, contributed to the death of Mary Lily Kenan Flagler Bingham. Her second husband may have been ambitious—even cold and calculating at times. He obviously expected to gain by marrying one of the wealthiest women in America. However, there is no evidence that, either by omission or commission, he contributed to her death. Moreover, I have found nothing in over a decade and a half of studying the life of Robert Worth Bingham to suggest that he possessed either the flawed character or criminal personality necessary to commit such an act. Over the years Bingham's independent and often liberal stances led many a cynical conservative enemy to revive the specter of a wife killer as a foil against the power and influence of the Binghams and their newspapers.[4]

Although I find little personal warmth in Bingham, this very active Kentuckian did not lack passion. Whether hunting, pursuing an editorial policy, or fighting for closer Anglo-American understanding, he entered everything with an intensity that belied the exterior appearances that Wilson Wyatt, Sr., and others observed. That vigor also unnerved lethargic politicians who, unlike Bingham, were tradition bound. Progressive and pragmatic to the end, whether as mayor, publisher, or diplomat, Bingham always viewed public life as a quest for something better and his newspapers as a "public trust."[5]

Everything in Robert Worth Bingham's life he filtered through his southern and Victorian prisms. He could not escape the Old South / New South mystique of his youth and would not in adulthood betray the values of the South that he believed to be paramount. But he had come a long way from the days of old Colonel Robert, his father, and the dreamworld of the Bingham School.

Robert Worth Bingham bequeathed to his son Barry a tradition of liberal political action and publishing excellence. Both father and son kept themselves above the mainstream of Kentucky society and politics. Their fortune and the newspaper monopoly in Louisville assured a certain level of independence that few other individuals could ever hope to have. All things considered, they used their resources wisely and for the benefit of the public.

Barry Bingham overcame the southern mystique. Under his leadership, and that of Mark Ethridge, the "Bingham" papers became leading voices of liberalism in the post–World War II era. John Egerton in his recent book about the South before desegregation, *Speak Now Against the Day: The Generation Before The Civil Rights Movement in the South,* credits the *Courier-Journal* in the early 1940s "as the South's most liberal newspaper—and probably its finest." That sea change would not have been possible without the foundation established by Robert Worth Bingham and his legacy of enlightened southern leadership.[6]

Notes

Preface

1. William E. Ellis, "Robert Worth Bingham and Louisville Progessivism, 1905–1910," *Filson Club History Quarterly* 54 (Apr. 1980): 169–95.

2. William E. Ellis, "Robert Worth Bingham and the Crisis of Cooperative Marketing in the Twenties," *Agricultural History* 56 (Jan. 1982): 99–116; idem, "The Bingham Family: From the Old South to the New South and Beyond," *Filson Club History Quarterly* 61 (Jan. 1987): 5–33.

3. *Courier-Journal Magazine*, 20 Apr. 1986.

4. Ibid.; David Leon Chandler and Mary Voelz Chandler, *The Binghams of Louisville: The Dark History behind One of America's Great Fortunes* (New York: Crown, 1987); Robert Ireland, review of *The Binghams of Louisville*, by Chandler and Chandler, *The Register of the Kentucky Historical Society* 86 (Summer 1988): 280–82. See also the critiques of Chandler and Chandler's *The Binghams of Louisville* by Samuel W. Thomas and James J. Holmberg in *Filson Club History Quarterly* 63 (July 1989): 307–85. In response to the proposed publication of the Chandlers' book by Macmillan, Barry Bingham, Sr., had prepared a refutation entitled "Memorandum to Macmillan Publishing Company from Barry Bingham, Sr., April 27, 1987, Re: *The Binghams of Louisville* by David Leon Chandler." This information was shared with me and is cited hereafter as Bingham memorandum to Macmillan. Gordon B. Davidson, Wyatt, Tarrant, and Combs to the author, 3 February 1989. The document is in my possession.

5. Marie Brenner, *House of Dreams: The Bingham Family of Louisville* (New York: Random House, 1988), 26.

6. Sallie Bingham, *Passion and Prejudice: A Family Memoir* (New York: Alfred A. Knopf, 1989). The reviewer of Bingham's book in *Time*, 30 Jan. 1989, p. 73, is R. Z. Sheppard. In response to the publication of Sallie Bingham's book, her father commissioned another response entitled "Summary of Response Document by Members of the Bingham Family to Sallie Bingham's *Passion and Prejudice* (hereafter cited as "Sum-

mary of Response to Bingham's *Passion and Prejudice*"). This document is in my possession. Mrs. Barry Bingham Sr. to the author, 10 March 1988.

7. Susan E. Tifft and Alex S. Jones, *The Patriarch: The Rise and Fall of the Bingham Dynasty* (New York: Summit Books, 1991).

1. From the Old South to the New

1. Robert Worth Bingham to Margaret Mitchell, 16 Feb. 1937, Robert Worth Bingham Papers, Manuscript Division, Library of Congress (hereafter cited as RWB-LC).

2. The motto of the Bingham School was prominently displayed on the school stationery.

3. George Bingham to RWB, 7 Mar. 1933, RWB-LC; RWB to R. Diamond, 4 Sept. 1905, Robert Worth Bingham Papers, The Filson Club (hereafter cited as RWB-FC); Robert Hamlin Stone, *A History of Orange Presbytery, 1770–1970* (Greensboro, N.C.: n.p., 1970), 49–50.

4. Ernest B. Goodwin, "The High Schools of Orange County" (M.A. thesis, University of North Carolina, Chapel Hill, 1927), 6–7; Bennett L. Steelman, "Robert Bingham," *Dictionary of North Carolina Biography* (Chapel Hill: University of North Carolina Press, 1979), 157–58.

5. *1840 Census*, North Carolina, Orange County, 212; *1850 Census*, North Carolina, Orange County, 219; *1860 Census*, North Carolina, Orange County, 11; RWB to Mitchell, 16 Feb. 1937, RWB-LC.

6. James Barry Bingham, *Descendants of James Bingham of County Down, Northern Ireland* (Baltimore: Gateway Press, 1980), 47–83.

7. Archibald Henderson, *The Campus of the First State University* (Chapel Hill: University of North Carolina Press, 1949), 43; Steelman, "Robert Bingham," 157–58.

8. Ruth Blackwelder, *The Age of Orange: Political and Intellectual Leadership in North Carolina, 1752–1861* (Charlotte: William Loftin, 1961), 174, 180; William S. Powell, *North Carolina: A Bicentennial History* (New York: W. W. Norton, 1977), 126–33; Carl N. Degler, *The Other South* (New York: Harper and Row, 1974), 165.

9. Peter Mitchell Wilson, *Southern Exposure* (Chapel Hill: University of North Carolina Press, 1927), 29–32; Bingham, *Descendants of James Bingham*, 58; RWB to Mitchell, 16 Feb. 1937, RWB-LC.

10. Blackwelder, *Age of Orange*, 122–23, 154.

11. RWB to Mitchell, 16 Feb. 1937, RWB-LC; Powell, *North Carolina*, 126–33.

12. Bingham, *Descendants of James Bingham*, 53–55; John G. Barrett, *The Civil War in North Carolina* (Chapel Hill: University of North Carolina Press, 1963), 125–26; RWB to Henrietta Bingham, 14 Mar. 1923, Robert Bingham Papers, Southern Historical Collection; Edwin B. Coddington, *The Gettysburg Campaign: A Study in Command* (New York: Charles Scribner's Sons, 1968), 101–2. The Philanthropic Society Records, Southern Historical Collection, University of North Carolina, Chapel Hill, contains a picture of Robert Bingham in his Confederate uniform. For a description of his prison experiences see typescript of Robert Bingham Papers, Diary of Imprisonment during Civil War, 2 vols., Southern Historical Collection, University of North Carolina at Chapel Hill (hereafter cited as Bingham Diary).

13. RWB to Mitchell, 16 Feb. 1937, RWB-LC; Wilson, *Southern Exposure,* 31–32; Bingham, *Descendants of James Bingham,* 57; Bingham Diary, 2:91–92.

14. Worth to Bingham, 16 Sept. 1864, in J. G. de Roulhac Hamilton, ed., *The Correspondence of Jonathan Worth,* vol. 1 (Raleigh, 1909), 330; Henry Steele Commager, *The Blue and the Gray* (Indianapolis: Bobbs-Merrill, 1950), 1016; RWB to Mitchell, 16 Feb. 1937, RWB-LC; Bruce Catton, *A Stillness at Appomattox* (New York: Doubleday, 1954), 241–53; R. A. Brock and Philip Van Doren Stern, *The Appomattox Roster* (New York: Antiquarian Press, 1962), 296.

15. R. D. W. Connor, William K. Boyd, and J. G. de Roulhac Hamilton, *History of North Carolina,* vol. 6, *North Carolina Biography* (Chicago: Lewis, 1919), 185; Bingham, *Descendants of James Bingham,* 57–58; Hugh Lefler and Paul Wager, eds., *Orange County, 1752–1952* (Chapel Hill: Orange Printshop, 1953), 324.

16. *Asheville Citizen,* 21 Nov. 1921, 19 Nov. 1933; *Greensboro Daily News,* 26 Dec. 1948; Bingham, *Descendants of James Bingham,* 58, 68.

17. RWB to Mitchell, 16 Feb. 1937, RWB-LC.

18. C. Vann Woodward, *Origins of the New South, 1877–1913,* vol. 9, *A History of the South,* ed. Wendell Holmes Stephenson and E. Merton Coulter (Baton Rouge: Louisiana State University Press, 1951), 1–3.

19. *Trial of William W. Holden,* vol. 3 (Raleigh: Sentinel Printing Office, 1871), 2537–47; RWB to Mitchell, 16 Feb. 1937, RWB-LC.

20. Richard L. Zuber, *North Carolina during Reconstruction* (Raleigh: State Department of Archives and History, 1969), 25–27; Otto H. Olsen, "The Ku Klux Klan: A Study in Reconstruction Politics and Propaganda," *North Carolina Historical Review* 39 (July 1962): 353–55; Powell, *North Carolina,* 161–62; Lefler and Wager, *Orange County,* 112–22; Degler, *Other South,* 250–51.

21. Allen W. Trelease, *White Terror: The Ku Klux Klan Conspiracy and Southern Reconstruction* (New York: Harper and Row, 1971), 192–200; Otto H. Olsen, *Carpetbagger's Crusade: The Life of Albion Winegar Tourgée* (Baltimore: Johns Hopkins Press, 1965), 156–57.

22. W. J. Cash, *The Mind of the South* (New York: Alfred A. Knopf, 1941), 102; Olsen, "Ku Klux Klan," 360–62; see preface.

23. Robin Brabham, "Defining the American University: The University of North Carolina, 1865–1875," *North Carolina Historical Review* 57 (Oct. 1980): 437–38; J. G. de Roulhac Hamilton, *Reconstruction in North Carolina* (1914; reprint, Gloucester, Mass.: Peter Smith, 1964), 626–27.

24. Bingham, *Descendants of James Bingham,* 58; RWB to Mitchell, 16 Feb. 1937, George Douglas Rouse to RWB, 7 Feb. 1935, RWB to Rouse, 25 Mar. 1935, all in RWB-LC; M. C. S. Noble to RWB, 24 Feb. 1933, Noble Papers, Southern Historical Collection.

25. *Raleigh News and Observer,* 10 Sept. 1882; Robert Bingham to Kemp P. Battle, 5 Sept. 1874, Battle Family Papers, Southern Historical Collection; Henderson, *Campus of the First State University,* 248; *Greensboro Daily News,* 7 Jan. 1940; Robert Bingham to J. A. Bryan, 29 May 1880, C. S. Bryan Papers, Southern Historical Collection.

26. "Bingham School Order of Exercises," in the C. S. Bryan Papers; Bingham School Ledger, 1890–1919, Southern Historical Collection.

27. Bennett L. Steelman, "Robert Worth Bingham," *Dictionary of North Carolina*

Biography, 158–59; Arthur Link, *The Papers of Woodrow Wilson,* vol. 3 (Princeton: Princeton University Press, 1967), 268–70.

28. Paul M. Gaston, *The New South Creed: A Study in Southern Mythmaking* (New York: Alfred A. Knopf, 1970), 9; F. Garvin Davenport, *The Myth of Southern History: Historical Consciousness in Twentieth-Century Southern Literature* (Nashville: Vanderbilt University Press, 1967), 4–7.

29. Willard B. Gatewood, Jr., "North Carolina and Federal Aid to Education: Public Reaction to the Blair Bill, 1881–90," *North Carolina Historical Review* 40 (Oct. 1963): 469; Robert Bingham, *The New South* (pamphlet, 15 Feb. 1884, in the North Carolina Collection), 10–14; Woodward, *Origins of the New South,* 63–64, 219, 400–401; Gatewood, "North Carolina and Federal Aid," 488; *Raleigh News and Observer,* 9 May 1927; David Alexander Lockmiller, "The Establishment of the North Carolina College of Agriculture and Mechanic Arts," *North Carolina Historical Review* 16 (July 1939): 284; Gaston, *New South Creed,* 190–203; Robert Bingham, *The Fifty Years between 1857 and 1907, and Beyond* (pamphlet, 3 June 1907, North Carolina Collection), 6, 10; idem, *Secession in Theory, as the Framers of the Constitution Viewed It; Secession as Practiced and as Sustained by the United States; Secession as Attempted by the Confederate States* (pamphlet, 13 Oct. 1908, North Carolina Collection), 4, 23, 29; idem, *The Status of the South in the Past; The Decadence of That Status; Its Restoration* (pamphlet, 14 Dec. 1904, North Carolina Collection), n.p.; idem, *Some Sectional Misunderstandings* (pamphlet, reprinted from *North American Review,* Sept. 1904), 5–6, 8–11; idem, *Fifty Years,* 6; Thomas L. Connelly and Barbara L. Bellows, *God and General Longstreet: The Lost Cause and the Southern Mind* (Baton Rouge: Louisiana State University Press, 1982), 73–81; George B. Tindall, *The Ethnic Southerners* (Baton Rouge: Louisiana State University Press, 1976), 233; Robert Bingham, *An Ex-Slaveholder's View of the Negro Question in the South* (pamphlet, reprinted from *Harper's,* July 1900), 5.

30. Bingham, *Ex-Slaveholder's View,* 8.

31. Charles Lee Raper, *The Church and Private Schools of North Carolina* (Greensboro: Josiah J. Stone, 1898), 76–84; *Asheville Citizen-Times,* 19 Nov. 1933; RWB to S. R. McKee, 25 Jan. 1923, RWB to W. R. Cobb, 23 Oct., 13 Dec. 1924, all in RWB-LC; Henderson, *Campus of the First State University,* 281.

32. Floyd C. Watkins, *Thomas Wolfe's Characters* (Norman: University of Oklahoma Press, 1957), 151–53; Thomas Wolfe, *The Hills Beyond* (New York: Harper and Row, 1941), 60–87; C. Hugh Holman and Sue Fields Ross, *The Letters of Thomas Wolfe to His Mother* (New York: Charles Scribner's Sons, 1943), 7.

33. Bruce Clayton, *The Savage Ideal* (Baltimore: Johns Hopkins Press, 1972), 44; Nicholas Worth, *The Southerner* (New York: Doubleday, Page, 1909), 37, 41, 56; Burton J. Hendrick, *The Training of an American: The Earlier Life and Letters of Walter Hines Page: 1855–1913* (Boston: Houghton, Mifflin, 1928), 23–25, 114–15, 176–81; John Milton Cooper, Jr., *Walter Hines Page: The Southerner as American, 1855–1918* (Chapel Hill: University of North Carolina Press, 1977), 10–11.

34. P. T. Penick, *A Memorial to Mrs. Robert Bingham* (1886); RWB to Mitchell, 16 Feb. 1937, RWB-LC.

35. Robert Bingham to Colonel [?] Caldwell, [1905], RWB-FC; Degler, *Other South,* 332; Woodward, *Origins of the New South,* 264. For a study of up-country Georgia, a

region similar to the Binghams' home in North Carolina, see Steven Hahn, *The Roots of Southern Populism* (New York: Oxford University Press, 1983).

36. *Catalogue of the Members of the Dialectic Society* (Chapel Hill, 1890), n.p.; *Durham Morning Herald*, 4 Oct. 1959; Archibald Henderson, *Robert Worth Bingham: A Memorial Address* (The Society of Transylvania, 1941), n.p.; RWB to Mrs. Albert Lee Thurman, 20 May 1935, RWB-LC.

37. Letter to "Hail Sir Knight Bingham," 9 Apr. 1933, RWB to Harrison Randolph, 8 July 1935, RWB to Ansley Coxe, 25 Feb. 1935, George Watts Hill to RWB, 27 Apr. 1935, Shepard Bryan to RWB, 4 Sept. 1936, all in RWB-LC; boxes 3, 9, and 24 in the Robert Worth Bingham Papers at The Filson Club, Louisville, Kentucky, contain much correspondence with old fraternity brothers Shepard Bryan and Harrison Randolph and concerning Alpha Tau Omega Fraternity matters over the years. RWB to Robert Bingham, 8 Jan. 1907; RWB to J. G. de R. Hamilton, 18 Feb. 1907, RWB-FC.

38. Kemp P. Battle, *History of the University of North Carolina*, vol. 2 (Raleigh: Edwards and Broughton, 1912), 450–51; RWB to *Louisville Anzeiger*, 2 June 1904, RWB to R. S. McRae, 22 Aug. 1906, RWB-FC; James J. Holmberg, oral-history interview, 2 July 1987, Eastern Kentucky University Archives.

39. The RWB-LC at the Library of Congress contains a large folder of Bingham-Young correspondence. RWB to Ansley Coxe, 25 Feb. 1935, RWB-LC; Hugh Young, *Hugh Young: A Surgeon's Biography* (New York: Harcourt, Brace, 1940), 504–8.

At some point in Rob's time at the University of Virginia he became friends with Mary Lily Kenan, a young woman who would later marry Henry Flagler and subsequently become Robert Worth Bingham's second wife.

40. RWB to "Cousin Louise," 30 Apr. 1937, RWB-LC; Barry Bingham, Sr., oral-history interviews, 17 Nov. 1983, 9 Apr., 24 Sept. 1987, Eastern Kentucky University Archives; *Courier-Journal*, 21 May 1896.

41. Miller Family File, RWB-FC; Bingham, oral-history interview, 17 Nov. 1983.

42. *The City of Louisville and a Glimpse of Kentucky* (Louisville: Committee on Industrial and Commercial Improvement of the Louisville Board of Trade, 1887), 125; Miller Family File, RWB-FC.

43. Miller Family File, RWB-FC; *Courier-Journal*, 3 Feb. 1895.

44. RWB to Henrietta Long Miller, [n.d.] 1896, RWB-FC.

45. Bingham, oral-history interviews, 17 Nov. 1983, 9 Apr., and 24 Sept. 1987.

46. *Courier-Journal*, 21 May 1986.

47. *National Cyclopedia*, vol. 34, 261; Bingham, oral-history interviews, 17 Nov. 1983, 9 Apr., and 24 Sept. 1987.

2. From the New South to Progressivism

1. Dewey W. Grantham, *Southern Progressivism: The Reconciliation of Progress and Tradition* (Knoxville: University of Tennessee Press, 1983), 82–83; Steven A. Channing, *Kentucky: A History* (New York: W. W. Norton, 1977), 164–85; Thomas D. Clark, *A History of Kentucky* (New York: Prentice-Hall, 1937), 605–24; Bingham, oral-history interviews, 3 Dec. 1980, 17 Nov. 1983.

2. For background of this era see: Hambleton Tapp and James C. Klotter, *Kentucky: Decades of Discord, 1865–1900* (Frankfort: Kentucky Historical Society, 1977),

and James C. Klotter, *William Goebel: The Politics of Wrath* (Lexington: University Press of Kentucky, 1977).

3. Bingham, oral-history interviews, 9 Apr. and 24 Sept. 1987; George H. Yater, *Two Hundred Years at the Falls of the Ohio: A History of Louisville and Jefferson County* (Louisville: Heritage Press, 1979), 118–44.

4. Yater, *Two Hundred Years,* 118–44.

5. RWB to Mrs. A. F. Callahan, 29 May 1905, A. F. Callahan to RWB, 5 Jan. 1907, RWB-FC; extensive Callahan-Bingham correspondence is located in box 11, RWB-FC.

6. RWB to A. S. Cleveland, 16 July 1906, W. Tharp to RWB, 9 Nov. 1906, RWB to W. A. Thomson, 17 June 1907, RWB to Katie Callahan, 11 May 1906, all in RWB-FC. See also Summary of Response to Bingham's *Passion and Prejudice,* for a description of the cause for an early conflict between Bingham and Abraham Flexner. Flexner would later become an archenemy of Bingham. Bingham, oral-history interview, 24 Sept. 1987.

7. Bingham, oral-history interviews, 9 Apr. and 24 Sept. 1987.

8. RWB to Major R. T. Grinnan, 8 May 1907, Thomas Wadley Raoul to RWB, 26 Apr. 1900, RWB-FC; *Courier-Journal,* 22 Sept. 1907.

9. Herbert Levy to RWB, 18 June 1906, RWB-FC; Bingham, oral-history interviews, 9 Apr. and 24 Sept. 1987. In *The Binghams of Louisville,* David Leon Chandler misinterpreted W. W. Davies's personal correspondence and concluded that Bingham in the nineties was given "to drink and carousing" (52–53). Davies replied to these charges: "good God-no!" Davies to William H. Taylor, 6 Aug. 1898, RWB-FC; Bingham memorandum to Macmillan.

10. RWB to Ravitch, 24 June 1905, RWB to H. Kaiser, 21 Oct. 1904; RWB to Robert Bingham, 25 Jan. 1900, Harrison Randolph to RWB, 16 Mar. 1904, RWB-FC; Bingham, oral-history interview, 24 Sept. 1987.

11. Bingham, oral-history interviews, 9 Apr., 24 Sept. 1987; Davies to RWB, 1 June 1903, RWB to Joseph P. Byers, 28 Jan. 1911, RWB to J. M. Terry, 12 Feb. 1902, RWB-FC. However, the dog could just as easily have belonged to Davies, as this correspondence copy was not signed.

12. Robert Bingham to RWB, 24 Oct. 1899, 20 Apr. 1900, 3 Feb. 1901, 5 Oct. 1902, 30 Mar. 1905, RWB to Robert Bingham, 1 Mar. 1902, 3, 11 May, 20 Sept. 1905, 20 Nov. 1906, 18 June 1907, Norwood Mordecai to RWB, 29 Sept. 1902, RWB-FC.

Just after the turn of the century Bingham became involved in a family and legal matter involving the disposition of the bankrupt Worth Manufacturing Company, a corporation that operated three textile mills in North Carolina. Bingham represented the children of his deceased mother, Dell Worth Bingham, in their bid to obtain something from shares of stock inherited from their mother. With the company in receivership, the matter became even more complicated when a change in the will of Dr. J. M. Worth, who formerly headed the firm, became contested in the courts. Bingham finally offered to sell his stock for fifty cents on the dollar, and the other heirs accepted this settlement. The Worth Company recovered slowly under receivership. For extensive correspondence on the Worth case see boxes 3, 4, and 5, RWB-FC.

13. RWB to J. A. Hiner, 11 Oct. 1899, J. H. Powers to RWB, 24 Feb. 1905, RWB-FC.

14. In the early days of their partnership, Bingham and Davies worked closely together, but as time went on, Bingham apparently concentrated more on politics and business than on the law practice. Bingham memorandum to Macmillan, 62; RWB to

Edward T. Harrington, [n.d.], RWB to Robert Bingham, 22 Feb. 1901, RWB to Shepard Bryan, 21 Mar. 1906, RWB to R. T. Grinnan, 13 Dec. 1905, RWB-FC.

See boxes 10, 13, 14, 15, and 30, RWB-FC, for examples of Bingham and Davies business accounts in the first decade of this century.

For more information about Davies see William E. Ellis, "Tenement House Reform: Another Episode in Kentucky Progressivism," *Filson Club History Quarterly* 55 (Oct. 1981): 375–82.

15. Files 333, 334, 335, 339, 340, 344, 346, 350, RWB to Judge J. H. Candler, 20 Nov. 1906, RWB-FC.

16. Files 313, 320, 328, 338, 377, 378, listing of office locations in Filson Club records, RWB to Alexander Gilmour, 25 May 1908, RWB to Slaughter and Gilmour, 17, 21, 26 Sept. 1901, all in RWB-FC.

17. File 290, box 30, RWB-FC.

18. Boxes 8, 9; Perrin Busby to RWB, 10 June 1905, William DeWitt to RWB, 2 Dec. 1902, RWB-FC. Davies's marriage to B. F. Avery's granddaughter also served as an entrée for the partners into that company.

19. Boody, McLellan and Co. to RWB, 24 Sept. 1901, RWB to Battery Park Bank, 19 Sept. 1902, Goldsmith, Wolf, and Lyons to RWB, 29 Apr., 20 May, 22 Aug. 1905, RWB to Davies, 23 Aug. 1905, T. L. Jefferson to RWB, 19 Oct. 1905, E. C. Hegan to RWB, 25 Oct. 1906, RWB to J. H. Haager, 3 Jan. 1909, RWB-FC.

Boxes 6 and 7 in RWB-FC contain an extensive record of transactions of RWB with W. L. Lyons and Company, J. J. B. Hilliard and Son, and other stock brokerages.

20. See boxes 11, 13, 14, RWB-FC; A. F. Callahan to RWB, 30 Aug. 1904, RWB-FC.

21. See box 12, RWB-FC; A. F. Callahan to RWB, 30 Apr. 1908, RWB-FC.

22. See boxes 8, 10, 15, 18, and 21, RWB-FC; Davies to C. B. Robinson, 11 Jan. 1907, RWB-FC.

23. Bingham also belonged to other fraternal organizations such as the Woodmen of the World, Knights of Pythias, Improved Order of Redmen, Benevolent and Protective Order of Elks, and Ancient Order of United Workmen. Robert H. Wiebe, *Businessmen and Reform: A Study of the Progressive Movement* (Cambridge: Harvard University Press, 1962), 18; Samuel S. Hill et al., *Religion and the Solid South* (Nashville: Abingdon Press, 1972), 51; William J. Watkins to RWB, 20 Jan. 1899, RWB to George C. Bender, 11 Mar. 1903, RWB to Charles Graves, 17 Jan. 1901, J. G. Jewell to RWB, 3 June 1901, Al Bourlier to Bingham and Davies, 26 Apr. 1900, RWB-FC.

24. Bingham's business affiliations included the Louisville Commercial Club, the Louisville Board of Trade, and the Louisville Bar Association. He also included such agencies as the YMCA, Kentucky Anti-Tuberculosis Association, and the State Forestry Association among his philanthropic interests. E. L. McDonald to RWB, 21 Jan. 1901, H. Dumesnil to RWB, 9 Sept. 1901, J. C. Van Pell to RWB, 5 Apr. 1899, RWB to R. V. Van Vreedenburgh, 8 Oct. 1901, T. Smith Milton to RWB, 4 Apr. 1903, J. S. Bell to RWB, 11 Dec. 1899, E. G. Routzahn to RWB, 15 Jan. 1908, RWB to J. C. W. Beckham, 16 Dec. 1905, RWB to Charles Speed, 19 Apr. 1900, RWB to Charles F. Price, 21 Jan. 1903, RWB-FC. See also box 27, RWB-FC; *Courier-Journal*, 5 June 1909.

25. W. R. Shackelford to RWB, 26 June 1908, RWB to R. C. Creal, 13 Feb. 1907, RWB-FC; Scrapbook, Program for the Dramatic Club, *School for Scandal*, 28 Apr. 1899, RWB-FC.

26. Herbert Levy to RWB, 18 June 1906, RWB to Charles W. Kent, 30 Sept. 1908, RWB-FC; See also box 27, RWB-FC, for voluminous correspondence relating to hunting and firearms; Holmberg, oral-history interview.

27. See Tindall, *Ethnic Southerners*, 143–47, and Grantham, *Southern Progressivism*, 410–22.

28. RWB to A. and H. Veeder, 20 Nov. 1908, RWB to Louis Summers, 6 Oct. 1908, L. L. [?] to RWB, 31 Jan. 1908, C. H. Huhlein to RWB, 22 June 1908, RWB to J. C. W. Beckham, 17 Feb. 1908, RWB to Earl D. Babst, 28 Jan., 9 Mar. 1908, National Biscuit Company to RWB, 27 Oct. 1908, RWB to Charles H. Kerr and Co., 26 May 1908, J. F. Buckner, Jr., to RWB, 28 Jan. 1903, RWB-FC; *Louisville Evening Post*, 14 Feb. 1908.

29. *Louisville Evening Post*, 4 Sept. 1907; *Courier-Journal*, 1, 6, 7, 13 Sept. 1907; J. V. Beckman to RWB, 6 Sept. 1907, Arthur M. Wallace to RWB, 5 Sept. 1907, RWB to T. J. Minary, 5 Sept. 1907, RWB-FC.

30. See George C. Wright, *Racial Violence in Kentucky, 1865–1940: Lynchings, Mob Rule, and "Legal Lynchings"* (Baton Rouge: Louisiana State University Press, 1990), chaps. 2–6, for a description of the full impact of racial intimidation in this era. Wright calculated 353 lynchings occurring in Kentucky from 1866 through 1934 in appendix A.

Tapp and Klotter, *Kentucky: Decades of Discord*, 10–18, 141–71; George C. Wright, *Life behind a Veil: Blacks in Louisville, Kentucky, 1865–1930* (Baton Rouge: Louisiana State University Press, 1985), part 2. In 1907 a leading Republican of Trigg County threatened to remove the Negroes' right to vote. *Courier-Journal*, 6 Sept. 1907; C. H. Parrish to RWB, 3 Sept. 1907, C. H. Bullock to RWB, 2 Oct. 1907, G. W. Ferguson to RWB, 14 Jan. 1908, J. A. Gooden to RWB, 4 Oct. 1910, RWB-FC.

31. Robert M. Crunden in *Ministers of Reform: The Progressives' Achievement in American Civilization, 1889–1920* (New York: Basic Books, 1982) discussed in chap. 1 the morality that impelled individuals like Bingham toward reform.

See box 28, RWB-FC, for an extensive file of correspondence on the Kentucky Children's Home Society. For many years Bingham handled legal matters for the society. RWB to William S. Pryor, 15 Sept. 1904, Joseph P. Byars to RWB, 31 Dec. 1902, Thomas D. Osborne to RWB, 27 Dec. 1907, RWB to John F. Kelly, 23 Jan. 1905, RWB-FC; *Courier-Journal*, 3 Dec. 1902.

32. Bingham, oral-history interview, 9 Apr. 1987; RWB to Harrison Randolph, 6 Dec. 1906, RWB to Charles L. Collins, 10 Apr. 1908, RWB to S. C. Warren, 1 Apr. 1908, RWB-FC.

33. *Courier-Journal*, 30 Oct., 4, 29, 30 Nov. 1907; *Louisville Evening Post*, 5, 23, 30 Sept. 1907; John Bryce Baskin to RWB, 16 Aug. 1907, RWB to M. P. Hunt, 11 Nov. 1907, Noel Gaines to RWB, 16 Jan. 1911, RWB-FC; Ferenc M. Szasz, *The Divided Mind of Protestant America, 1880–1930* (University: University of Alabama Press, 1982), xi–xiii.

34. Robert Bingham to Colonel [?] Caldwell, [1905], Commission as Democratic committeeman for the forty-third precinct, forty-eighth legislative district, 1898, RWB-FC.

35. RWB to Alfred W. Davis, 4 Nov. 1899, RWB to John H. Leathers, 4 Oct. 1901, John H. Page to RWB, 18 Oct. 1901, RWB to Mayor Charles F. Grainger, 10 Apr. 1902, RWB-LC.

36. *Louisville Times,* 18 Nov. 1903; *Courier-Journal,* 9 Nov. 1904; Irvine Hampton to RWB, 27 Mar. 1902, RWB to Robert Bingham, 12 Dec. 1903, RWB to Clarence M. Finn, 28 Nov. 1904, RWB-FC.

37. For a full description of Beckham's years as governor see Nicholas C. Burckel, "From Beckham to McCreary: The Progressive Record of Kentucky Governors," *The Register of the Kentucky Historical Society* 76 (Oct. 1978): 285–306. Box 30, RWB-FC, contains extensive Bingham material for his years as county attorney.

38. Executive Committee, Mutual Protective Association, to RWB, 17 Apr. 1906, RWB to J. C. Boardman, 18 Apr. 1906, RWB to George Braden, 23 May 1906, RWB to Beckham, 23 May 1906, RWB to T. Kennedy Helm, 23 May 1906, RWB to N. B. Hays, 4 Feb. 1907, Beckham to RWB, 28 Feb. 1907, J. N. Prestridge to RWB, 6 Mar. 1907, RWB-FC.

39. Thomas D. Clark, *Helm Bruce, Public Defender: Breaking Louisville's Gothic Political Ring, 1905* (Louisville: Filson Club, 1973), 20; Tapp and Klotter, *Kentucky: Decades of Discord,* 98, 340–47.

40. Clark, *Helm Bruce,* 32–44; *Courier-Journal,* 8, 9 Nov. 1905.

41. RWB to F. R. Bishop, 7, 11 Sept. 1905, RWB to Robert Bingham, 3 Oct., 22 Nov. 1905, Davies to RWB, 10 Aug. 1905, RWB-FC.

42. *Courier-Journal,* 8, 9 Nov. 1905, 2 Nov. 1986.

43. Clark, *Helm Bruce,* 43–50.

44. Ibid., 45–48; RWB to Dr. R. H. Rhea, 21 Feb. 1906, Bingham and Davies to Percy Haly, 24 Feb. 1906, Haly to Bingham and Davies, 2 Mar. 1906, RWB to all Democratic officeholders in Jefferson County, 4 Apr. 1907, R. F. Peck to RWB, 18 Oct. 1910, RWB to Peck, 19 Oct. 1910, RWB-FC.

45. Clark, *Helm Bruce,* 43–50.

46. RWB to W. A. Moffett, 25 May 1907, RWB-FC.

3. ". . . And Politics—The Damnedest in Kentucky"

The title comes from a quote from "In Kentucky," a poem by Jim Mulligan, from John Wilson Townsend, *"In Kentucky" and Its Author Jim Mulligan* (Lexington: John Bradford Club, 1935), 9.

1. Clark, *Helm Bruce,* 50.

2. Robert Bingham to RWB, 29 June 1907, RWB-FC; *Courier-Journal,* 28, 30 June, 14 July 1907; *Louisville Evening Post,* 28 June 1907; *Louisville Herald,* 28, 29 June 1907; *Louisville Times,* 28 June 1907.

3. Norman H. Clark, *Deliver Us from Evil: An Interpretation of American Prohibition* (New York: W. W. Norton, 1976), 13.

Clark's monograph is representative of a new, more sympathetic view toward prohibition among historians. For other examples see K. Austin Kerr, *Organized for Prohibition: A New History of the Anti-Saloon League* (New Haven: Yale Univeristy Press, 1985); David E. Kyvig, *Repealing National Prohibition* (Chicago: University of Chicago Press, 1979); and particularly John C. Burnham, *Paths into American Culture: Psychology, Medicine, and Morals* (Philadelphia: Temple University Press, 1988).

4. Harrison Dickson, "The Battle of the Bottle: The Obituary of Kentucky and the Epitaph of Tennessee," *Saturday Evening Post,* 28 Dec. 1907, 15–17, 29.

5. Examples of support included the editor of the *Western Recorder,* a weekly Southern Baptist newspaper; a resolution of support from the Kentucky Baptist General Association annual meeting; letters from assorted Baptist, Disciples of Christ, Lutheran, Presbyterian, and Methodist ministers; and the endorsement of the Kentucky Anti-Saloon League. See box 31, RWB-FC. *Courier-Journal,* 28 June, 1, 8 July 1907; T. T. Eaton to RWB, 27 June 1907, Walker W. Watson to RWB, 28 June 1907, C. L. Collins to RWB, 29 June 1907, RWB-FC.

6. *Courier-Journal,* 30 June 1907.

7. *Courier-Journal,* 1, 7, 8, 9, 17 July 1907; *Louisville Evening Post,* 1 July 1907; *Louisville Herald,* 1, 2 June 1907; "Special Proclamation to Saloons," Chief of Police Sebastian Gunther to RWB, 1 July 1907, RWB-FC.

8. *Courier-Journal,* 30 June, 6, 14, 26 July, 1, 6 Aug. 1907.

9. *Courier-Journal,* 2, 3, 5, 9, 15 July 1907; James T. Wills, "Louisville Politics, 1891–1897" (M.A. thesis, University of Louisville, 1966), 88; Ben LaBree to RWB, 25 June 1907, E. L. Powell to RWB, 28 June 1907, Abner Harris to RWB, 12 July 1907, RWB-FC.

10. *Courier-Journal,* 29 June, 12, 21 July 1907.

11. Ibid., 13, 16, 18, 20, 23 July 1907.

12. E. H. Chase, Jr., to RWB, 3 July 1907, John Niman to RWB, 14 July 1907, RWB-FC.

13. *Courier-Journal,* 18 July, 4, 18, 19 Aug., 8 Sept. 1907; *Louisville Evening Post,* 5 Aug. 1907.

14. *Louisville Evening Post,* 22 July, 5, 6 Aug. 1907.

15. *Courier-Journal,* 7 July, 14, 21 Aug., 15, 18, 26, 28 Sept., 9, 24, 28 Oct., 9 Nov. 1907, 9, 10 June 1908.

16. *Louisville Evening Post,* 26, 27 Sept. 1907.

17. *Courier-Journal,* 10, 22, 23 Oct. 1907.

18. Ibid.

19. Ibid., 24 July, 7, 8 Aug. 1907.

20. Ibid., 21, 24, 27, 28 Aug., 8, 9 Sept., 30 Oct. 1907; "Joint Resolution" appointing the Audit Company of New York to investigate the "affairs" of the Louisville Water Company, 20 Aug. 1907, RWB-FC.

21. *Courier-Journal,* 13 Aug., 17 Sept., 22 Oct., 10, 12, 16 Nov., 1, 4 Dec. 1907; *Louisville Evening Post,* 16 Sept. 1907; William Marshall Bullitt to RWB, 24 Aug. 1907, RWB to Charles F. Grainger, 13 Sept. 1907, Grainger to RWB, 16 Sept. 1907, RWB-FC; Yater, *Two Hundred Years,* 147.

22. Helm Bruce to RWB, 18 Sept. 1907, RWB to N. B. Hays, 9 Oct. 1907, Hays to RWB, 10, 14 Oct. 1907, R. L. Page to Hays, 16 Oct. 1907, Hays to Page, 19 Oct. 1907, RWB-FC.

23. *Louisville Evening Post,* 8 July 1907.

24. *Courier-Journal,* 6, 7, 8, 9, 10 July 1907; A. B. Lipscomb to RWB, 5 July 1907, RWB-FC; Bingham, oral-history interview, 6 Jan. 1977.

25. *Courier Journal,* 9, 10, 30 July 1907; *Louisville Evening Post,* 20 Aug., 4 Sept. 1907.

26. *Louisville Evening Post,* 3, 9, 20 Aug., 4 Sept. 1907; William Bosler to RWB, 8 July 1907, John F. Kelly to RWB, 12 July 1907, W. E. Richards to Governor Beckham, 1

Aug. 1907, J. M. Lansing to RWB, 16 Aug. 1907, Neville S. Bullitt to RWB, 17 Aug. 1907, W. T. Ellis to RWB, 14 Aug. 1907, RWB-FC.

For more information about the political ambitions of Beckham, see Burckel, "From Beckham to McCreary."

27. *Courier-Journal*, 27, 28, 29 July 1907.

28. Ibid., 30, 31 July, 10, 31 Aug., 17 Sept. 1907; *Louisville Evening Post*, 29 July, 7, 26, 31 Aug., 13 Sept. 1907; Lewis C. Humphrey to RWB, 25 Sept. 1907, RWB to Eames MacVeagh, 8 Aug. 1910, RWB-FC.

29. *Courier-Journal*, 19 Sept. 1907.

30. *Louisville Evening Post*, 14, 15, 16, 17 Aug. 1907; James P. Helm to RWB, 14 Aug. 1907, RWB-FC.

31. *Courier-Journal*, 21 Aug. 1907; *Louisville Times*, 21 Aug. 1907.

32. *Louisville Herald*, 22 Aug. 1907; *Courier-Journal*, 23, 24, 25 Aug. 1907; *Louisville Evening Post*, 21 Aug. 1907; Helm Bruce to RWB, 23 Aug. 1907, RWB-FC.

33. *Courier-Journal*, 17 Sept. 1907.

34. *Louisville Evening Post*, 7 Aug., 18, 23 Sept. 1907; *Louisville Herald*, 4, 5 Nov. 1907; *Courier-Journal*, 27 Aug., 22 Sept., 9, 13 Oct. 1907.

35. *Courier-Journal*, 11 Aug., 2, 8 Sept., 4 Oct. 1907; "To the Public," 30 Aug. 1907, RWB-FC.

36. *Louisville Times*, 14, 18, 19 Sept. 1907; *Courier-Journal*, 19 Sept. 1907.

37. *Louisville Evening Post*, 19 Sept. 1907.

38. *Courier-Journal*, 1 Oct., 3, 6 Nov. 1907; "Louisville Police Department, Office of the Chief, Instructions to the Police Force Relative to Their Duties at the Election to be Held, 5 Nov. 1907," RWB-FC.

39. Peyton H. Hoge, "The Kentucky Election," *The Outlook* 87 (30 Nov. 1907), 751–52; *Courier-Journal*, 3, 10 Nov. 1907.

40. *Courier-Journal*, 3, 10 Nov. 1907; Watterson to RWB, 30 Oct. 1907, RWB-FC.

41. *Louisville Evening Post*, 2, 3 Nov. 1909; *Louisville Herald*, 2, 3 Nov. 1909; *Courier-Journal*, 4, 5, 7, 8 Oct., 1, 3, 4 Nov. 1909; RWB to Eames MacVeagh, 8 Aug. 1910, RWB-FC.

42. *The Reason*, pamphlet published by the Crescent Hill Independent League in support of Bingham, file 257, RWB-FC; *Courier-Journal*, 16 Aug. 1907.

43. RWB to W. T. Ellis, 13 Sept. 1910, RWB-FC.

44. *Courier-Journal*, 21 Sept. 1910; RWB to M. H. Thatcher, 23 Sept. 1910, RWB-FC.

45. RWB to "Dear Sir," 1 Oct. 1910, Zeno Wall to RWB, 21 Sept. 1910, RWB-FC. One file in box 7, RWB-FC, contains a four-page list of names of independent voters to whom Bingham mailed his circular letter.

46. *Courier-Journal*, 16 Aug. 1910; Frank B. Russell to James W. Brown, 13 Oct. 1910, Russell to Charles L. Scholl, 19 Oct. 1910, Russell to Bingham, 21 Oct. 1910, P. S. Collins to RWB, 24 Oct. 1910, Bingham to Curtiss Publishing Company, 21 Oct. 1910, RWB-FC.

47. *Courier-Journal*, 9 Nov. 1910; RWB to H. W. Jackson, 26 Nov. 1910, Bingham to Governor Augustus E. Willson, 22 Nov. 1910, Shepard Bryan to RWB, 22 Aug. 1910, Bryan to RWB, 14 Nov. 1910, RWB-FC.

48. RWB to Senator W. O. Bradley, 29 Nov. 1910, Temple Bodley to RWB, 12 Jan. 1911, William Heyburn to RWB, 6 June 1913, RWB-FC.

49. RWB to Herbert Hoover, 28 May 1917, RWB to H. N. Lukins, 21 Dec. 1916, both in RWB-FC; *Louisville Times,* 7 Nov. 1917.

4. Founding a Dynasty

1. *Courier-Journal,* 28, 29 April 1913; Bingham, oral-history interview, 9 Apr. 1987; Bingham memorandum to Macmillan; *Louisville Evening Post,* 29 Apr. 1913.

2. Bingham, oral-history interview, 9 Apr. 1987; Barry Bingham, Sr., to Mrs. Joseph H. Durham, Jr., 25 May 1982, RWB-FC; *Courier-Journal,* 28 Apr. 1913; Bingham memorandum to Macmillan; Bingham, *Passion and Prejudice,* 138–40.

3. Bingham, oral-history interview, 9 Apr. 1987; newspaper clippings in box 3 and miscellaneous items in box 10, RWB-FC; Samuel W. Thomas, ed., *Barry Bingham: A Man of His Word* (Lexington: University Press of Kentucky, 1993), 29–30.

4. George Cary Tabb to RWB, 21 Oct. 1918, RWB-LC; M. H. Miller to RWB, [Dec. 1914], RWB to Mrs. S. A. Miller, 2 Dec. 1914, RWB to George J. Long, 18 Jan., 17 Apr. 1916, RWB-FC; F. W. Paul, "His Excellency The Hon. Robert Worth Bingham, LL.D.," *The Landmark* 17 (Aug. 1935): 401–4; Bingham memorandum to Macmillan.

5. *New York Herald,* 6 Nov. 1916; Josephus Daniels, *Tar Heel Editor* (Chapel Hill: University of North Carolina Press, 1939), 68; Tifft and Jones, *Patriarch,* 32; Thomas, *Barry Bingham,* 202.

6. Sidney Walter Martin, *Florida's Flagler* (Athens: University of Georgia Press, 1949), 90, 186, 190–201, 248–51; Edward N. Akin, *Flagler: Rockefeller Partner and Florida Baron* (Kent, Ohio: Kent State University Press, 1988), 148–49.

7. Martin, *Florida's Flagler,* 190–93; Alvaretta Kenan Register, *The Kenan Family* (Statesboro, Ga.: Kenan Print Shop, n.d.), n.p.; Samuel W. Thomas, interview by author, 13 Aug. 1987; Akin, *Flagler,* 227–29; Brenner, *House of Dreams,* 102.

Sallie Bingham suggested that Owen Kenan played a role in the death of Henry Flagler. Bingham, *Passion and Prejudice,* 151.

David Leon Chandler declared in *Henry Flagler* (New York: Macmillan, 1986), 189, that Mary Lily "picked up a liking for bourbon whiskey and for laudanum" during her years with Flagler. In *The Binghams of Louisville* (116), published a year later, he contended that "there is no indication she used narcotics" when she married Bingham. This is a good example of Chandler's twisting of facts and contortion of arguments into support of any thesis he feels necessary to attack Robert Worth Bingham. Summary of Response to Bingham's *Passion and Prejudice,* 14.

8. *New York Herald,* 6 Nov. 1916; T. S. Kenan III, "Mary Lily Kenan Flagler Bingham," *Dictionary of North Carolina Biography,* ed. William S. Powell, vol. 1 (Chapel Hill: University of North Carolina Press, 1979), 157.

Sallie Bingham and Chandler charge that Robert Worth was encouraged to push for a romance with the eligible Mrs. Flagler by his creditors, owing one million dollars in debts for unsuccessful political campaigns and business ventures. They cite no proof. As a matter of fact, Chandler cited Sallie Bingham as his source in *The Binghams of Louisville,* 103, and Bingham recited the charge in *Passion and Prejudice,* 143.

9. *New York Herald,* 15, 16 Nov. 1916.

10. Thomas, interview by author; Bingham, oral-history interview, 24 Sept. 1987.

11. *Courier-Journal*, 6, 13, 27 May 1917; Bingham memorandum to Macmillan; RWB to John Russell Pope, 25 Jan. 1917, RWB-FC; Thomas, interview by author.

12. *Courier-Journal*, 27, 28 July 1917; *Raleigh News and Observer*, 28 July 1917.

13. *New York Times*, 28 July 1917; Certificate of Death, Bingham memorandum to Macmillan; S. T. G. Smith to RWB, 28 July 1917, Ethel Thacker to RWB, 5 Aug. 1917, RWB-FC.

14. *Raleigh News and Observer*, 9 June 1963; Michael Lesy, *Real Life: Louisville in the Twenties* (New York: Pantheon, 1976), 152–55.

15. Thomas S. Kenan III to Barry Bingham, Sr., 2 Apr. 1987, Bingham memorandum to Macmillan, 42, 78–81, 121–25; *Louisville Evening Post*, 4 Sept. 1917; Akin, *Flagler*, 228–29. One of the gossipers may have been Abraham Flexner, a Louisvillian who became a national leader in higher education, with whom Bingham had a disagreement over a school attended by young Robert and run by Flexner in the early part of the century. Flexner would make these same accusations in 1933 when Bingham's nomination to the Court of St. James's came before the U.S. Senate. Thomas, interview by author; Bingham, oral-history interviews, 9 Apr., 24 Sept. 1987; enclosure from Hugh H. Young to Mrs. Robert Worth Bingham, 14 Feb. 1940, RWB-FC. See Abraham Flexner, *Abraham Flexner: An Autobiography* (New York: Simon and Schuster, 1960) for a full description of his professional career.

16. Bingham memorandum to Macmillan, 78, 94–96, 121; Summary of Response to Bingham's *Passion and Prejudice*, 14.

17. *Courier-Journal*, 5 Sept., 19 Nov. 1917; *Louisville Evening Post*, 21 Dec. 1917; Thomas, interview by author.

18. *Louisville Herald* and *Courier-Journal*, 5 Sept. 1917; *Louisville Evening Post*, 23 Nov. 1917; Summary of Response to Bingham's *Passion and Prejudice*, item 10.

19. *Courier-Journal*, 22, 23, 26 Sept. 1917; *Louisville Herald* and *Louisville Times*, 21 Sept. 1917.

20. *Courier-Journal*, 24, 25, 26, 27, 28 Sept., 3 Oct. 1917; *Louisville Herald*, 21, 24 Sept. 1917; *Louisville Times*, 21, 25 Sept. 1917; *Louisville Herald Post*, 22 Sept. 1917.

21. Emily Dawson to RWB, 19 May [1918], RWB-LC; RWB to B. Broderick, 1 Nov. 1917, RWB-FC; *Courier-Journal*, 24, 25 Sept., 3 Oct. 1917; *Louisville Evening Post*, 24, 26 Sept. 1917.

22. *Courier-Journal*, 7 Apr., 28 July 1918, 17 July 1987; Tifft and Jones, *Patriarch*, 66–68.

23. Chandler and Chandler, *Binghams of Louisville*, 211; Bingham, *Passion and Prejudice*, 134; Brenner, *House of Dreams*, 73, 107; Thomas, *Barry Bingham*, 196. Nothing in Robert Worth Bingham's medical records indicates that he had ever had syphilis. Grover M. Hutchins, Professor of Pathology, The Johns Hopkins University School of Medicine, to Mark M. Wilson, 31 Mar. 1987, Summary of Response to Bingham's *Passion and Prejudice*, item 7.

24. George M. Ward to RWB, 19 July 1917, RWB-FC.

25. *Courier-Journal*, 17 July 1987; Thomas, interview by author; enclosure from Joe Ward to author, 22 July 1987.

Copies of the Young manuscripts located in Bingham memorandum to Macmillan, 30–39, include a statement dated 13 March 1933 and a letter to Mrs. RWB, 14 Feb.

1940. In the latter Young mentioned that he was submitting his memoirs to the publisher and that he would not describe the death of Mary Lily and the controversy with the Kenans. See Young, *Hugh Young.* Another physician also corroborated Young's testimony.

While trying to overcome the first effects of his son's addiction to alcohol, Bingham mentioned to his daughter that when he found out about "poor M.L." (Mary Lily's alcoholism) he made "a real study of the disease and I know now a great deal about it from a scientific standpoint." RWB to Henrietta Bingham, 12 Nov. [1922], RWB-FC.

26. Young manuscripts in Bingham memorandum to Macmillan, 30–31; Samuel W. Thomas, "Let the Documents Speak: An Analysis of David Leon Chandler's Assessment of Robert Worth Bingham," *Filson Club History Quarterly* 63 (July 1989): 334–37. Brenner claimed that Hugh Young lied in order to protect his friend Bingham, but offered no direct proof of this charge. For some reason she also quoted Thomas S. Kenan III as referring to Mary Lily Kenan Flagler as "my great grandmother," when, of course, she had no children. Brenner, *House of Dreams,* 79, 129; RWB to Herbert Hoover, 28 May 1917, RWB-FC.

27. Young manuscripts, Bingham memorandum to Macmillan, 30–39; Much of the argument made for Bingham's complicity in the death of Mary Lily by David Leon Chandler in *Binghams of Louisville* is based on allegedly having been informed by Thomas S. Kenan III of what is contained in the "Confidential Autopsy Report" and "Confidential Kenan family private detective report, August and September, 1917." See pages 116, 122, 130, and 161 for specific examples of these documents to support the theses of Mr. Chandler. Thomas S. Kenan III, however, stated to Barry Bingham, Sr., Samuel W. Thomas, and me that Chandler personally saw neither the autopsy nor the private detective report in possession of the Kenan family in Chapel Hill, North Carolina, nor was there any such arrangement as Chandler described in his book. Thomas S. Kenan III to the author, 3 Feb. 1988; Kenan to Samuel Wilson Thomas, 5 Mar. 1987, Bingham memorandum to Macmillan; Thomas, interview by author; Bingham, oral-history interview, 24 Sept. 1987.

Chandler also based much of his evidence of a Bingham conspiracy on a letter in the files of The Filson Club. The author of *The Binghams of Louisville* incorrectly dated the letter from the wife of Hugh Young, who was in Europe as of 27 May 1917, when internal and external evidence indicates that the correct date is 27 May 1918. In the letter Bess Young asked for Bingham to reinvest some of his money with her brother. If the date had been in 1917, it would have supported the thesis of Chandler that a rapacious Bingham was plotting the death of Mary Lily. However, the date is obviously 1918 because she designates the day as "Monday, May 27th," which occurred in 1918 and not 1917. James J. Holmberg, "The Use of Filson Club Manuscripts in *The Binghams of Louisville,*" *Filson Club History Quarterly* 63 (July 1989): 382–83.

See reviews of the Chandler book by Mary K. Bonsteel Tachau in the *Courier-Journal,* 10 Jan. 1988, and Robert M. Ireland, in *The Register of the Kentucky Historical Society* 86 (Summer 1988): 280–82.

28. *Courier-Journal,* 28 July 1918; Alex P. Humphrey to C. T. Collins, 28 May 1918, RWB to Humphrey, 18 Feb. 1920, RWB-LC; W. A. Blount to Helm Bruce, 26 Apr., 23 May 1918, Bruce to A. P. Humphrey, 22 May 1918, Humphrey to RWB, 19 Aug. 1918,

W. R. Kenan, Jr. to Humphrey, 2 Jan. 1919, Kenan receipt from RWB, 31 July 1919, RWB-FC.

29. *Courier-Journal*, 2, 9, 25, 27 Oct., 14 Dec. 1917, 8 Apr. 1918, 8, 9 Oct., 22 Nov. 1919, 26 May, 31 July 1920; *New York Times*, 12 Aug. 1917.

30. *Courier-Journal*, 10 Oct., 30 Nov. 1917, 9 June, 24 Oct. 1918, 9, 17 July 1919; *Louisville Post*, 29 Jan. 1923.

31. J. A. Sullivan to RWB, 15 Aug. 1918, Robert Worth Bingham Papers, microfilm, reel 1, The Filson Club, Louisville, Kentucky (hereafter cited as *RWB Papers;* all references are to reel 1 unless otherwise indicated); *New York Herald*, 6 Nov. 1916.

32. RWB to Adjutant General, War Department, Washington, D.C., 13 Feb. 1917, RWB-LC; Davies to RWB, 21 July 1918, *RWB Papers;* Young to RWB, 16 July 1917, Levi to RWB, 16, 30 Sept. 1917, RWB-FC; RWB to Henrietta Bingham, 15 Aug. 1914, Major J. S. Battle to RWB, 26 Apr. 1917, RWB-FC.

33. Arthur Krock, *Memoirs: Sixty Years on the Firing Line* (New York: Funk and Wagnalls, 1968), 47–48.

34. Bingham, oral-history interviews, 17 Nov. 1983, 4 Apr. 1987; Krock to RWB, 19 July 1918, RWB-LC; Thomas, interview by author. Much of Chandler's argument for Bingham's complicity in the death of his wife is based on the mistaken idea that Bingham needed money fast in order to put in a bid for the newspapers. See Chandler and Chandler, *Binghams of Louisville*, 121–22.

35. Krock to RWB, 19 July 1918, RWB-LC; Krock, *Memoirs*, 44–48; Dennis Charles Cusick, "Gentleman of the Press: The Life and Times of Walter Newman Haldeman" (M.A. thesis, University of Louisville, 1987), 201–9; Bruce Haldeman to Henry Watterson, 6 Mar. 1915, Haldeman Family Papers, The Filson Club; Thomas, *Barry Bingham*, 53.

36. *Courier-Journal*, 3 Sept. 1914, 7, 10 Apr. 1917, 16 Jan. 1987.

37. Cusick, "Gentleman of the Press," 209; *Louisville Times*, 23 June, 14, 28 July 1917; *Courier-Journal*, 17 June, 24, 25 July 1917; *Louisville Evening Post*, 20 June 1917.

38. Cusick, "Gentleman of the Press," 211–12; *New York Times*, 7 Aug. 1917, 28 July, 7 Aug. 1918; *Courier-Journal*, 6, 7 Aug. 1918; Option Document, 1 July 1918, RWB-FC; Thomas, *Barry Bingham*, 206.

39. *Courier-Journal*, 31 July 1919, 1 May 1920, 24 Apr. 1983.

40. *Courier-Journal*, 7 Aug. 1918, 24 Apr. 1983; Joseph Frazier Wall, *Henry Watterson: Reconstructed Rebel* (New York: Oxford University Press, 1956), 315–16, 320–21; Thomas, *Barry Bingham*, 206.

41. Woods to RWB, 16 Sept. 1918, Sullivan to RWB, 15 Aug. 1918, Mullins to RWB, 8 Aug. 1918, Powell to RWB, 7 Aug. 1918, RWB-LC.

42. W. A. McLean to RWB, 7 Aug. 1918, Breckinridge to RWB, 8 Aug. 1918, John Stites to RWB, 25 July 1918, A. Y. Ford to RWB, 6 Aug. 1918, John J. Barret to RWB, 7 Aug. 1919, Bagley to RWB, 20 Sept. 1918, Burlingame to RWB, 24 July 1918, RWB-LC. As a result of World War I and the unsavory character of a small section of Green Street as a site for houses of prostitution, the street name was changed to Liberty. Yater, *Two Hundred Years*, 170.

43. Edwin Emery and Michael Emery, *The Press and America: An Interpretive History of the Mass Media*, 5th ed. (Englewood Cliffs, N.J.: Prentice-Hall, 1984), 281–367.

·44. Krock, *Memoirs,* 42, 48–50, 59; Krock to RWB, 15 Mar. 1923, RWB-LC; Robert E. Hughes to Bruce Haldeman, 4 Mar. 1918, Haldeman Family Papers, The Filson Club; RWB to Henrietta Bingham, [Feb. 1923], 14 Mar. [1923], RWB-FC.

45. Norburne Robinson to RWB, 15 Nov. 1918, RWB to W. S. Lockhart, 29 Aug. 1918, Lockhart to RWB, 11 Sept. 1918, RWB to Zorn, 27 Jan. 1919, J. M. Vollmer to RWB, 13 Sept. 1919, RWB-LC.

46. Robert E. Hughes to RWB, 15 Oct. 1918, RWB-LC.

47. Krock, *Memoirs,* 36, 49; RWB to Lee Richardson, 5 Sept. 1918, RWB-LC.

48. Krock, *Memoirs,* 50; Henry M. Johnson to RWB, 9 Aug. 1918, RWB-LC.

49. Mrs. Bruce Haldeman to RWB, n.d., 1918, *RWB Papers;* Harper to RWB, 28 Aug., 6 Sept. 1918, Catt to RWB, 3 Sept. 1918, RWB-LC.

50. RWB to Trammell, 4 Feb. 1919, South to RWB, 30 Aug. 1918, RWB-LC.

51. Wall, *Henry Watterson,* 323, 327–38; Krock to Watterson, 26 Jan. 1918, Henry Watterson Papers, The Filson Club (hereafter cited as HW-FC); Tumulty to RWB, 4 Nov. 1918, 20 June 1919, Oscar Underwood to RWB, 19 Dec. 1919, Wilson to RWB, 1 Jan. 1922, RWB-LC; Woodrow Wilson to Krock, 30 Jan. 1919, RWB to Wilson, 17 June 1919, Wallace to RWB, 24 Dec. 1918, *RWB Papers.*

52. *Courier-Journal,* 2 Mar. 1919, 2 Apr., 19 May 1948; Watterson to RWB, 3, 22 Mar., 27 May 1919, *RWB Papers;* RWB to Watterson, 18 Mar., 5 Apr. 1919, HW-FC; Isaac F. Marcosson, *"Marse Henry": A Biography of Henry Watterson* (New York: Dodd, Mead, 1951), 234–35.

53. Wall, *Henry Watterson,* 328; Watterson to RWB, 22 Mar., 27 May 1919, Tom Wallace to RWB, 24 Dec. 1918, *RWB Papers;* RWB to Watterson, 5 Apr. 1919, HW-FC.

54. RWB to Woodrow Wilson, 17 June 1919, Oscar W. Underwood to RWB, 19 Dec. 1919, Joseph Tumulty to RWB, 4 Nov. 1918, Tumulty to RWB, 20 June 1919, RWB-LC.

55. *Courier-Journal,* 2 Mar. 1919.

56. Bingham, oral-history interview, 3 Dec. 1980. For a description of race relations in the Progressive Era on a national scale, see Jack Temple Kirby, *Darkness at the Dawning: Race and Reform in the Progressive Era* (Philadelphia: Temple University Press, 1972).

57. *Courier-Journal,* 28 Mar. 1920; RWB to Henrietta Bingham, 4 Mar. [1922], 14 June [1923], RWB-FC.

58. Wright, *Life behind a Veil,* 3, 262–63, 265, 281; James Bond to Lewis Humphrey, 26 Oct. 1923 (copy), *RWB Papers,* reel 2; RWB to A. Eugene Thomson, 1 Aug. 1923, RWB to George Colvin, 24 Sept. 1923, Ragland to RWB, 10 Dec. 1923, 25 Nov. 1924, RWB-LC.

59. RWB to John H. Cowles, 1 Feb. 1923, RWB to Luce, 16 Oct. 1926, RWB-LC; RWB to A. Eugene Thomson, 11 Oct. 1922, *RWB Papers,* reel 2; Wright, *Life behind a Veil,* 283–85.

60. RWB to W. T. C. Carpenter, 1 Nov. 1918, RWB to C. S. Nunn, 22 Nov. 1920, RWB-LC.

61. Bingham, oral-history interviews, 9 Apr., 24 Sept. 1987; Thomas, interview by author; Yater, *Two Hundred Years,* 106; Thomas, *Barry Bingham,* 205.

62. For examples of Bingham's investments, see box 6 in RWB-FC; RWB to H. J. Angenier, 20 Oct. 1918, W. P. Bewley, 18 Dec. 1918, J. Fred Miles to RWB, 8 May 1919, RWB to Swiss Oil Company, 17 July 1919, RWB to Jose and E. S. Stern, Inc., 18

Sept. 1919, *RWB Papers;* Southern Motors Company sales receipt duplicate, 23 Aug. 1917, RWB-FC; RWB to Peter and Burghard Stone Company, 5, 17 Sept. 1918, RWB-LC.

63. RWB to Walter E. Hughes, 29 Apr. 1918, Elwood Street to RWB, 13 Dec. 1918, RWB-LC; RWB to Robert Bingham, 2 Dec. 1920, *RWB Papers; Courier-Journal,* 27 May 1928.

64. RWB to Benjamin Proctor, 31 Aug. 1918, RWB to Vance C. McCormick, 20 Oct. 1918, Arthur Krock to RWB, 17 Apr. 1920, RWB-LC; RWB to Clarence E. Woods, 20 Sept. 1918, Democratic National Committee, receipt, 12 Nov. 1918, E. M. Parks, Cashier, *RWB Papers.*

5. *"My Great Plan": A Case Study in Business Progressivism*

1. Grantham, *Southern Progressivism,* 410–22.

2. Ibid., 413, 416–17; George Brown Tindall, *Emergence of the New South, 1919–1945* (Baton Rouge: Louisiana State University Press, 1967), 224–30.

3. Gilbert C. Fite, *American Farmers: The New Minority* (Bloomington: Indiana University Press, 1981), 34–36; Gilbert C. Fite, *Cotton Fields No More: Southern Agriculture, 1865–1980* (Lexington: University Press of Kentucky, 1984), 103–5; Jack Temple Kirby, *Rural Worlds Lost: The American South, 1920–1960* (Baton Rouge: Louisiana State University Press, 1987), 275–77.

4. William H. Nicholls, *Price Policies in the Cigarette Industry* (Nashville: Vanderbilt University Press, 1951), 209–14.

5. *Courier-Journal,* 21 Dec. 1920, 5, 7 Jan. 1921; *Lexington Herald,* 2, 4 Jan. 1921.

6. *Courier-Journal,* 21 Dec. 1920.

7. Ibid.; RWB to Baruch, 13 Feb. 1923, RWB-LC; McVey to RWB, 23 July 1923, *RWB Papers,* reel 2.

8. Grace H. Larsen and Henry E. Erdman, "Aaron Sapiro: Genius of Farm Co-Operation Promotion," *Mississippi Valley Historical Review* 49 (Sept. 1962): 242–68; RWB to Reinhardt Dempwolf, 23 Mar. 1922, *RWB Papers,* reel 2; *Courier-Journal,* 21 Dec. 1920.

9. Ewell Paul Roy, *Cooperatives: Today and Tomorrow* (Danville, Ill.: Interstate Printers and Publishers, 1969), 82–83; Edwin G. Nourse, "The Place of the Cooperative in Our National Economy," in *Agricultural Cooperation: Selected Readings,* ed. Martin A. Abrahamsen and Claud L. Scroggs (Minneapolis: University of Minnesota Press, 1957), 425; RWB to W. J. Smith, 20 Feb. 1924, *RWB Papers,* reel 3; RWB to Henrietta Bingham, 24 Nov. 1922, RWB-FC.

10. RWB to J. W. Stoll, 3 Apr. 1923, *RWB Papers,* reel 2; H. S. McElroy to RWB, 21 June 1923, RWB-LC.

11. The so-called Burley Belt consisted of most of central and northern Kentucky along with a few counties in Ohio, West Virginia, and Indiana. The immediate area surrounding Lexington, Kentucky dominated the market. *Courier-Journal,* 21 Dec. 1920, 25, 26, 27, 28, 30 May, 18 Nov. 1921; *Lexington Herald,* 19 May 1921.

12. *Courier-Journal,* 15 Nov. 1921; *Burley Tobacco Grower,* May 1922.

13. C. Hallmeyer to RWB, 6 Dec. 1922, RWB-LC; *Courier-Journal,* 16 Nov. 1921; W. F. Axton, *Tobacco and Kentucky* (Lexington: University Press of Kentucky, 1975), 103–4.

14. O. B. Jesness, *The Cooperative Marketing of Farm Products* (Philadelphia: J. B. Lippincott, 1923), 124–27; copy of Burley Tobacco Growers' Cooperative Association marketing contract, RWB-LC.

15. RWB to Henrietta Bingham, 21 Oct. 1921, RWB-FC.

16. *Courier-Journal,* 17 Nov. 1921.

17. Axton, *Tobacco and Kentucky,* 105.

18. Ibid.; Harold A. Ruby, ed., *An Outline of Co-operative Marketing* (Hopkinsville, Ky.: Tobacco Planter, 1923), 61.

19. *Burley Tobacco Grower,* May 1922.

20. Roy, *Cooperatives,* 215, 254; Theodore Saloutos, "Robert Worth Bingham," in *Great American Cooperators,* ed. Joseph G. Knapp et al. (District of Columbia: American Institute of Cooperation, 1967), 71–73; *Burley Tobacco Grower,* June 1922; *Tobacco Planter,* Mar. 1928.

21. *Courier-Journal,* 5 Mar. 1922; *Burley Tobacco Grower,* Sept. 1922; RWB to Passoneau, 4 Feb. 1922, John T. Reynolds to RWB, 11 May 1922, Charles B. Forbes to RWB, 3 May 1922, Sapiro to RWB, 10 Oct. 1922, RWB to John Wilson, 20 Oct. 1921, Passoneau to RWB, 12 May, 10 June 1922, Bradshaw to RWB, 5 Nov. 1922, RWB to Bradshaw, 7 Nov. 1922, RWB-LC; *Robertson County Times* (Springfield, Tenn.), 29 Aug. 1922; *Tobacco Planter,* Dec. 1922.

22. RWB to Senator Arthur Capper, 26 Oct. 1922, RWB to Henry C. Wallace, 26 Oct. 1922, RWB-LC; RWB to President Warren G. Harding, 26 Oct. 1922, *RWB Papers,* reel 2.

23. Harry Barth, "Cooperation in the Blue Grass," *Journal of Political Economy* 33 (Aug. 1925): 455–65; *Burley Tobacco Grower,* Sept. 1923.

24. RWB to George F. Chipman, 12 Mar. 1924, *RWB Papers,* reel 3; *Burley Tobacco Grower,* June 1922; Nicholls, *Price Policies,* 216; H. B. Price et al., "Outlook for Cooperative Marketing of Tobacco" (Paper presented at the Twenty-Third Annual Meeting of the American Farm Economics Association, Cincinnati, Ohio, Dec. 1932), 10.

25. James C. Stone to RWB, 14 Oct. 1922, RWB-LC; Julius Klein to RWB, 27 Feb. 1923, Henry C. Wallace to RWB, 8 Feb. 1922, Meyer to RWB, 23 Dec. 1922, *RWB Papers,* reel 2.

26. W. F. Bradshaw to RWB, 17 Apr. 1923, RWB-LC.

27. Nicholls, *Price Policies,* 216; Price, "Outlook for Cooperative Marketing," 11–12; Helen Morris Bleidt, "History of the Development of Growers' Organizations and Tobacco Pools in the Burley District of Kentucky, 1902–1927" (M.A. thesis, University of Kentucky, 1932), 66.

28. Fite, *American Farmers,* 38–39; idem, *Cotton Fields No More,* 105–11.

29. Reavis Cox, *Competition in the American Tobacco Industry, 1911–1932* (New York: Columbia University Press, 1933), 165; RWB to Stone, 28 Oct. 1923, RWB-LC; RWB to Lady Astor, 25 Apr. 1924, RWB to David Lloyd George, 25 Apr. 1924, RWB to Lord Robert Cecil, 25 Apr. 1924, RWB to Lord Burnham, 25, 26 Apr. 1924, Oliver J. Sands to RWB, 1 May 1924, *RWB Papers,* reel 2.

30. Sands to Bingham, 16 Sept. 1924, *RWB Papers,* reel 3; *Tobacco Planter,* Feb. 1927; Axton, *Tobacco and Kentucky,* 58; Verna Elsinger, "The Burley Tobacco Growers Experiment," *American Cooperation* 2 (1928): 563–77.

31. Bingham to W. T. Jackson, 10 Feb. 1923, Edward M. House to RWB, 11 Feb., 17 Mar. 1923, RWB to House, 16 Feb., 4 Mar. 1923, *RWB Papers,* reel 2; RWB to House,

15 Feb. 1923, RWB-LC; RWB to Henrietta Bingham, 25 Jan. 1923, RWB-FC; Joseph G. Knapp, "Cooperative Expansion Through Horizontal Integration," in *Agricultural Co-operation,* ed. Martin A. Abrahamsen and Claud L. Scroggs (Minneapolis: University of Minnesota Press, 1957), 361.

32. Richard B. Tennant, *The American Cigarette Industry* (New Haven: Yale University Press, 1930), 220.

33. RWB to Sapiro, 3 Mar. 1924, RWB-LC.

34. Elsinger, "Burley Tobacco Growers," 563–69; Grace Larsen, "Aaron Sapiro: Cooperative Evangelist," in Knapp, *Great American Cooperators,* 453–54; RWB to R. L. McKellar, 9 Nov. 1926, *RWB Papers,* reel 5.

35. RWB to Sapiro, 23 Oct. 1923, Harold A. Ruby to RWB, 22 Jan. 1924, RWB-LC.

36. Sapiro to RWB, 6 Feb. 1923; Sapiro to William F. Bradshaw, 7 Feb. 1923, Passoneau to RWB, 28 Dec. 1922, Sapiro to Passoneau, 17 Jan. 1923, RWB-LC; RWB to W. F. Bradshaw, 4 Feb. 1924, R. M. Barker to RWB, 7 Mar. 1924, *RWB Papers,* reel 3,

37. Peteet to RWB, 18 Aug. 1926, *RWB Papers,* reel 5; Joseph C. Robert, *The Story of Tobacco in America* (New York: Alfred A. Knopf, 1949), 205; RWB to Sapiro, 19 Oct. 1926, Peteet to RWB, 8 Jan. 1926, RWB-LC.

38. Larsen and Erdman, "Aaron Sapiro," 265–66; E. Fred Koller, "Oscar B. Jesness," in Knapp, *Great American Cooperators,* 263–64; RWB to Dark Tobacco Association Board of Directors, 29 Sept. 1924, RWB-LC.

39. Robert, *Story of Tobacco,* 205, RWB to Samuel R. Guard, 24 Oct. 1924, RWB-LC; RWB to Bernard Baruch, 29 Nov. 1924, *RWB Papers,* reel 3.

40. Grant McConnell, *The Decline of Agrarian Democracy* (New York: Atheneum, 1969), 61; *Dearborn Independent,* 3 Nov. 1923; *New York Times,* 1 Apr. 1927; Sapiro to RWB, [?] 1923, 10 Jan. 1924, 26 Jan., 9 Feb. 1926, RWB-LC. At the time of his death Bingham had an unpaid note for twenty-two thousand on Sapiro in his safety-deposit box. RWB-FC.

Sapiro was later indicted but acquitted for racketeering and bribery in Illinois and New York and disbarred. Thomas, *Barry Bingham,* 209.

41. Bleidt, "History of the Development," 58–62; RWB to T. F. Durham, 27 Nov. 1924, *RWB Papers,* reel 3; *Tobacco Planter,* Aug. 1928; Elsinger, "Burley Tobacco Growers," 577–81.

42. See Fite, *American Farmers,* chap. 3; McConnell, *Decline of Agrarian Democracy,* 58–64.

43. James C. Klotter, *The Breckinridges of Kentucky, 1760–1981* (Lexington: University Press of Kentucky, 1986), 234–35.

William Purcell Dennis Haly (1875–1937), a "protégé" of William Goebel, later served as adjutant general in the administration of Governor J. C. W. Beckham. Because of his fondness of Woodrow Wilson, he and Bingham became political allies. Thomas, *Barry Bingham,* 213–14. See also James C. Klotter, *Kentucky: Portrait in Paradox, 1900–1950* (Frankfort: Kentucky Historical Society, 1996), 203–9.

6. The 1920s: Publisher, Businessman, Father

1. The economic history of the 1920s is capably developed in George Soule, *Prosperity Decade, from War to Depression: 1917–1929* (New York: Harper Torchbook, 1968); Bingham, oral-history interviews, 17 Nov., 8 Dec. 1983.

2. *Who's Who in Kentucky, 1936,* 419; Wallace to RWB, [?]1922, [?] 1923, *RWB Papers,* reel 2; Bingham, oral-history interview, 9 Apr. 1987.

3. Krock to RWB, 15 Mar. 1923, Robertson to RWB, 25 Mar. 1923, *RWB Papers,* reel 2; Krock to RWB, 8 June 1923, RWB-LC; John Herchenroeder, oral-history interviews, 16 Sept., 23 Oct. 1980, 24 Sept. 1987; *Courier-Journal,* 1 Apr. 1923; Thomas, *Barry Bingham,* 212–13.

4. RWB to Robert E. Hughes, 19 Aug. 1920, Harrison Robertson to RWB, 25 Mar. 1923, *RWB Papers,* reel 2; RWB to Harold Ruby, 19 Oct. 1926, RWB-LC; *Courier-Journal,* 7 May 1926; RWB to Henrietta Bingham, 1 Apr. 1923, RWB-FC.

5. RWB to Anthony Woodson, 1 July 1924, RWB-LC; RWB to Henrietta Bingham, [Feb. 1923], RWB-FC.

6. Brainard Platt to RWB, 5 July 1923, Ulric Bell to RWB, 5 May, 22 Nov. 1926, *RWB Papers,* reel 2; J. Fremont Frey to RWB, 4 July 1923, RWB to Frey, 9 July 1923, RWB to Sallie Graham Stice, 29 Nov. 1924, RWB-LC; Herchenroeder, oral-history interviews, 16 Sept., 23 Oct. 1980, 24 Sept. 1987, 7 Apr. 1988; RWB to Henrietta Bingham, [Feb. 1923], RWB-FC; Thomas, *Barry Bingham,* 207–8.

7. RWB to Josephus Daniels, 7 Jan. 1920, *RWB Papers;* Loring Pickering to RWB, 3 May 1926, *RWB Papers,* reel 5; RWB to Lewis R. Atwood, 17 Mar. 1920, RWB to Fred R. Martin, 4 Oct. 1920, Daniels to RWB, 8 Jan. 1926, Loring Pickering to RWB, 3 May 1926, RWB-LC.

8. *Courier-Journal,* 17, 18, 19 July 1922; Terry L. Birdwhistell, "WHAS Radio and the Development of Broadcasting in Kentucky, 1922–1942," *Register of the Kentucky Historical Society* 79 (Autumn 1981): 333–34.

9. *Courier-Journal,* 17 July 1922, 4–17 Feb., 23, 24 July 1925, 18 July 1962; *Courier-Journal Magazine,* 5 July 1987; Thomas, *Barry Bingham,* 57–58.

10. Credo Harris to Robert L. Porter, 3 Mar. 1926, *RWB Papers,* reel 5; RWB to McHenry Rhoads, 1 July 1924, Rhoads to RWB, 15 July 1924, RWB-LC; Birdwhistell, "WHAS Radio," 341–46.

11. *Courier-Journal,* 17, 18 May 1928; Herchenroeder, oral-history interview, 7 Apr. 1988; *Shelby Sentinel-News,* 5 Dec. 1990.

12. Emery and Emery, *Press and America,* 340; Frank E. Gannett to RWB, 14 June, 14 July 1924, A. Brisbane to RWB, 20 June 1924, William Allen White to RWB, 8 July 1924, *RWB Papers,* reel 3.
White later claimed Hearst to be "the most vicious influence in America—bar none." Walter Johnson, *William Allen White's America* (New York: Henry Holt, 1947), 346, 452.

13. *Who's Who in Kentucky, 1936,* 52–53; Bunk Gardner to RWB, 26 Jan. 1924, *RWB Papers,* reel 3; Yater, *Two Hundred Years,* 188–91.

14. Emanuel Levi to RWB, 29 Aug. 1926, RWB-LC; Lesy, *Real Life,* 67–80, 86–89.

15. RWB to Irving Fisher, 24 Sept., 20 Nov. 1920, RWB-LC; RWB to J. F. Galbreath, 9 July 1923, *RWB Papers,* reel 2.

16. Bingham, oral-history interviews, 17 Nov., 8 Dec. 1983; RWB to E. C. Walton, 12 June 1922, RWB to Wayne Wheeler, 26 Oct. 1923, *RWB Papers,* reel 2; A. C. Graham to RWB, 5 Nov. 1924, RWB-LC.

17. E. Y. Mullins to RWB, 26 June 1923, RWB to Mullins, 5 July 1923, *RWB Papers,* reel 2.

18. RWB to Ulric Bell, 22 Nov. 1926, RWB-LC.

19. RWB to John H. Cowles, 5 May 1924, *RWB Papers,* reel 3; RWB to W. J. Puckett, 16 Oct. 1926, RWB-LC; Stanley Ousley, "The Kentucky Irish American," *Filson Club History Quarterly* 53 (Apr. 1979): 189–90.

20. William E. Ellis, "The Kentucky Evolution Controversy of the Twenties" (M.A. thesis, Eastern Kentucky University, 1967), chap. 1; Alonzo Fortune, "The Kentucky Campaign against the Teaching of Evolution," *Journal of Religion* 2 (May 1922): 227–35; Frank McVey, *The Gates Open Slowly* (Lexington: University of Kentucky Press, 1949), 122; Arthur M. Miller, "Kentucky and the Theory of Evolution," *Science* 55 (17 Mar. 1922): 178–80.

21. RWB to J. W. Porter, 21 Apr. 1923, RWB-LC.

22. M. P. Hunt to RWB, 5 May 1923, *RWB Papers,* reel 2; RWB to E. Y. Mullins, 21 Dec. 1926, *RWB Papers,* reel 5; J. W. Porter to RWB, 9 Apr. 1923, RWB-LC.

23. C. F. Huhlein, 20 June 1923, *RWB Papers,* reel 2; *Courier-Journal,* 18 June 1923, 16, 26, June 1924; James Bond to Lewis Humphrey, 26 Oct. 1923 (copy), LeRoy Percy to RWB, 16 May 1923, Thomas Fitzgerald to RWB, 26 Oct. 1926, RWB to Fitzgerald, 16 Nov. 1926, RWB-LC; William E. Ellis, H. E. Everman, and Richard D. Sears, *Madison County: 200 Years in Retrospect* (Richmond: Madison County Historical Society, 1985), 306.

24. Wright, *Life behind a Veil,* 262–82; George Colvin to RWB, 23 Aug. 1923, RWB to Colvin, 24 Sept. 1923, *RWB Papers,* reel 2.

25. A. Eugene Thompson to RWB, 1 Aug., 26 Sept. 1923, J. M. Ragland to RWB, 13 Nov. 1923, RWB to Ragland, 24 Dec. 1923, *RWB Papers,* reel 2; P. M. Wood to RWB, 21 Aug. 1923, RWB to Wood, 24 Sept. 1923, *RWB Papers,* reel 3; *Courier-Journal,* 24 July 1925; C. C. Stoll to RWB, 8 June, 10 Nov. 1923, Alma Schmitt to RWB, 27 Feb. 1924, J. M. Ragland to RWB, 25 Nov. 1924, RWB to John E. Roberts, 2 May 1926, RWB to Ragland, 25 May 1926, RWB-LC.

26. Bingham, oral-history interview, 9 Apr. 1987.

27. *Courier-Journal,* 27 Dec. 1926, 25 Oct. 1927; J. H. Brewer to RWB, 5 July 1923, *RWB Papers,* reel 2; Bingham to Brewer, 9 July 1923, RWB to T. F. Durham, 27 Nov. 1924, RWB to M. H. Thatcher, 2 July 1924, RWB-LC.

28. Day-letter telegram sent to all U.S. senators, 11 Mar. 1920, John Sharp Williams to RWB, 12 Mar. 1920, Bernard M. Baruch to RWB, 18 Oct. 1920, *RWB Papers;* Woodrow Wilson to RWB, 1 Jan. 1922, *RWB Papers,* reel 2.

29. RWB to Irving Fisher, 2 Nov. 1920, *RWB Papers;* Claud Perry to RWB, 30 July 1923, William H. Short to RWB, 23 Nov. 1923, James G. McDonald to RWB, 16, 17 Mar. 1923, *RWB Papers,* reel 2; RWB to Philip Bennett, 2 July 1924, *RWB Papers,* reel 3; RWB to Charles G. Bauer, 5 Feb. 1926, *RWB Papers,* reel 4; RWB to Charles Stewart Davison, 11 Aug. 1920, RWB to John H. Finley, 9 July 1923, Claud Perry to RWB, 30 Mar. 1923, RWB-LC; *Courier-Journal,* 18 June, 21 Aug. 1924.

30. RWB to Sir John Fraser, 8 Sept. 1920, *RWB Papers;* RWB to Attilla Cox, 4 Dec. 1923, *RWB Papers,* reel 2; RWB to F. W. Paul, 20 Mar. 1920, RWB to W. T. Jackman, 10 Feb. 1923, Sir Campbell Stuart to RWB, 6 June 1924, RWB to Colonel Hugh B. Protheroe-Smith, 11 Nov. 1924, RWB-LC; *Courier-Journal,* 13 June 1924.

31. *Courier-Journal,* 20, 21, 22 Oct. 1923; A. J. Sylvester to RWB, 10 July 1923, Frederic M. Sackett to RWB, 11 Oct. 1923, David Lloyd George to RWB, 27 Oct. 1923, RWB-LC; Yater, *Two Hundred Years,* 174.

32. *New York Times*, 21 Aug. 1924; *Courier-Journal*, 21 Aug. 1924; Bingham, oral-history interview, 17 Nov. 1983; will of Robert Worth Bingham, Bingham memorandum to Macmillan, item B; Ante-Nuptial Contract copy, 18 Aug. 1924, RWB-FC.

33. RWB to Dr. S. R. McKee, 25 Jan., 30 May, 7 June 1923, *RWB Papers*, reel 2; W. R. Cobb to Emily Overman, 23 Oct., 13 Dec. 1924, Lillian Taylor to RWB, 8 Mar. 1924, RWB to Mr. [?] Embs, 21 Jan. 1924, *RWB Papers*, reel 3.

34. Sadie Bingham Grinnan to Miss Overman, 27 Feb. 1926, RWB to Sadie Grinnan, 4 Mar., 27, 30 May, 1 July 1926, *RWB Papers*, reel 4; *Asheville Times*, 9 May 1927; Bingham, oral-history interview, 17 Nov. 1983.

35. RWB to George M. Ward, 5 May 1922, RWB-LC; Bingham, oral-history interviews, 17 Nov., 8 Dec. 1983; Herchenroeder, oral-history interviews, 16 Sept., 23 Oct. 1980, 24 Sept. 1987, 7 Apr. 1988; RWB to Henrietta Bingham, 17 Sept., 22, 30 Oct. 1922, 15 Jan. [1923], 24 June 1923, RWB-FC; Thomas, *Barry Bingham*, 41, 204.

36. *Courier-Journal*, 18 June 1968; Henrietta Bingham to RWB, 24 Mar., 14, 24 June, 23 Oct., 24 Nov., 31 Dec. 1926, Edith R. Isaacs to RWB, 25 Mar. 1926, *RWB Papers*, reel 4.

37. *The Louisville Skyline*, 4 Sept. 1985; Frances Partridge, *Love in Bloomsbury* (Boston: Little, Brown, 1981), 99; RWB to Sadie Grinnan, 17 Nov. 1924, *RWB Papers*, reel 3; RWB to Henrietta Bingham, 22 Oct. 1922, 12, 15 Jan., 24 Feb. 1923, RWB-FC.

38. RWB to Henrietta Bingham, 25 Mar., 1 Apr. 1923, RWB-FC.

39. Bingham, oral-history interview, 9 Apr. 1987; Herchenroeder, oral-history interview, 16 Sept. 1980; J. H. Richmond to RWB, 20 Nov. 1920, RWB to George M. Ward, 6 May 1922, W. P. Raymond to RWB, 24 Mar. 1923, RWB to Aaron Sapiro, 25 Mar. 1923, Maurice Firuski to RWB, 3 Apr. 1923, *RWB Papers*, reel 2; B. M. Brigman to RWB, 8 Feb. 1924, *RWB Papers*, reel 3; Sam F. Trelease to RWB, 11 July 1924, RWB-LC; Thomas, *Barry Bingham*, 15, 32, 37, 203.

40. Bingham, oral-history interviews, 8 Dec. 1983, 9 Apr. 1987; Herchenroeder, oral-history interviews, 16 Sept. 1980, 24 Sept. 1987; Thomas, *Barry Bingham*, 2, 41–44, 48–51, 54–59.

41. RWB to Larkin W. Glassbrook, 1, 27 Apr. 1920, *RWB Papers;* RWB to John Paul Marsh, 16 Apr. 1923, RWB to H. C. Gelnow, 21 Nov. 1923, RWB to Annin and Company, 24 June 1924, RWB to George E. Roberts, 1 Nov. 1926, RWB-LC.

42. Bingham, oral-history interviews, 3 Dec. 1980, 17 Nov. 1983, 9 Apr. 1987; Thomas, interview by author; *Courier-Journal*, 6 July 1924, 8, 11 June 1933; Lafon Allen to RWB, 15 June 1925, 7 June 1926, *RWB Papers*, reel 4; E. T. Hutchins to RWB, 8 Dec. 1923, *RWB Papers*, reel 2; RWB to W. H. Evans, 2 Oct. 1926, RWB-LC.

43. Young, *Hugh Young*, 504–7; RWB to D. Fenton, 18 Oct. 1926, RWB to Major Ivan Guthrie, 19 Apr. 1926, *RWB Papers*, reel 4.

44. *Courier-Journal*, 18 July 1929; *Atlanta Constitution*, 21 Jan. 1934; Hugh Young to RWB, 28 Dec. 1936, George Cary Tabb to Emanuel Levi, 13 Sept. 1923, RWB-LC; RWB to Henrietta Bingham, [Feb. 1923], RWB-FC; Thomas, *Barry Bingham*, 208.

45. Bingham, oral-history interviews, 3 Dec. 1980 and 9 Apr. 1987; RWB to Richard Ernst, 25 May 1926, RWB to Major Ivan Guthrie, 19 Apr., 22 May 1926, *RWB Papers*, reel 4; John Dymond, Jr., to RWB, 29 Jan. 1920, G. W. Grimes to RWB, 15 Feb. 1926, Ralph Gilbert to RWB, 10 May 1926, RWB-LC; Thomas, *Barry Bingham*, 208.

46. Bingham memorandum to Macmillan, item A; *Courier-Journal*, 24 July 1925; Bingham, oral-history interview, 3 Dec. 1980.

47. M. E. Vaughn to RWB, 25 Sept., 14, 18 Oct. 1922, RWB to A. Y. Ford, 9 July 1923, *RWB Papers*, reel 2; RWB to John H. Cowles, 14 Jan., 3 May 1924, RWB to Enterprise Publishing Company, 24 Jan. 1924, George L. Sehon to RWB, 12 May 1924, William Carter to RWB, 1 July 1924, *RWB Papers*, reel 3; RWB to President William J. Hutchins, 27 Feb. 1926, RWB to Joe W. Ervin, 2 Mar. 1926, RWB to Dr. Edwin A. Alderman, 2 June 1926, RWB to C. E. Heberhart, 12 Oct. 1926, *RWB Papers*, reel 4; RWB to George L. Sehon, 12 Feb. 1923, RWB to A. Y. Ford, 9 July 1923, RWB to E. O. Griffenhagen, 12 Oct. 1923, RWB to Ethel Brownsberger, 4 Mar. 1924, RWB to Edwin A. Alderman, 21 July 1924, Lucy Furman to RWB, 18 Oct. 1924, RWB to A. H. Patterson, 20 Oct. 1926, RWB-LC.

48. RWB to Rebecca E. Watterson, 13 Feb. 1923, Watterson to RWB, 15 Feb. 1923, reel 2; RWB to Ethel Brownsberger, 4 Mar. 1924, Emily Overman to Mary Park Beard, 1 Mar. 1926, reel 3; RWB to John R. Downing, 10 Aug. 1926, reel 4, all in *RWB Papers*.

49. Emily Overman to Equitable Trust Company, 17 Apr. 1923, Stock Options, 20 May 1920, Overman to Frank Fehr Company, 13 May 1920, *RWB Papers;* Overman to J. J. B. Hilliard and Son, 21 Apr. 1923, James C. Wilson to RWB, 2 June 1922, *RWB Papers*, reel 2; Guaranty Trust Company to RWB, 19 Jan. 1926, *RWB Papers*, reel 4; RWB to Charles F. Huhlein, 11 Jan. 1923, Leon Isaccsen to RWB, 30 Mar. 1923, RWB-LC.

50. RWB to Henrietta Bingham, 8 Mar., 24 June 1923, RWB-FC; RWB to H. J. Graham, 19 Feb. 1924, *RWB Papers*, reel 3; Overman to Elwood Hamilton, 6 Feb. 1925, RWB-LC.

51. Overman to John E. Buckingham, 9 Apr. 1923, J. W. M. Stewart to Directors, The Standard Petroleum Company, Ashland, 29 Oct. 1923, *RWB Papers*, reel 2; RWB to L. E. Owens, 1 Feb. 1923, RWB to Mrs. A. M. Fetter, 29 Mar. 1923, J. W. M. Stewart to RWB, 6 Mar. 1926, RWB to Stewart, 8 Mar. 1926, J. J. Hayes to RWB, 8 Oct. 1926, RWB-LC.

52. Herchenroeder, oral-history interview, 16 Sept. 1980; *Who's Who in Kentucky, 1936,* 52–53; Yater, *Two Hundred Years,* 190–94; Overman to National Bank of Kentucky, 27 Feb., 13 Mar., 11 Apr., 11, 21 Aug. 1923, *RWB Papers*, reel 2; RWB to Richard Bean, 13 Feb. 1924, Oscar Fenley to RWB, 18 Feb. 1924, *RWB Papers*, reel 3; RWB to Richard Bean, 13 Feb. 1924, RWB-LC.

53. John Berry McFerrin, *Caldwell and Company: A Southern Financial Empire* (1939; reprint, Nashville: Vanderbilt University Press, 1969), 57–58; List of Directors, Inter-Southern Life Insurance Co., *RWB Papers*, reel 4.

54. RWB to Ralph H. Barker, 23 Jan. 1926, Attilla Cox to RWB, 30 Jan. 1926, RWB to Edward H. Hilliard, 5 Jan., 2 Feb. 1926, Rogers Caldwell to RWB, 10, 15 Feb. 1926, RWB to Caldwell, 17 Feb., 9, 13 Mar., 19 Apr. 1926, Emanuel Levi to RWB, 19 Mar. 1926, RWB to Bernard Baruch, 6 Nov. 1926, *RWB Papers*, reel 4; RWB to Clark Patterson, 1 Feb. 1926, *RWB Papers*, reel 5; Rogers Caldwell to RWB, 23 Apr. 1926, RWB-LC.

7. Politics in the Twenties: The "Damnedest" Again

1. RWB to Judge William C. Halbert, 26 June 1926, *RWB Papers*, reel 4.

2. RWB to H. G. Garrett, 22 Nov. 1920, RWB to Hancock Taylor, 17 Nov. 1922, RWB to Loring Pickering, 18 Dec. 1923, RWB-LC.

3. *Lexington Leader,* 16 Nov. 1920; RWB to House, 1 May, 21 June 1926, House to RWB, 25 May 1926, *RWB Papers*, reel 4.

4. RWB to Will H. Hays, 15 Mar. 1920, Homer Cummings to RWB, 5 Apr. 1920, *RWB Papers;* RWB to Basil Richardson, 7 Jan. 1920, RWB to Frank O. Lowden, 12 July 1923, *RWB Papers,* reel 2; RWB to W. W. Marsh, 23 Sept., 9 Oct. 1920, RWB-LC.

5. Nicholas C. Burckel, "J. C. W. Beckham," in *Kentucky's Governors, 1792–1985,* ed. Lowell H. Harrison (Lexington: University Press of Kentucky, 1985), 118; Arthur Krock to RWB, 17 Apr., 17, 27 Sept. 1920, RWB to W. W. Davies, 27 Oct. 1920, *RWB Papers;* RWB to James M. Cox, 25 July 1920, RWB-LC.

6. *Courier-Journal,* 1, 3 Nov. 1920; RWB to John L. Grayot, 25 Oct. 1920, *RWB Papers,* reel 2; RWB to Grayot, 5 Aug. 1920, Lewis Humphrey to RWB, 1 Nov. 1920, RWB-LC.

7. *Courier-Journal,* 5 Nov. 1920; John H. Fenton, *Politics in the Border States* (New Orleans: Hauser Press, 1957), 46–47.

8. *Courier-Journal,* 10 Oct. 1920; Herbert Parsons to RWB, 14 Oct. 1920, *RWB Papers;* RWB to Bernard M. Baruch, 10 Mar. 1926, *RWB Papers,* reel 4; Memoranda for Judge Bingham [1926], RWB-LC; John Ed Pearce, *Divide and Dissent: Kentucky Politics, 1930–1963* (Lexington: University Press of Kentucky, 1987), 26; Fenton, *Politics in the Border States,* 47–49.

9. Thomas H. Appleton, Jr., "Augustus Owsley Stanley," in *Kentucky's Governors,* 124–25; Klotter, *Breckinridges of Kentucky,* 234–35.

10. Elwood Hamilton to Emily Overman, 12 Feb. 1923, *RWB Papers,* reel 2.

11. RWB to Desha Breckinridge, 19 Nov. 1920, RWB-LC.

12. Thomas H. Appleton, Jr., "Augustus Everett Willson," in *Kentucky's Governors,* 118–22; Melba Porter Hay, "Edwin Porch Morrow," in *Kentucky's Governors,* 128–32; *Courier-Journal,* 6 Aug. 1920; Morrow to RWB, 10, 19, 27 Aug. 1920, Bingham to Morrow, 26 Mar., 12 Aug. 1920, Vance Armentrout to RWB, 4 Aug. 1920, RWB to Armentrout, 5 Aug. 1920, *RWB Papers;* Willson to RWB, 8 July 1922, *RWB Papers,* reel 2; RWB to Richard P. Ernst, 22 Dec. 1923, 23 Jan., 8 July 1924, RWB-LC.

13. *Courier-Journal,* 16 Oct. 1927; RWB to John D. Carroll, 15 Nov. 1920, *RWB Papers;* memorandum from Brainard Platt to RWB, [1923], RWB to Edward T. Sanford, 20 Nov. 1924, *RWB Papers,* reel 3; RWB to Basil Richardson, 7 Jan. 1920, 30 Nov. 1926, Richardson to RWB, 29 Nov. 1926, RWB to Frederic W. Upham, 19 Oct. 1923, RWB-LC.

14. Robert F. Sexton, "The Crusade against Parimutuel Gambling: A Study of Southern Progressivism in the 1920's," *Filson Club History Quarterly* 50 (Jan. 1976): 47–57.

15. Letterhead of The Kentucky Anti-Race Track Gambling Commission, *RWB Papers,* reel 2.

16. Logan B. English to RWB, 17 Apr. 1923, M. J. Winn, 18 Sept. 1922, *RWB Papers,* reel 2; W. F. Bradshaw to James B. Brown, 12 Mar. 1923, Bradshaw to RWB, 15 Mar. 1923, Frank B. Russell to RWB, 2 Apr. 1925, RWB-LC.

17. Klotter, *Breckinridges of Kentucky,* 235–37; Bingham, oral-history interview, 9 Apr. 1987; Pearce, *Divide and Dissent,* 26–27; Hubert Meredith to Arthur Krock, 24 Jan. 1923, *RWB Papers,* reel 2; RWB to Bernard Baruch, 13 Feb. 1923, Baruch to RWB, 26 June 1923, RWB-LC.

18. Fenton, *Politics in the Border States,* 48–49; George W. Robinson, "The Making of a Kentucky Senator: Alben W. Barkley and the Gubernatorial Primary of 1923," *Filson Club History Quarterly* 40 (Apr. 1966): 123–35.

19. Pearce, *Divide and Dissent*, 26–27; Robinson, "Making of a Kentucky Senator," 123–35; Fenton, *Politics in the Border States*, 48–52.

20. *Courier-Journal*, 12 Apr. 1923; RWB to Alice Lloyd, 24 Mar. 1923, Lloyd to RWB, 26 Mar. 1923, M. P. Hunt to RWB, 12 Apr. 1923, H. S. McElroy, 21 June 1923, RWB to McElroy, 25 June 1923, *RWB Papers*, reel 2; M.P. Hunt to RWB, 12 Apr. 1923, RWB to Elwood Hamilton, 5 July 1923, Dr. H. L. Driskell to RWB, 9 Aug. 1923, RWB to Driskell, 26 Sept. 1923, Platt memorandum to RWB [1923], Joe Richardson to RWB, 7 July 1923, RWB-LC; RWB to Henrietta Bingham, 24 June [1923], RWB-FC.

21. Robinson, "Making of a Kentucky Senator," 123–35; Sexton, "Crusade against Parimutuel Gambling," 194–206.

22. Fenton, *Politics in the Border States*, 48–51 and map; James K. Libbey, *Dear Alben: Mr. Barkley of Kentucky* (Lexington: University Press of Kentucky, 1979), 42; RWB to Elwood Hamilton, 14 Aug. 1923, *RWB Papers*, reel 2.

23. *Courier-Journal*, 9 Sept. 1923; William E. Ellis, "William Jason Fields," in *Kentucky's Governors*, 132–35; William Goodell Frost to RWB, 15 Aug. 1923, RWB to Frost, 26 Sept. 1923, A. Y. Aronson to Brainard Platt, 19 Sept. 1923, RWB-LC.

24. *Courier-Journal*, 6, 8 Nov. 1923.

25. Ibid., 3, 4, 9 Jan. 1924.

26. Ibid., 4, 11 Feb. 1924; Clark, *History of Kentucky*, 444.

27. Ulric Bell to RWB, telegram, 9 Sept. 1923, *RWB Papers*, reel 3; Ellis, "William Jason Fields," 132–35.

28. Bingham to E. O. Griffenhagen, 12, 18 Oct. 1923, Griffenhagen to RWB, 23 Oct. 1923, *RWB Papers*, reel 2; Harry Giovannoli to RWB, 15 Nov. 1924, RWB to Giovannoli, 20 Nov. 1924, *RWB Papers*, reel 3; RWB to Colonel Robert McBryde, 12 Sept. 1923, RWB to Eustice L. Williams, 24 Sept. 1923, Harry A. Sommers to RWB, 2 July 1923, RWB to Sommers, 21 Dec. 1923, Griffenhagen to RWB, 29 Jan. 1924, "The Greater Kentucky Committee of the Kentucky Good Roads Association" to "Fellow Kentuckian," 24 Oct. 1924, RWB-LC.

29. *Courier-Journal*, 25, 29 Jan. 1924; RWB to Eustice L. Williams, 24 Sept. 1923, J. Guthrie Coke to RWB, 18 Oct. 1926, RWB-LC.

30. *Lexington Herald*, 4 Nov. 1924; Klotter, *Breckinridges of Kentucky*, 266–38; Harry Sommers to RWB, 20 Dec. 1923, *RWB Papers*, reel 2.

31. *Courier-Journal*, 29 Feb., 4, 5, 18 Mar. 1924; Denhardt to RWB, 4 Mar. 1924, RWB to Denhardt, 13 Mar. 1924, RWB-LC; Denhardt to Robert L. Page, 5 Mar. 1924, *RWB Papers*, reel 3.

32. *Courier-Journal*, 19 Feb. 1924; RWB to Fields, 20 Jan., 22 Feb. 1924, Fields to RWB, 20, 26 Feb. 1924, RWB-LC.

33. *Courier-Journal*, 24, 28 Feb., 21 Mar. 1924.

34. S. W. Rogers to RWB, 25 Feb. 1924, *RWB Papers*, reel 3; Augustus E. Willson to RWB, 7 Mar. 1924, RWB to Willson, 12 Mar. 1924, *RWB Papers*, reel 4.

35. William T. Baker to RWB, 25 Feb. 1924, Louis Bower to RWB, 26 Feb. 1924, RWB to Mrs. H. H. Cherry, 29 Nov. 1924, RWB to R. H. Clagett, 16 Dec. 1924, Robert T. Caldwell, 6 May 1924, RWB to R. A. Chiles, 6 Mar. 1924, *RWB Papers;* R. P. Taylor to RWB, 13 Mar. 1924, RWB to Taylor, 11 Apr. 1924, RWB-LC.

36. Frost to RWB, 28 Feb. 1924, James Tandy Ellis to RWB, 26 Feb. [1924], RWB to

F. H. Yates, 1 Mar. 1924, B. L. Curry, 10 Mar. 1924, RWB to Wayland Rhoads, 12 March 1924, RWB-LC.

37. *Courier-Journal*, 10 May, 1, 2, 3, 5, 10, 15 July 1924; John Stewart Bryan to RWB, 2 May 1924, RWB to Bryan, 9 May 1924, Sapiro to RWB, 5 July 1924, Sapiro to Baruch, James Cox, Franklin Roosevelt, George M. Brennan, Joe Robinson, etc., telegrams, 6 July 1924, *RWB Papers*, reel 3.

38. *Courier-Journal*, 10 May, 16, 26 June, 1, 2, 3, 5, 10, 15 July 1924; Mark Sullivan to RWB, 28 Nov. 1923, RWB to Sullivan, 19 Dec. 1923, RWB to Ben V. Smith, 19 Apr., 5 May 1924, Smith to RWB, 26 Apr. 1924, RWB to Thomas D. Taylor, 3 May 1924, RWB to Sapiro, 7 July 1924, RWB-LC.

39. *Courier-Journal*, 9 Aug. 1924; Bernard V. Burke, "Senator and Diplomat: The Public Career of Frederic M. Sackett," *Filson Club History Quarterly* 61 (Apr. 1987): 185–92; RWB To Bernard Baruch, 13 Feb. 1923, *RWB Papers*, reel 2; Attilla Cox to RWB, 4 Oct. 1924, RWB to Cox, 6 Oct. 1924, RWB-LC; Robert F. Sexton, "Frederic Mosley Sackett," *Kentucky Encyclopedia*, 791.

40. *Courier-Journal*, 2, 3, 4, 5, 6 Nov. 1924; Ellis, "William Jason Fields," 134–35; *Courier-Journal Magazine*, 2 July 1950; RWB to Attilla Cox, 6 Oct. 1924, RWB to John W. Davis, telegram, 9 July 1924, Davis to RWB, 2 Aug., 26 Sept., 24 Oct. 1924, *RWB Papers*, reel 3; RWB to Judge Robert H. Winn, 10 Nov. 1924, James W. Gerard to RWB, 10 Nov. 1924, RWB to Wayne B. Wheeler, 12 Nov. 1924, RWB-LC.

41. *Courier-Journal*, 5 Nov. 1924; A. C. Graham to RWB, 5 Nov. 1924, *RWB Papers*, reel 3; RWB to Wayne B. Wheeler, 12 Nov. 1924, RWB to Edward T. Sanford, 28 Nov. 1924, RWB to R. H. Clagett, 16 Dec. 1924, RWB-LC.

42. RWB to R. H. Clagett, 16 Dec. 1924, RWB to Justice Edward T. Sanford, 28 Nov. 1924, RWB-LC; A. C. Graham to RWB, 5 Nov. 1924, *RWB Papers*, reel 3; RWB to Robert H. Winn, 10 Nov. 1924, *RWB Papers*, reel 4.

43. Certificate of appointment to Louisville Memorial Commission, 20 Apr. 1920, *RWB Papers;* RWB to John J. Barret, 19 Nov. 1924, *RWB Papers*, reel 3; W. E. Morrow to RWB, 5 Mar. 1926, *RWB Papers*, reel 5; Mayor Huston Quin to RWB, 24 Apr. 1922, RWB to Thomas Hastings, 16 Dec. 1926, RWB-LC.

44. *Courier-Journal*, 3, 5 Nov. 1925; RWB to John J. Barret, 19 Nov. 1924, RWB-LC; Herchenroeder, oral-history interviews, 16, 23 Sept. 1980.

45. RWB to Alice Lloyd, 2, 3, 27 Feb. 1926, RWB to Harry Giovannoli, 16 Dec. 1926, *RWB Papers*, reel 4; RWB to Ralph Beaver Strassberger, 16 Oct. 1926, RWB-LC.

46. Daniels to RWB, 7 May 1926, RWB to Daniels, 26 June 1926, *RWB Papers*, reel 4.

47. Pearce, *Divide and Dissent*, 26; Emily Overman to Elwood Hamilton, 21, 25 Oct. 1926, Hamilton to RWB, 6 Nov. 1926, RWB to Hamilton, 8 Nov. 1926, Thomas Fitzgerald to RWB, 26 Oct. 1926, RWB to Fitzgerald, 16 Nov. 1926, *RWB Papers*, reel 4; Hamilton to RWB, 5 Nov. 1926, RWB-LC.

48. *Courier-Journal*, 3, 4 Nov. 1926; Libbey, *Dear Alben*, 48; RWB to Elwood Hamilton, 8 Nov. 1926, RWB-LC; Barkley to RWB, 30 Nov. 1926, *RWB Papers*, reel 4.

49. Beckham to RWB, 3 Dec. 1926, *RWB Papers*, reel 4; Fenton, *Politics in the Border States*, 50.

50. Pearce, *Divide and Dissent*, 26–27; Robert F. Sexton, "Flem D. Sampson," in *Kentucky's Governors*, 135–38; Sexton, "Crusade against Parimutuel Gambling," 194–206; Fenton, *Politics in the Border States*, 49–55.

51. *Louisville Herald-Post,* 31 Aug., 2, 4, 7, 10, 13, 15,18, 19, 20, 25, 28, 29 Sept. 1927; Fenton, *Politics in the Border States,* 53–54; *Courier-Journal,* 1, 7, 9 Nov. 1927.

52. *Courier-Journal,* 9 Nov. 1927.

53. Bernard Baruch to RWB, 17 Oct., 4 Nov. 1926, RWB to Baruch, 20 Oct. 1926, *RWB Papers,* reel 4; personal interview with Clements, 2 Oct. 1980; FDR to Patrick Henry Callahan, 23 Aug. 1928, FDR Papers, 1928 Campaign Correspondence, Roosevelt Library, Hyde Park, New York (hereafter cited as FDR Papers); *Courier-Journal,* 30 Aug. 1928.

54. *Courier-Journal,* 5, 6 Nov. 1928; RWB to FDR, 31 Aug. 1928, FDR to RWB, 8 Oct. 1928, FDR Papers.

55. *Courier-Journal,* 5, 6 Nov. 1928; RWB to FDR, 31 Aug. 1928, FDR to RWB, 8 Oct. 1928, FDR Papers; Jasper B. Shannon and Ruth McQuown, *Presidential Politics in Kentucky: 1824–1948* (Lexington: University of Kentucky Press, 1950), 104–6.

56. William E. Ellis, "Labor-Management Relations in the Progressive Era: A Profit Sharing Experience in Louisville," *The Register of the Kentucky Historical Society* 78 (Spring 1980): 140–56; *New York Times,* 24 Nov. 1930; George T. Blakey, *Hard Times and New Deal in Kentucky: 1929–1939* (Lexington: University Press of Kentucky, 1986), 8–11.

57. Robert T. Fugate, Jr., "The BancoKentucky Story," *Filson Club History Quarterly* 50 (Jan. 1976): 370–87; McFerrin, *Caldwell and Company,* 183; David E. Hamilton, "The Causes of the Banking Crisis of 1930: Another View," *Journal of Southern History* 51 (Nov. 1985): 590; Herchenroeder, oral-history interviews, 16, 23 Sept. 1980; Transcript of Ray Riebel interview, n.d., RWB-FC.

58. Donald W. Whisenhunt, "The Great Depression in Kentucky: The Early Years," *Register of the Kentucky Historical Society* 67 (Jan. 1969): 55–62.

59. William E. Ellis, "Ruby Laffoon," in *Kentucky's Governors,* 138–42.

8. Kentuckian in Knee Breeches

1. RWB to FDR, 31 Aug. 1928, FDR to RWB, 8 Oct. 1928, 1928 Campaign Correspondence, Roosevelt to The Century Association, 6 Apr. 1929, RWB to FDR, 22 Sept. 1931, Private Correspondence, 1928–32, all in FDR Papers; FDR to RWB, 29 Sept. 1931 in Elliott Roosevelt, ed., *FDR: His Personal Letters, 1928–1945,* 4 vols. (New York: Duell, Sloan and Pearce, 1950), 1:219.

2. Frank Freidel, *Franklin D. Roosevelt: The Triumph* (Boston: Little, Brown, 1956), 17, 278, 291, 336; James MacGregor Burns, *Roosevelt: The Lion and the Fox* (New York: Harcourt, Brace, and World, 1956), 130; Arthur M. Schlesinger, Jr., *The Age of Roosevelt: The Crisis of the Old Order* (Boston: Houghton, Mifflin, 1957), 280; Bingham to Shepard Bryan, 24 Oct. 1932, Shepard Bryan Papers, #2969, Southern Historical Collection, University of North Carolina, Chapel Hill; *New York Times,* 27 Sept. 1938.

3. *Courier-Journal,* 1, 4, 7, 9, 10 Nov. 1932; FDR to RWB, 3 Dec. 1932, Aileen Bingham to FDR, 10 Dec. 1932, Private Correspondence, 1928–32, FDR Papers.

4. Raymond Moley, *After Seven Years* (New York: Harper and Brothers, 1939), 111–12; *New York Times,* 4 Dec. 1932; *Times* (London), 24 Feb., 2 Mar. 1933; Schlesinger, *Age of Roosevelt,* 467–68; Frank Freidel, *Franklin D. Roosevelt: Launching the New Deal* (Boston: Little, Brown, 1973), 144.

5. Bingham to Shepard Bryan, 24 Oct. 1932, Southern Historical Collection, University of North Carolina, Chapel Hill.

6. *Courier-Journal*, 4 Sept. 1957; Burns, *Roosevelt*, 176; Cordell Hull, *The Memoirs of Cordell Hull*, 2 vols. (New York: Macmillan, 1948), 1:181; John Gunther, *Roosevelt in Retrospect* (New York: Harper and Brothers, 1950), 276; Arnold A. Offner, *American Appeasement: United States Foreign Policy in Germany, 1933–1938* (Cambridge, Mass.: Belknap Press of Harvard University Press, 1969), 54–55; Josephus Daniels, *Shirt-Sleeve Diplomat* (Chapel Hill: University of North Carolina Press, 1947), 291.

7. Frank Freidel, *Franklin D. Roosevelt: A Rendezvous With Destiny* (Boston: Little, Brown, 1990), 107; Bingham to Edmund F. Traube, 4 Dec. 1923, Bingham to Reverend R. W. Paul [n.d. 1933, RWB-LC; *Times* (London), 16 Mar. 1933; Eleanor Roosevelt to Mrs. R. W. Bingham, 23 Sept. 1937, Eleanor Roosevelt Correspondence, Personal letter, FDR Papers; *Bournemouth Daily Echo*, 18 May 1933.

8. Freidel, *Launching the New Deal*, 360; Hull to Embassy, Great Britain, 7 Mar. 1933, telegram, 123 Bingham, Robert W./1, Department of State Papers, National Archives (hereafter cited as Dept. of State Papers); Andrew W. Mellon to Hull, 9 Mar. 1933, 123 Bingham, Robert W./2, Dept. of State Papers.

9. Key Pittman to Hull, 16 Mar. 1933, RBW-LC; *Louisville Herald-Post*, 18, 27, 29 Sept. 1927; *Chicago Daily Tribune*, 14 Mar. 1933.

10. *New York Times*, 23 Mar. 1933; Roosevelt to King George V, 25 Mar. 1933, RWB-LC; *Newsweek*, 27 May 1933.

11. *New York Times*, 25 Mar. 1933; Bingham to Atherton, 14 Mar. 1933, RWB-LC.

12. Bingham, oral-history interview, 3 Dec. 1980; *Times* (London), 24 Mar., 19 May 1933; Bingham to Dr. Hugh H. Young, 31 Oct. 1933, Young to Bingham, 22 May, 6 June, 27 Nov. 1933, RWB-LC; *New York Times*, 11 May 1933.

13. *New York Times*, 18, 20 May 1933; Dr. Edward H. Linnehan to "Dear Doctor," 16 May 1933, Dr. William F. Rienhoff, Jr., to Bingham, 9 June 1933, RWB-LC; *London Daily Express*, 18 May 1933; Bingham to Hull, 10 Apr. 1933, 123 Bingham, Robert W./14, Dept. of State Papers; Herbert O. Hengstler to Roosevelt Steamship Line, n.d., 123 Bingham, Robert W./26, Dept. of State Papers.

14. Bingham, oral-history interview, 3 Dec. 1980; Hull to Embassy, Paris, 24 Mar. 1933, 123 Bingham, Robert W./32, Dept. of State Papers; *New York Times*, 20 May 1933.

15. *Times* (London), 24 May 1933; *Portsmouth Evening News*, 11 Nov. 1933; Bingham to W. W. Davies, 16 Nov. 1933, RWB to Shepard Bryan, 12 Nov. 1933, Southern Historical Collection; Bingham to Homer Cummings, 28 June 1937, RWB-LC.

In his diaries kept during his years in London, Bingham often noted the names of people who visited the embassy each day, sometimes with telling notations. For example, he wrote one day: "Saw a pestiferous old man named Rosenfield, from Chicago at 11:15." Bingham Diaries, vol. 1, 105, RWB-LC.

16. William B. Phillips to Bingham, 11, 21 Nov. 1933, Bingham to Alfred Budge, 1 June 1933, RWB-LC.

17. Bingham to Roosevelt, 1 Nov. 1934, 11 May 1937, RWB-LC; Bingham to Hull, 1 Aug. 1936, PSF, Diplomatic, GB:1933–35, FDR Papers; Young to Bingham, 22 May 1933, J. Hanbury Williams to Bingham, 24 May 1934, RWB-LC; Bingham to Roosevelt, 7 June 1937, PSF, GB:RWB, Roosevelt to Bingham, 18 June 1937, PSF, GB:RWB, FDR Papers.

18. *Louisville Times,* 30 June, 25 Nov. 1933; *Courier-Journal,* 23 Oct. 1934, 24 June 1937; Bingham to Shepard Bryan, 15 Dec. 1936, 13 July 1937, Southern Historical Collection, University of North Carolina at Chapel Hill; Emily Overman to Alice Fox Pitts, 31 July 1937, RWB-LC; Bingham to Hull, 9 Sept. 1933, 123 Bingham, Robert W./42, Dept. of State Papers; Bingham Diaries, vol. 2, 22 Oct. 1934, RWB-LC.

Apparently, Bingham played bridge as he did everything else—to win. Betty Cranborne to Bingham, [1934], RWB-LC.

19. Robert D. Schulzinger, *American Diplomacy in the Twentieth Century* (New York: Oxford University Press, 1984), 150–53; Robert Dallek, *Franklin D. Roosevelt and American Foreign Policy, 1932–1945* (New York: Oxford University Press, 1979), 23–34; Wayne S. Cole, *Roosevelt and the Isolationists* (Lincoln: University of Nebraska Press, 1983), 23, 108, 123–24.

20. Lloyd C. Gardner, et al., *Creation of the American Empire* (Chicago: Rand, McNally), 385.

21. Jordan A. Schwarz, *The Speculator: Bernard M. Baruch in Washington, 1927–1965* (Chapel Hill: University of North Carolina Press, 1981), 5, 22, 273–74.

22. Gardner, *Creation of the American Empire,* 399–400; H. G. Nicholas, *The United States and Britain* (Chicago: University of Chicago Press, 1975), 84–85; John E. Wiltz, *From Isolation to War, 1931–1941* (New York: Thomas Y. Crowell Company, 1968), 3–17; David Reynolds, *The Creation of the Anglo-American Alliance, 1937–1941* (Chapel Hill: University of North Carolina Press, 1981), 7–23.

23. Gardner, *Creation of the American Empire,* 387; Dallek, *FDR and American Foreign Policy,* see part 1; Reynolds, *Creation of the Anglo-American Alliance,* 25; *Chicago Daily Tribune,* 8 May 1933; Howard Jablon, *Crossroads of Decision: The State Department and Foreign Policy, 1933–1937* (Lexington: University Press of Kentucky, 1983), 138.

In a session of the 1985 annual meeting of the Southern Historical Association a panel concluded that "Roosevelt himself never had a coherent foreign policy and thus found it difficult to defend his policies to those who disagreed with him. Moreover, Roosevelt did not perform well the role of educating America on foreign policy issues as he did with domestic issues via his fireside chats." David A. Shannon, "The Fifty-First Annual Meeting," *Journal of Southern History* 52 (May 1986): 235.

24. Reprint from *London Daily Herald* in *Chicago Daily Tribune,* 8 May 1933.

25. *New York Times,* 31 May 1933.

26. Edgar B. Nixon, ed., *Franklin D. Roosevelt and Foreign Affairs,* vol. 1, *January 1933–February 1934* (Cambridge, Mass.: Belknap Press of Harvard University Press, 1969), 193; *Foreign Relations, 1933,* vol. 1 (Washington: Dept. of State, 1950), 166–68; Burns, *Roosevelt,* 189.

27. Burns, *Roosevelt,* 189.

28. *Raleigh News and Observer,* 31 May 1933.

29. Ray Atherton to Hull, telegram, 23 Mar. 1933, 123 Bingham, Robert W./6, Dept. of State Papers; "George R. I." to Bingham, 30 May 1933, Pilgrim's Dinner Speech, 30 May 1933, Speech File, RWB-LC; *Times* (London), 24, 31 May 1933.

30. Copy of speech, 30 May 1933, 123 Bingham, Robert W./35, Dept. of State Papers.

31. *Chicago Herald-Examiner,* 4 June 1933; Emanuel Levi to Bingham, 5 June 1933, RWB-LC; Rodney P. Carlisle, *Hearst and the New Deal* (New York: Garland, 1979), 9, 19;

Bingham to Roosevelt, 26 May, 11 June 1933, OF 491, FDR Papers; *New York Times,* 1, 7, 22 June 1933; W. A. Swanberg, *Citizen Hearst* (New York: Charles Scribner's Sons, 1961), 473; Cole, *Roosevelt and the Isolationists,* 23, 108, 123–24.

32. *London Daily Mail,* 5 June 1933; *London Daily Telegraph,* 31 May 1933; Bingham Diaries, vol. 1, 21 June 1933; Bingham to Ulric Bell, 27 Oct. 1934, Bingham to Grover Page, 23 June 1933, RWB-LC; Nixon, ed., *FDR and Foreign Affairs,* 1:238.

A self-made Canadian-born millionaire, Lord Beaverbrook (William Maxwell Aitken) built a newspaper empire in the 1920s after becoming a power in the Conservative party. He followed a somewhat "erratic" course in his publishing policies but, owing to his Canadian origins, remained a steadfast advocate of free trade and generally followed an isolationist path until the beginning of World War II. Francis Williams, "Challenge by the Press Lords," in *The Baldwin Age,* ed. John Raymond (London: Eyre and Spottiswoode, 1960), 164–67.

33. Offner, *American Appeasement,* 21–29, 37, 50; Wiltz, *From Isolation to War,* 45.

34. Nicholas, *United States and Britain,* 84–89; Maurice Cowling, *The Impact of Hitler: British Politics and British Policies, 1933–1940* (London: Cambridge University Press, 1975), 65.

35. Robert A. Divine, *The Reluctant Belligerent: American Entry into World War II,* 2d ed. (New York: Alfred A. Knopf, 1979), 3.

36. Gardner, *Creation of the American Empire,* 385–87; Bingham Diaries, vol. 1, 6, 14, 17 June 1933, 1 July 1933, RWB-LC; Nixon, ed., *FDR and Foreign Affairs,* 1:207, 226–27, 243–44.

37. Divine, *Reluctant Belligerent,* 3–4; Moley, *After Seven Years,* 241.

38. Bingham Diaries, vol. 1, 5 Mar., 12, 19, 22, 30 June, 6 July 1933, RWB-LC.

39. Moley, *After Seven Years,* 243; Herbert Feis, *1933: Characters in Crisis* (Boston: Little, Brown, 1966), 204–7; Ted Morgan, *FDR: A Biography* (New York: Simon and Schuster, 1985), 393; Freidel, *Launching the New Deal,* 491–92; Schwarz, *Speculator,* 277–78.

40. Offner, *American Appeasement,* 37–40; Bingham Diaries, vol. 1, 29 June 1933, RWB-LC; Nixon, ed., *FDR and Foreign Affairs,* 1:268–69.

41. Moley, *After Seven Years,* 327.

42. Bingham Diaries, vol. 1, 13, 14, 23, 24 June, 2, 6, 12, 26, 28 July 1933, Bingham to Lincoln MacVeagh, 11 Sept. 1933, RWB-LC.

43. Moley, *After Seven Years,* 327; Richard N. Kottman, *Reciprocity and the North Atlantic Triangle, 1932–1938* (Ithaca: Cornell University Press, 1968), 76; Daniels, *Shirt-Sleeve Diplomat,* 20; RWB to FDR, 8 Sept. 1933, PPF 716, FDR Papers; Bingham to Josephus Daniels, 25 Aug. 1933, RWB-LC; William E. Leuchtenburg, *Franklin D. Roosevelt and the New Deal* (New York: Harper and Row, 1963). 202.

44. Dallek, *FDR and American Foreign Policy,* 57; *New York Times,* 28 June, 14 July 1933; Bingham Diaries, vol. 1, 4, 15, 24 July 1933, RWB-LC.

45. *Courier-Journal,* 12 Sept., 19 Oct. 1933; Bingham Diaries, vol. 1, 11 Sept. 1933, 17 May, 2 June, 1934; vol. 2, 16–23 Aug. 1934, RWB-LC.

46. *New York Times,* 19 Oct., 2 Dec. 1933; Speech File, 13, 18 Oct. 1933, RWB-LC; *London Morning Post,* 23 Nov. 1933; Bingham Diaries, vol. 1, 30 Nov. 1933, RWB-LC; speech, 24 Oct. 1933, 123 Bingham, Robert W./43, Thanksgiving Day Speech, 30 Nov. 1933, 123 Bingham, Robert W./53, both in Dept. of State Papers.

47. *New York Times,* 25 Oct., 10, 12, 25 Nov., 5 Dec. 1933; FDR to RWB, 13 Nov. 1933, Ulric Bell to Bingham, 27 July 1933, RWB-LC.

48. FDR to RWB, 15 Apr., 15 Dec. 1933, RWB to FDR, 22 May 1933, OF 491, FDR Papers.

49. Offner, *American Appeasement,* 279; FDR to RWB, 13 Nov. 1933, Bingham to Mrs. Sara Delano Roosevelt, 29 Aug. 1933, PSF, GB:RWB, FDR Papers; Dallek, *FDR and American Foreign Policy,* 57, 510; Bingham Diaries, vol. 1, 21 Mar., 10 Aug.–early Sept., 3, 17 Nov., 6 Dec. 1933, RWB-LC.

50. Bingham Diaries, vol. 1, 21 Mar. 1933, Bingham to Sir William Wiseman, 24 Aug. 1933, RWB-LC.

51. Elliott Roosevelt, ed., *FDR Letters,* 1:371; "George R.I." to Roosevelt, 25 Nov. 1933, PSF, GB:1933–36, FDR Papers; Dallek, *FDR and American Foreign Policy,* 57; Bingham Diaries, vol. 1, 24 July 1933, RWB-LC.

52. *New York Times,* 21 Nov., 13, 15, 16, 22, 23, 24, 31 Dec. 1933, 14 Jan. 1934; FDR to RWB, 10 Nov. 1933, OF 491, Marvin McIntyre memo for M. LeHand, 12 Dec. 1933, PPF 716, FDR Papers; Bingham Diaries, vol. 1, 22 Dec. 1933, RWB-LC.

9. A World Closer to War and Battles on the Home Front

1. *New York Times,* 24 Feb., 6 Mar. 1934; RWB to Lord Salvesen, 27 Oct. 1934, Grace Radford to RWB, 1 Nov. 1934, RWB to Joseph Hume, 2 Oct. 1934, RWB to Lord Denbigh, 4 Dec. 1934, RWB-LC.

2. RWB to Katie Callahan, 16 July 1934, RWB-LC.

3. *Courier-Journal,* 15 Mar. 1934; *New York Times,* 16 Mar. 1934; *London Daily Mirror,* 17 Mar. 1934; RWB to Armentrout, 3 May 1934, William B. Belknap to RWB, 16 June 1934, RWB to Belknap, 16 July 1934, RWB-LC; House of Representatives, Commonwealth of Kentucky, 15 Mar. 1934 Resolution, signed by J. Erwin Sanders, Clerk, House of Representatives, 123 Bingham, Robert W./59, Dept. of State Papers.

4. Joseph P. Lash, *Eleanor and Franklin* (New York: W. W. Norton, 1971), 587; Eleanor Roosevelt to RWB, 8, 27 Jan. 1934, RWB to Eleanor Roosevelt, 14 Jan. 1934, Eleanor Roosevelt Correspondence, FDR Library; Eleanor Roosevelt to Miss LeHand, 31 Jan. 1934, OF 491, FDR Papers; Emma Saurer and Chester Hicks to FDR, 16 Mar. 1934, 123 Bingham, Robert W./61, Dept. of State Papers; William Green to RWB, 16 Jan. 1934, RWB to Green, 13 Feb. 1934, RWB-LC.

5. Dallek, *FDR and American Foreign Policy,* 26, 35–37, 76.

6. *New York Times,* 6 Apr., 1 May, 22 Sept., 1934, 26 Mar. 1935; *Courier-Journal,* 3 May, 20, 22 Sept. 1934; Speech of RWB at American Chamber of Commerce, 5 Apr. 1934, 123 Bingham, Robert W./62, Speech of RWB at meeting of Royal Institute of International Affairs, 30 Apr. 1934, 123 Bingham, Robert W./66, Speech of RWB at Barnstaple, 21 Sept. 1934, 123 Bingham, Robert W./73, all in Dept. of State Papers; "Address of the American Ambassador . . . at the Royal Institute of International Affairs," Press Release, RWB-LC.

7. Dallek, *FDR and American Foreign Policy,* 76–77; Offner, *American Appeasement,* 9, 13, 97; Bingham Diaries, vol. 1, 20 Feb. 1934, 1 Mar. 1934; vol. 2, 16 July, 7 Nov. 1934, RWB-LC; RWB to FDR, 8 May 1934, PSF, GB:1933–36, FDR Papers.

8. *Foreign Relations, 1934,* vol. 1 (Washington: Dept. of State, 1951), 264; Bingham

Diaries, "Memorandum of Conversation Between Prime Minister MacDonald and Norman H. Davies," 2 Mar. 1934, inserted in vol. 1, 22 June 1934, RWB-LC; vol. 2, 16 July, 18–19 June, 19 Nov., 13 Dec. 1934, RWB-LC; Cordell Hull to RWB, 30 June 1934, OF 491, FDR Papers.

9. *New York Times,* 6, 29 Mar., 27 Apr., 6 May 1934; *Cambridge Daily News,* 3 Dec. 1934; Bingham Diaries, vol. 1, 26, 30 Apr. 1934; vol. 2, 24–25 Aug. 1934, 9–16 Oct. 1934, RWB-LC.

10. *New York Times,* 24, 25, 29, 30, 31 Oct. 1934; *London Evening Standard,* 9 Nov. 1934; RWB to Lord Queensborough, 14 Apr. 1934, 28 Oct. 1937, Queensborough to RWB, 27 Oct. 1937, RWB to William E. Dodd, 29 Oct. 1934, 16 Apr. 1935, RWB to Mary M. French, 7 May 1935, copy of *Fortune* magazine article from Ulric Bell, 25 June 1934, Sir Lewis Bayly to RWB, 11 May 1934, RWB to Bayly, 1 Oct. 1934, RWB-LC; Bingham Diaries, vol. 1: 12 Apr. 1934; vol. 2: 10 Apr. 1935; vol. 4: 27 Oct., 4 Dec. 1936, RWB-LC; Anne Trotter, *Britain and East Asia, 1933–1937* (London: Cambridge University Press, 1975), 170–72.

11. *New York Times,* 12 Oct. 1934; *Courier-Journal,* 15, 16, 17, 21, 23 Oct. 1934.

12. RWB to Barry Bingham, 15 Oct. 1934, Lee L. Miles to RWB, 17 Oct. 1934, RWB to Berry V. Stoll, cablegram, n.d., Stoll to RWB, 30 Oct. 1934, all in RWB-LC; A. B. Chandler, oral-history interview, 7 Oct. 1980, Eastern Kentucky University Archives.

13. *Courier-Journal,* 25, 30 Oct. 1934; *New York Times,* 26 Oct. 1935; "Address to Edinburgh Philosophical Institution," 23 Oct. 1934, RWB-LC; Speech, Edinburgh Philosophical Institution, 23 Oct. 1934, 123 Bingham, Robert W./80, Dept. of State Papers.

14. Cordell Hull to George Holden Trinkam, 16 Jan. 1935, Bingham, Robert W./87, Dept. of State Papers; RWB to Lawrence K. Callahan, 26 Oct. 1934, RWB-LC; *Manchester Daily Express,* 24 Oct. 1934; Bingham Diaries, vol. 2: 23 Oct. 1934, 162–63.

15. *Courier-Journal* and *New York Times,* 24 Nov. 1934; speech, Plymouth branch of the English-Speaking Union, 23 Nov. 1934, 123 Bingham, Robert W./81, Rollin R. Winslow to Cordell Hull, 27 Nov. 1934, 123 Bingham, Robert W./82, both in Dept. of State Papers; Lord Mildmay to RWB, 24 Nov. 1934, RWB-LC; William R. Rock, *Chamberlain and Roosevelt: British Foreign Policy and the United States, 1937–1940* (Columbus: Ohio State University Press, 1988), 24.

16. M. A. LeHand to RWB, 20 Apr. 1934, OF 491, RWB to FDR, 15 June 1934, OF 208q, Marvin McIntyre to Homer S. Cummings, 19 Sept. 1934, OF 491, FDR Papers; *London Star,* 5 June 1934, RWB-LC; Stanley Reed to RWB, 27 Oct. 1934, RWB to Reed, 12 Nov. 1934, FDR to RWB, 3, 23 Nov. 1934, RWB to FDR, 31 Dec. 1934, RWB-LC.

17. Credo Harris to Marvin McIntyre, 12 Nov. 1934, OF 200-J, FDR to RWB, 5 July 1935, OF 491, RWB to FDR, 6 Dec. 1935, PSF, GB:RWB, FDR Papers; Admiral A. C. Dickens to RWB, 31 July 1935, RWB-LC; Elliott Roosevelt, ed., *Roosevelt Letters* 1:449.

18. Howe to RWB, 29 Aug. 1934, telegram, 123 Bingham, Robert W./71, RWB to Howe, 30 Aug. 1934, 123 Bingham, Robert W./72, both in Dept. of State Papers; Morgan, *FDR: A Biography,* 442.

A sympathetic biographer does not mention this incident, which may have coincided with Howe's efforts to find money for congressional elections in 1934. During this time Howe's health declined. Early the next year he entered a hospital where he remained until he died in April 1936. The White House period was "bitter years" for the old aide of FDR. Though intensely loyal to his boss, Howe soon became a liability to the administration because of his constant meddling in policy. Moreover, "he could make money—real money—for the first time in his life," at one time getting nine hundred dollars per minute for a pro–New Deal radio program. This sudden opportunity may have led to pleas for "SECRET CODE" money from Bingham. Alfred B. Rollins, Jr., *Roosevelt and Howe* (New York: Alfred A. Knopf, 1962), 406, 411, 417, 422–23, 427–32.

19. *Courier-Journal*, 2, 25 Dec. 1934; *New York Times*, 2, 3, 4, 5, 7, 15, 23, 24, 25 Dec. 1934; interview with RWB in the *Observer*, 2 Dec. 1934, 123 Bingham, Robert W./83, Dept. of State Papers.

20. *Courier-Journal*, 25 Dec. 1934.

21. Offner, *American Appeasement*, 106–16, 130–31; RWB to Sir Austen Chamberlain, 16 Feb. 1935, RWB-LC; Cowling, *Impact of Hitler*, 86.

22. Offner, *American Appeasement*, 132.

23. RWB to FDR, 26 Mar. 1935, PPF 716, FDR to RWB, 11 July 1935, PSF, GB:RWB, FDR Papers.

24. *New York Times*, 28 Feb., 16, 23 Mar., 11 Apr., 2, 7 May 1935.

25. Bingham Diaries, vol. 2: 25 Mar., 17, 24 Apr. 1935, RWB-LC; RWB telegram, 9 Apr. 1935, 862.20/870, Dept. of State Papers; Joseph Landau to RWB, 5 July 1933, William E. Dodd to RWB, 29 May 1935, RWB to Sir Lewis Bayly, 9 June 1935, Bayly to RWB, 6 July 1935, 1 June 1936, RWB-LC; Trotter, *Britain and East Asia*, 172–87.

26. *Courier-Journal*, 26 Mar. 1935; RWB to Cordell Hull, 28 June 1935, Sir John Reith to RWB, 28 Feb., 26 Apr. 1935, RWB to Reith, 17 Apr. 1935, Reith to Ray Atherton, 27 Mar. 1935, RWB-LC.

27. Bingham Diaries, vol. 2: 14 May, 29 July 1935; vol. 3: 28 Oct., 19 Dec. 1935, RWB-LC; Baldwin to RWB, 26 Sept. 1934, 11 Mar. 1937, RWB to R. P. Taylor, 16 Oct. 1934, RWB to Hoare, 24 Oct. 1935, RWB-LC; RWB to FDR, 1 June 1935, PSF, GB:RWB, FDR Papers.

28. Dallek, *FDR and American Foreign Policy*, 101–6; Cowling, *Impact of Hitler*, 79–91, 226.

29. *Courier-Journal*, 7 Aug. 1935; RWB to Barry Bingham, 8 Apr. 1935, RWB-LC.

30. RWB to Barry Bingham, 16 Oct. 1935, RWB to Ulric Bell, 3 July 1935, both in RWB-LC; Dallek, *FDR and American Foreign Policy*, 111; *New York Times*, 25 July, 1, 7, 8, 12, 30 Aug., 11 Sept. 1935.

31. Edgar B. Nixon, ed., *Franklin D. Roosevelt and Foreign Affairs*, vol. 3, *September 1935–January 1937* (Cambridge, Mass.: Belknap Press of Harvard University Press, 1969), 16–17; Offner, *American Appeasement*, 129; Cowling, *Impact of Hitler*, 99–104; Charles Loch Mowat, *Britain between the Wars, 1918–1940* (Chicago: University of Chicago Press, 1955), 556–63; *New York Times*, 20 Sept., 17 Dec. 1935; RWB to Hugh Young, 22 Oct. 1935, RWB to Arthur Peter, 28 Oct. 1935, RWB to William F. Rienhoff, 9 Dec. 1935, RWB-LC; Bingham Diaries, vol. 3: 10 Sept., 8, 17 Oct. 1935, RWB-LC.

32. *New York Times*, 30 July 1935.

33. Elliott Roosevelt, ed., *FDR Letters*, 1:473–74; Nixon, ed., *FDR and Foreign Affairs*, 3:45–47, 88–90; RWB to FDR, 9 May 1935, PSF, GB:RWB, FDR Papers; Bingham Diaries, vol. 2, 21 Feb. 1935, RWB-LC; *Foreign Relations, 1935* (Washington: Dept. of State), 1:772–73.

34. Offner, *American Appeasement,* 120–21; Dallek, *FDR and American Foreign Policy,* 90; RWB to FDR, 28 June 1935, PSF, GB:RWB, FDR Papers; *Foreign Relations, 1935,* 1:129; Bingham Diaries, vol. 1, 80–96; vol. 2, 9 July 1935, RWB-LC.

35. Dallek, *FDR and American Foreign Policy,* 90; Davis to RWB, 12, 27 Jan. 1935, RWB to Barry Bingham, n.d., Family Correspondence, 1935, RWB-LC.

36. Bingham Diaries, vol. 3, 28 Oct., 17 Nov. 1935, 23-page insertion; vol. 4, 25 Jan. 1936, RWB-LC; Elliott Roosevelt, ed., *FDR Letters,* 1:525–27; Hull to RWB, 19, 23 Nov. 1936, PPF 716, "Memo for Secretary of State," n.d., PSF Confidential, Dept. of State Papers.

37. Bingham, oral-history interviews, 17 Nov., 3 Dec. 1983, 9 Apr. 1987; *Courier-Journal,* 31 Dec. 1965; Barry Bingham to RWB, 3 Oct. 1935, RWB to Thomas J. Watson, 30 July 1935, Helen Jacobs to RWB, 31 Dec. 1935, Eleanor Agar to RWB, n.d., 1936, RWB-LC.

Jabobs won four U.S. Open singles titles and one Wimbledon singles title in the 1930s. Will Grimsley, *Tennis: Its History, People and Events* (Englewood Cliffs, N.J.: Prentice-Hall, 1971), 188.

Henrietta's escapades during her father's tenure as ambassador apparently included actor-director John Houseman. The latter reported in his memoirs a romance with Henrietta in the mid-thirties. "Looking back through the mists, of hope, ambition and frustrated yearning with which I surrounded her," Houseman explained, "I find it impossible to separate the memory of the real Henrietta Bingham, with whom I fell in love my first Christmas in America and with whom I finally lost my virginity in a seaside hotel with a crystal chandelier and red damask walls sixteen months later, from the fantasy of her that I created in the loneliness of my first wander-years in America." Moreover, Houseman's romantic attachment to the Louisvillian lasted for several years, and he recalled writing "endless yearning letters to Henrietta." His "obsessive romantic fantasy" finally subsided, but apparently not the memories, as Henrietta is again mentioned prominently in Houseman's second autobiography. *Courier-Journal,* 5 July 1987; John Houseman, *Run-Through: A Memoir* (New York: Simon and Schuster, 1972), 46, 56, 61, 134, 143, 219, 313; John Houseman, *Front and Center* (New York: Simon and Schuster, 1979), 108–10, 305.

38. Bingham, oral-history interview, 9 Apr. 1987; RWB to Barry Bingham, 1 Oct. 1934, RWB-LC.

39. RWB to Barry Bingham, 8 Mar. 1935, Emanuel Levi to RWB, 12, 25 Oct. 1935, RWB to Levi, 15, 28 Oct. 1935, RWB-LC; C. J. P. Lucas to Marvin McIntyre, 3 Aug. 1935, OF 491, FDR Papers.

40. *Who Was Who,* vol. 7, 1971–1980 (1980), 8; Herbert S. Agar, *The People's Choice: From Washington to Harding; A Study in Democracy* (New York: Houghton Mifflin, 1933); RWB to Mrs. Henry G. Bennett, 1 Oct. 1934, RWB to Agar, 27 Jan. 1935, Agar to RWB, 2 Feb. 1935, RWB to Barry Bingham, 2 Nov. 1935, RWB-LC.

41. RWB to Robertson, 23 Apr., 19 July 1935, 5 July 1937, Robertson to RWB, 12 Aug. 1935, 20 June 1937, RWB-LC.

42. Barry Bingham to RWB, 12 Nov. 1935, RWB to Edith Callahan, 26 Nov. 1935, RWB-LC; William E. Ellis, *Patrick Henry Callahan: Progressive Catholic Layman in the American South* (Lewiston, N.Y.: Edwin Mellen Press, 1989), 101–2.

43. Bingham, oral-history interviews, 8 Dec. 1983, 9 Apr., 24 Sept. 1987.

44. Bingham, oral-history interview, 9 Apr. 1987; RWB to Plaschke, 4 Dec. 1935, Page to RWB, 29 Aug. 1935, RWB to Levi, 24 Oct. 1933, Levi to RWB, 22 Sept. 1934, 12, 27 Aug., 18 Nov. 1935, RWB to George Cary Tabb, 26 July 1934, RWB to Thomas J. Watson, 30 Apr. 1935, RWB-LC; RWB to Henrietta Bingham, 16 Mar. 1935, RWB-FC; Thomas, *Barry Bingham*, 211.

45. Neville Miller to RWB, 16 Nov. 1933, RWB to Miller, 22 Sept. 1936, 7 July 1937, RWB to E. Levi, 19 Oct. 1934, RWB-LC; Wilson Wyatt, Sr., oral-history interview, 26 July 1986, Eastern Kentucky University Archives; Thomas, *Barry Bingham*, 213.

46. RWB to FDR, 4 Nov. 1934, PPF 716, FDR Papers.

47. RWB to FDR, telegram, 20 May 1933, OF 491, RWB to Louis Howe, 8, 28 Sept. 1933, OF 491, Ulric Bell to Steven Early, 14 Sept. 1933, PPF 2409, RWB to Henry Morgenthau, Jr., 15 Aug. 1935, OF 491, RWB to FDR, 13 Aug. 1935, PSF, GB:RWB, "Confidential Memo left with Mr. Howe from Judge Bingham of Kentucky" to FDR, 25 Sept. 1933, OF 400, FDR Papers; RWB to Manny Levi, 10 June, 9 Sept. 1933, 20 July 1934, RWB to Homer Cummings, 30 Aug. 1934, Frederick A. Wallis to RWB, 1 Aug. 1934, RWB to Wallis, 30 Aug. 1934, RWB to R. P. Taylor, 22 Sept. 1934, RWB to J. E. Crider, Jr., 4 June 1934, Ulric Bell to RWB, 10 July 1935, RWB-LC.

48. Charles J. Turck to RWB, 22 June 1934, RWB to Turck, 20 July 1934, RWB-LC; James Duane Bolin, "Bipartisan Combine," *Kentucky Encyclopedia*, 81.

49. RWB to R. P. Taylor, 6 June, 3 July 1935, RWB to Percy Haly, 22 Sept. 1934, RWB-LC.

50. John Y. Brown, Sr., oral-history interview, 19 Nov. 1979, Eastern Kentucky University Archives; RWB to Marvin McIntyre, telegram, 2 May 1935, OF 491, FDR Papers; Haly to RWB, 5 Jan., 1 Feb., 2 May, 5 Nov. 1934, 12 Jan. 1935, RWB to Haly, 2 May 1934, RWB to Barry, (n.d.) 1934, John Y. Brown to RWB, 27 Aug. 1934, Neville Miller to RWB, 31 July 1935, Ulric Bell to RWB, 27 Apr., 2 May 1935, telegrams, RWB-LC.

51. *Lexington Herald*, 17 Apr. 1935; Bingham Diaries, vol. 2, 21, 25 Feb. 1935, RWB-LC; RWB to FDR, 10 May 1935, PSF, GB:RWB, FDR Papers.

52. Harry F. Walters and Coleman Wright to Marvin McIntyre, 13 Apr. 1935, OF 300, Jim Farley to McIntyre, 23 Apr. 1935, OF 300, RWB to FDR, 10 May 1935, PSF, GB:RWB, FDR to Frances Perkins, 24 May 1935, OF 491, FDR Papers; Percy Haly to RWB, 27, 30 Apr. 1935, Elwood Hamilton to RWB, 9 July 1935, RWB to Barry Bingham, 24 Apr., 3 May 1935, Barry Bingham to RWB, 25, 29 Apr. 1935, RWB to Ulric Bell, 8 Nov. 1934, 24 Apr. 1935, Bell to RWB, telegram, 20 Apr. 1935, RWB-LC; Lowell H. Harrison, "John Crepps Wickliffe Beckham," *Kentucky Encyclopedia*, 65.

53. Blakey, *Hard Times and New Deal in Kentucky*, 176–77.

54. Bingham Diaries, vol. 3, 8–29 Aug. 1935, RWB to Barry Bingham, 10 May 1935, Barry Bingham to RWB, 24 June 1935, RWB to Ralph Barker, 4 June 1935, Bell to RWB, 26 June 1935, RWB to Bell, 8 July 1935, RWB-LC.

55. Blakey, *Hard Times and New Deal in Kentucky*, 178–80; RWB to FDR, 13 Aug. 1935, OF 491, "Memorandum for Mr. McIntyre from Judge Bingham by way of Ulric Bell," 15 Aug. 1935, OF 491, FDR Papers.

56. *New York Times*, 28 Sept. 1935; RWB to Marvin McIntyre, 13 Aug. 1935, OF 491, FDR Papers; RWB to Howard Henderson, 25 Sept. 1935, Carlisle Crutcher to Miss Overman, 26 Sept. 1935, Barry Bingham to RWB, 3 Oct. 1935, A. B. Chandler to RWB, 6 Oct. 1935, RWB-LC; A. B. Chandler, oral-history interview, 7 Oct. 1980.

Robert J. Leupold, in "The Kentucky WPA: Relief and Politics, May-November 1935," *Filson Club History Quarterly* 49 (Apr. 1975): 152–69, maintains that the increase actually came so late as not to make much difference in the fall general election.

57. Percy Haly to RWB, 15 Nov. 1935, RWB-LC.

58. Chandler oral-history inteview, 7 Oct. 1980; Bingham Diaries, vol. 4, 19–23 Mar. 1936, RWB to Lee L. Miles, 11 Nov. 1935, RWB to Barry Bingham, 12 Nov. 1935, RWB to Emanuel Levi, 9 Nov. 1935, Levi to RWB, 22 Nov. 1935, RWB to J. C. W. Beckham, 19, 29 Nov. 1935, Beckham to RWB, 8 Nov. 1935, RWB to Chambers Roberts, 11 Nov. 1935, RWB to Ralph C. Gifford, 29 Nov. 1935, all in RWB-LC.

59. Bingham Diaries, vol. 3, 30 Oct. 1935; RWB to Lorenzo Martin, 17 Oct. 1935, Martin to RWB, 2 Nov. 1935, 1935 Thanksgiving Day Speech, all in RWB-LC.

60. Bingham Diaries, vol. 3, 16 Dec. 1935, memorandum, 9 Jan. 1936, RWB-LC; RWB to FDR, 24 Dec. 1935, PSF, GB:RWB, FDR Papers; *Foreign Relations, 1935,* 1:722–23.

10. Turning Points

1. Joseph L. Morrison, *Josephus Daniels: The Small-d Democrat* (Chapel Hill: University of North Carolina Press, 1966), 196; Fred L. Israel, "Breckinridge Long," *Dictionary of American Biography,* Supplement Six (1980), 387–88; *DAB,* s.v. "William Edward Dodd," "Claude Gernade Bowers"; Bingham Diaries, vol. 1, 23 Feb. 1934, RWB-LC; Robert B. Moseley to RWB, 7 July 1934, RWB to Vernon Bartlett, 8 Dec. 1934, RWB to Osmond Long Barringer, 10 Aug. 1936, House to RWB, 3 May 1937, RWB-LC; Bingham, oral-history interview, 11 Nov. 1983.

2. Bingham, oral-history interview, 4 Apr. 1987; *Northamptonshire Evening Telegraph,* 22 Nov. 1933; Bingham Diaries, vol. 3, 17 Dec. 1935, vol. 4, 19 Mar. 1936, RWB-LC.

3. House to FDR, 17 Nov. 1936, PPF 222, FDR to House, 9 Dec. 1936, OF 491, FDR Papers; "An American for America Only" to RWB, 11 Oct. 1935, Barry Bingham to RWB, 18 Nov. 1936, Charles Edward Russell et al. to Cordell Hull, 8 June 1936, 123 Bingham, Robert W./123, Dept. of State Papers; RWB to Barry Bingham, 4 Dec. 1936, RWB-LC.

Frederick W. Marks III, suggests in *Wind over Sand: The Diplomacy of Franklin Roosevelt* (Athens: University of Georgia Press, 1988), that House "helped [Bingham] hold his job in 1936 and 1937" (49). I have found no such evidence. As a matter of fact, Bingham appeared to have had no intention of staying on much past the second inauguration of Roosevelt.

4. Howard Jablon, *Crossroads of Decision: The State Department and Foreign Policy, 1933–1937* (Lexington: University Press of Kentucky, 1983), 131–38; Bingham Diaries, vol. 2, 29 Mar. 1935, RWB-LC.

5. *Foreign Relations, 1936,* 1:296–98, 304–5; Kottman, *Reciprocity,* 133, 143, 272–79.

6. RWB to FDR, 4 Sept. 1936, 21 July 1937, FDR to RWB, telegram, 14 Sept. 1936, PSF, GB:RWB, FDR Papers; RWB to Lady Grogan, 28 July 1936, 1 Oct. 1937, RWB-LC.

7. RWB to Sir Lewis Bayly, 28 Feb. 1936, 12 July 1937, RWB-LC; Bingham Diaries, vol. 4, 9 July, 6 Oct. 1936, RWB-LC.

8. Offner, *American Appeasement,* 139, 141, 246; Bingham Diaries, vol. 4, 8, 15 Apr., 14, 21 May, 6 Nov. 1936, RWB-LC; Robert Dallek, *Democrat and Diplomat: The Life of William E. Dodd* (New York: Oxford University Press, 1968), 257–317.

9. Speech to Association of British Chambers of Commerce, 30 Apr. 1936, 123 Bingham, Robert W./119, Dept. of State Papers.

10. *New York Times,* 26 June 1936; Bingham Diaries, vol. 4, 10–17 June 1936, 330–31, "Remarks of the American Ambassador at the American Society Dinner in London on July 4, 1936," RWB-LC.

11. Offner, *American Appeasement,* 154; *New York Times,* 15 July 1936; Michael J. Ryan to FDR, 5 July 1936, OF 491, FDR Papers; Celei Lyman to Cordell Hull, 9 July 1936, 123 Bingham, Robert W./126, *Ottawa Journal,* editorial, 123 Bingham, Robert W./127, Speech, English-Speaking Garden Party, 7 Aug. 1936, 123 Bingham, Robert W./130, all in Dept. of State Papers.

12. Herchenroeder, oral-history interview, 23 Sept. 1980; *Courier-Journal,* 12 Nov. 1936; Barry Bingham to Ulric Bell, 17 Apr. 1935, OF 300, FDR Papers; Bingham Diaries, vol. 2, 25 July 1935, vol. 3, 7 Aug. 1935, RWB-LC; RWB to Barry Bingham, 10 Oct. 1934, Barry Bingham to RWB, 12 Nov. 1936, RWB to H. W. Stodghill, 15 Oct. 1934, 21 May 1935, memo to RWB, 14 Mar. 1936, RWB-LC.

13. Arthur Peter to RWB, 20 Apr. 1935, Wilson Wyatt to Emily Overman, 17 Aug. 1936, RWB-LC; Wyatt, oral-history interview, 26 July 1986; Thomas, *Barry Bingham,* 212–13.

14. Barry Bingham to RWB, 9 Apr. 1936, Bingham Diaries, vol. 4, 4, 14 Mar. 1936, RWB-LC; Anthony Newberry, "Mark Foster Ethridge," *Kentucky Encyclopedia,* 299–300.

Barry Bingham, Sr., disputed the claim that FDR suggested that Ethridge join the Louisville papers. He maintained that he first came in contact with Ethridge through his wife Mary's relatives in Richmond, Virginia. Bingham, oral-history interviews, 3 Dec. 1980, 8 Dec. 1983.

15. RWB to Louis Brandeis, 26 Sept. 1936, Bingham Diaries, vol. 4, 17, 24 Mar., 15 Apr. 1936, RWB-LC; Wyatt, oral-history interview, 26 July 1986; Herchenroeder, oral-history interview, 7 Apr. 1988; Thomas, *Barry Bingham,* 213.

16. Mark Ethridge to RWB, [Sept. 1936], [Nov. 1936], 3 Dec. 1936, 8 Mar. 1937, RWB to Ethridge, 22 Sept., 16 Oct. 1936, 23 Mar. 1937, Barry Bingham to RWB, 23 Nov., 10 Dec. 1936, RWB to Barry Bingham, 10 Dec. 1936, Lisle Baker, Jr., to RWB, 29 Oct., 28 Nov. 1936, RWB-LC; Barry Bingham, Sr., to Michael Powell, 25 Feb. 1980, RWB-FC.

17. RWB to Barry Bingham, 7 Apr., 10 Aug., 22 Sept. (two letters), 7 Nov. 1936, Barry Bingham to RWB, 27 July, 30 Oct., 2 Dec. 1936, RWB to Lisle Baker, Jr., 22 Sept. 1936, Baker to RWB, 7, 29 Oct., 12 Nov. 1936, Barry Bingham to Emily Overman, 14 Aug. 1936, Arthur Peter to RWB, 8 Oct. 1936, Bingham Diaries, vol. 2, 3 Feb. 1936, RWB-LC.

18. Wyatt, oral-history interview.

19. Barry Bingham to RWB, 26 Dec. 1936, RWB-LC.

20. *Courier-Journal,* 5, 23 Aug. 1936; Barry Bingham to RWB, 9 Apr., 14 Sept. [1936], RWB to Barry Bingham, 22 Apr. 1936, RWB to Haly, 6 Oct. 1936, RWB to Chandler, 22 Sept. 1936, Bingham Diaries, vol. 4, 5–8 June 1936, RWB-LC; Chandler, oral-history interview, 7 Oct. 1980; Thomas, *Barry Bingham,* 214.

Apparently, the funds to pay Cutler came from a special "reserve for secret service and other purposes," according to Bingham. Out of this reserve came the allowance for son Robert and on one occasion a payment of five hundred dollars in cash to J. Guthrie Coke. RWB to Barry Bingham, 22 Apr., 14 Sept. 1936, RWB-LC.

21. *Courier-Journal*, 1, 5, 6 Aug. 1936; Mary Bingham to Emily Overman, 3 Aug. 1936, J. Guthrie Coke to RWB, 1 Sept. 1936, RWB to Coke, 14 Sept. 1936, RWB-LC.

22. *Courier-Journal*, 5 Aug. 1936; Barry Bingham to RWB, 4, 8 Aug. 1936, RWB to Ulric Bell, 16 Oct. 1936, RWB-LC.

23. Blakey, *Hard Times and New Deal in Kentucky*, 41–48, 182–88; *DAB*, s.v. "Harry Flood Byrd."

24. Morgan, *FDR: A Biography*, 442; RWB to Howe, 16 Mar. 1936, RWB to FDR, 19 Mar. 1936, PSF, GB:RWB, FDR Papers; Bingham Diaries, vol. 4, 18 Mar. 1936, RWB-LC.

Howe died on 18 April 1936, the evening of the annual Gridiron Dinner, where FDR delivered a speech. Lela Stiles, *The Man behind the President: The Story of Louis McHenry Howe* (Cleveland: World Publishing, 1954), 300.

25. Barry Bingham to RWB, 9 Apr. 1936, RWB to Barry Bingham, 22 Apr. 1936, RWB-LC; FDR to RWB, 4 May 1936, RWB to FDR, 5 May 1936, PSF, GB:RWB, FDR Papers; FDR to Jesse I. Straus, 4 May 1936, in Elliott Roosevelt, ed., *FDR Letters*, 1:585–86.

26. Betty Houchin Winfield, *FDR and the News Media* (Urbana: University of Illinois Press, 1990), 129; *Courier-Journal*, 20 May 1936; *New York Times*, 2 June 1936; FDR to Jesse I. Straus, 8 June 1936, in Elliott Roosevelt, ed., *FDR Letters*, 1:593; RWB to FDR, 13 July 1936, Bingham Diaries, vol. 4, 21–26 June 1936, RWB-LC.

27. Bingham Diaries, vol. 4, 2 June 1936, RWB-LC.

28. Bell to RWB, 6 Sept., 6 Oct. 1936, Bingham Diaries, vol. 4, 5 Aug., 16 Sept. 1936, RWB-LC; FDR to RWB, 14 Sept. 1936, telegram, 123 Bingham, Robert W./132, Dept. of State Papers; Dallek, *FDR and American Foreign Policy*, 125.

29. Steve Early—memorandum for the president, 17 Sept. 1936, PPF 2409, FDR Papers; RWB to FDR, telegram, 15 Sept. 1936, 123 Bingham, Robert W./133, Dept. of State Papers; FDR to RWB, 14 Sept. 1936, Elliott Roosevelt, ed., *FDR Letters*, 1:614; RWB to Bell, 22 Sept. 1936, W. Forbes Morgan to RWB, 27 Oct. 1936, RWB to Bell, telegram, 27 Oct. 1936, RWB-LC.

30. *Courier-Journal*, 2, 4, 5 Nov. 1936; RWB to FDR, [Nov. 1936], RWB-LC; RWB to FDR, 13 Nov. 1936, PSF, GB:RWB, FDR Papers.

31. RWB to FDR, 13 Nov. 1936, PSF, GB:RWB, FDR Papers; RWB to Major James S. Iredell, 11 Nov. 1936, RWB to Barry Bingham, 14 Dec. 1936, RWB-LC; FDR to George VI, 19 Dec. 1936, 123 Bingham, Robert W./125, Dept. of State Papers.

32. *Courier-Journal*, 26 Nov. 1937; *Foreign Affairs, 1936*, 450–51; Nixon, ed., *FDR and Foreign Affairs*, 3:412–13; Bingham Diaries, vol. 4, 2 Dec. 1936, Sir Evelyn Wrench to RWB, 5 Nov. 1936, RWB to Wrench, 6 Nov. 1936, Roy Howard to RWB, 1 Sept. 1936, RWB to Howard, 9 Sept. 1936, RWB-LC.

33. Bingham Diaries, vol. 4, 19 Sept., 26 Oct. 1936, RWB to Cordell Hull, 7 Apr. [1936], RWB-LC; Hull to FDR, 1 Aug. 1936, PSF, GB:1933–36, RWB to Kenneth de Courcy, 5 Oct. 1936, de Courcy to RWB, n.d. [1936], OF 491, FDR to RWB, 27 Oct. 1936, OF 491, FDR Papers; Nixon, ed., *FDR and Foreign Affairs*, 3:449–52.

34. *London Spectator,* 18 Dec. 1936; *Times* (London), 16 Dec. 1936; J. Taylor Peddie to RWB, 17 Jan. 1936, OF 491, FDR Papers; Nixon, ed., *FDR and Foreign Affairs,* 3:461–62, 484–86, 547–49.

11. "A Good Friend Lost"

1. Divine, *Reluctant Belligerent,* 47; Kenneth Rose, *King George V* (New York: Alfred A. Knopf, 1984), 391–92, 401–5; John W. Wheeler-Bennett, *King George VI: His Life and Reign* (New York: St. Martin's, 1958), 264–89.

2. Bingham Diaries, vol. 4, 28–29 Oct. 1936, RWB-LC; RWB to FDR, [late 1936], PSF, GB:RWB, FDR Papers; Wheeler-Bennett, *King George VI,* 282; Frances Donaldson, *Edward VIII* (Philadelphia: J. B. Lippincott, 1974), 272–81.

3. Nixon, ed., *FDR and Foreign Affairs,* 3:568–69; Donaldson, *Edward VIII,* 300–316; John Cudahy to FDR, 11 Dec. 1936, GB:1933–36, FDR Papers; Bingham Diaries, vol. 4, 6–10 Dec. 1936, RWB-LC.

4. Morgan, *FDR: A Biography,* 486; RWB to Shepard Bryan, 15 Dec. 1936, RWB-LC; RWB to FDR, 5 Jan. 1937, PSF, Diplomatic, GB:1937–38, FDR Papers. The pro-German sentiments of the Duke and Duchess of Windsor have been recently debated in the following books: Peter Allen, *The Windsor Secret: New Revelations of the Nazi Connection* (New York: Stein and Day, 1984); Charles Higham, *The Duchess of Windsor: The Secret Life* (New York: McGraw-Hill, 1988), 89, 100, 117–18; and Philip Ziegler, *King Edward VIII* (New York: Alfred A. Knopf, 1991), 333–45.

5. *New York Times,* 4 May 1937; RWB to Sir John Wilson Taylor, 18 May 1937, RWB to the Spanish ambassador, 22 Apr. 1937, FDR to RWB, 18 June 1937, RWB to FDR, 5 July 1937, RWB-LC.

6. Nixon, ed., *FDR and Foreign Affairs,* 3:568–69; Offner, *American Appeasement,* 157, 177–79.

7. *Times* (London), 29 Apr., 20 May 1937; Offner, *American Appeasement,* 178, 195–96; Peter Lowe, *Great Britain and the Origins of the Pacific War: A Study of British Policy in East Asia, 1937–1941* (Oxford: Clarendon Press, 1977), 18, 22; RWB to FDR, 5 Jan. 1937, PSF, GB:RWB, RWB to Cordell Hull, 6 July 1937, PSF, Diplomatic, GB:1937–38, FDR Papers; *Foreign Affairs, 1937,* vol. 2, 22–23, 81; RWB to Cordell Hull, 30 Apr. 1937, Hull to RWB, 25 Sept. 1937, RWB to Ulric Bell, 6 Apr. 1937, RWB to William Murray, 11 Mar. 1937, RWB to Lady Reading, 14 Oct. 1937, Robert Boothby to RWB, 11 Nov. 1937, RWB-LC.

8. *London Evening Standard,* 28 Oct. 1937; *New York Times,* 31 Aug. 1937; George R. Baldwin to Cordell Hull, 25 Mar. 1937, 123 Bingham, Robert W./148, Dept. of State Papers; RWB to Lord Beaverbrook, 1 Nov. 1937, Beaverbrook to RWB, 1 Nov. 1937, J. H. Harris, to RWB, [1937], RWB to John N. Wheeler, 8 Mar. 1937, RWB to Editor, *Financial Times,* 6 Nov. 1937, "Baron von Munschenhausen" [*sic*] to RWB, n.d. [1937], FDR to RWB, 23 July 1937, RWB-LC.

9. RWB to FDR, 11 Mar., 1 Aug. 1937, RWB-LC; Elliott Roosevelt, ed., *FDR Letters,* 1:702; RWB to FDR, 12 Aug. 1937, PSF, GB:RWB, FDR Papers.

10. RWB to R. P. Taylor, 1 Apr. 1937, RWB to Will H. Shippen, 1 Aug. 1937, RWB to FDR, [Aug. 1937], RWB-LC; RWB to Kent Cooper, 9 Sept. 1937, PSF, GB:RWB, RWB to FDR, 20 Sept. 1937, OF 491, FDR Papers.

11. Offner, *American Appeasement,* 181–82; Bingham Diaries, vol. 4, 10, 27 Mar. 1936, RWB-LC; RWB to FDR, 22 May 1937, PSF, GB:RWB, RWB to FDR, 1 July 1937, PSF, Diplomatic, GB:1937–38, memorandum, FDR to Secretary of State, 10 July 1937, OF 491, FDR to RWB, 16 July 1937, PSF, Diplomatic, GB:1937–38, FDR to RWB, 2 Aug. 1937, PSF, Diplomatic, GB:1937–38, RWB to Davis, 1 July 1937, PSF, GB:RWB, FDR Papers.

12. *Courier-Journal Magazine,* 18 Jan. 1987.

13. Ibid.

14. Ibid.; RWB to Fred B. Bate, 8 Mar. 1937, RWB to P. H. Callahan, 26 Jan. 1937, RWB-LC.

15. *New York Times,* 27 Jan., 2 Feb. 1937; memorandum of telephone conversation between RWB and Hull, 25 Jan. 1937, 123 Bingham, Robert W./142, Dept. of State Papers.

16. Wyatt, oral-history interview, 26 July 1986; *Courier-Journal,* 17 Feb. 1937; Bingham Diaries, vol. 4, 22 Jan., 17 Feb. 1937, RWB to Grace Radford, 9 Mar. 1937, Ulric Bell to RWB, 23 Apr. 1937, Breaux Ballard to RWB, 28 June 1937, RWB to Ballard, 12 July 1937, RWB-LC.

17. *Courier-Journal,* 16, 17 Feb. 1937; *Times* (London), 17 Mar. 1937.

18. RWB to Barry Bingham, telegram, 22 Jan. 1937, Heywood Broun to RWB, telegram, 12 Mar. 1937, RWB to Broun, telegram, 15 Mar. 1937, Ethridge to RWB, 10 June, 10 July, 19 Aug. 1937, RWB to Ethridge, 22 June, 27 July 1937, statement by Barry Bingham, 16 Mar. 1937, RWB-LC.

19. Clinton Davidson to RWB, 1 Apr. 1937, RWB-FC; RWB to Baker, 23 Nov. 1936, RWB-LC.

20. File 17, The *Louisville Times* Company, Minutes, 20 Sept. 1937, Wilson W. Wyatt to Barry Bingham, 1 July 1937, RWB-FC; Barry to RWB, 4 Oct. 1935, RWB to Barry, 4 Dec. 1936, Arthur Peter to RWB, 18 May 1937, RWB-LC.

21. Divine, *Reluctant Belligerent,* 48–50; Bingham Diaries, vol. 4, 20 Mar. 1937, RWB-LC; Sumner Welles, memorandum, 9 Oct. 1937, PSF, Welles, 1937–38, FDR Papers; Anthony Eden, *Facing the Dictators* (Boston: Houghton Mifflin, 1962), 598–603, 612; RWB to Lady Reading, 1 Oct. 1937, RWB-LC; John Harvey, ed., *The Diplomatic Diaries of Oliver Harvey, 1937–1940* (New York: St. Martin's, 1970), 44.

22. Hull, *Memoirs,* 1:510–12; Dallek, *FDR and American Foreign Policy,* 143; *Foreign Relations,* 1937, vol. 1, 317–18, 342–43; RWB to Cordell Hull, 14 July 1937, PSF, Diplomatic, GB:1937–38, memorandum for the Secretary of State from FDR, 7 July 1937, PSF, Confidential, State Department:1937–38, FDR Papers.

23. *New York Times,* 20 May 1937.

24. *Times* (London), 6 July 1937; *New York Times,* 6, 7 July 1937; *Louisville Times,* 6 July 1937. I have found no copy of the speech in either the Robert Worth Bingham file of the Dept. of State Papers, the Roosevelt Library, or the Bingham Papers at the Library of Congress. The accounts of his speech come entirely from newspaper sources.

25. *Louisville Times,* 6, 7 July 1937; William E. Dodd to Hull, 7 July 1937, 123 Bingham, Robert W./151, Dept. of State Papers.

26. *Chicago Daily Tribune,* 8 July 1937; "An American Tourist" to RWB, 12 July 1937, William Seymour to RWB, 12 July 1937, John V. Hynes to RWB, 22 July 1937, A. Jukes-Ham to "R. Worthless Bingham," 17 Aug. 1937, M. S. Watts to RWB, 22 Aug. 1937,

RWB-LC; Lady Lister Kaye to Hull, 11 Aug. 1937, 123 Bingham, Robert W./155, Dept. of State Papers.

27. Welles to FDR, 7 July 1937, FDR, Confidential memorandum, 8 July 1937, PPF 716, FDR Papers; Pierrepont Moffat to Welles, 23 July 1937, 123 Bingham, Robert W./152, Dept. of State Papers; FDR to RWB, 23 July 1937, RWB-LC.

28. RWB to Jan Masaryk, 6 July 1937, RWB to Jess Pope, 20 Aug. 1937, RWB to F. W. Paul, 2 Aug. 1937, RWB to William E. Chilton, 12 Nov. 1937, RWB to Ralph E. Moreton, 23 July 1937, RWB to Dr. William Rienhoff, Jr., 19 Aug. 1937, RWB to Raymond Buell, 15 July 1937, RWB-LC.

29. *Times* (London), 16 Aug. 1937; Daniels, *Shirt-Sleeve Diplomat*, 471; Speech, Dedication of the Chapel at American Military Cemetery, Brookwood, Surrey, 15 Aug. 1937, 123 Bingham, Robert W./157, Dept. of State Papers.

30. *Courier-Journal*, 31 Aug. 1937; *Louisville Times*, 30 Aug. 1937; *Times* (London), 15 July, 23 Aug., 1, 2, 18 Sept., 13 Oct. 1937; *New York Times*, 1, 2, 17 Sept., 21 Oct. 1937.

31. RWB to Brady Institute, 28 Aug. 1937, RWB to Marvin McIntyre, 9 Oct. 1937, OF 491, FDR Papers; Louise Peter to RWB, telegram, 19 Oct. 1937, RWB to Sir Lewis Bayly, 6 Nov. 1937, RWB-LC.

32. Divine, *Reluctant Belligerent*, 48; Offner, *American Appeasement*, 189–90; Wiltz, *From Isolation to War*, 62.

33. James Roosevelt to RWB, telegram, 11 Oct. 1937, RWB-LC; RWB to FDR, telegram, 6 Oct. 1937, OF 491, FDR Papers; Nicholas, *United States and Britain*, 87.

34. *New York Times*, 27 Oct. 1937; *Times* (London), 25, 26 Oct. 1937; RWB to FDR, 17 Oct. 1937, PSF, GB:RWB, FDR Papers; RWB to FDR, telegram, 11 Nov. 1937, 123 Bingham, Robert W./174, FDR to RWB, 11 Nov. 1937, 123 Bingham, Robert W./175, Hull to RWB, telegram, 16 Nov. 1937, copy of telephone conversation between RWB and Hull, 123 Bingham, Robert W./176, Dept. of State Papers.

35. *New York Times*, 20, 26, 28 Nov. 1937; *Times* (London), 20, 26 Nov. 1937.

36. *New York Times*, 9, 10 Dec. 1937; David E. Koskoff, *Joseph P. Kennedy: A Life and Times* (Englewood Cliffs, N.J.: Prentice-Hall, 1974), 114–15, 512; Cole, *Roosevelt and the Isolationists*, 276; Barry Bingham to FDR, 11 Dec. 1937, PPF 716, FDR Papers; RWB to FDR, 8 Dec. 1937, RWB-LC.

Ironically, Joe Kennedy paid Arthur Krock "large sums of money" to act as a "public advocate" in the press. Krock lobbied with Roosevelt and the administration for Kennedy's nomination. Nigel Hamilton, *JFK: Reckless Youth* (New York: Random House, 1992), 212–13.

37. *New York Times*, 15, 16, 19 Dec. 1937; *Times* (London), 15 Dec. 1937.

The medical records and autopsy of Robert Worth Bingham performed at the Johns Hopkins Hospital indicated early bouts with scarlet fever, diphtheria, and malaria. An attack of jaundice came in 1904. Radiotherapy was administered for "Neuroeczema" in 1921. An appendectomy in 1924 and the aforementioned "saddle sore," or ulcer on the buttock, probably caused by the radiotherapy, came at the time he entered diplomatic service. Even more serious was his case of nephritis (kidney inflammation) and continuing hypertension and neuroeczema during his stay in Great Britain. His death was determined to be the result of Hodgkin's disease. Previous records indicated that he had never had syphilis. Grover M. Hutchins, Professor of Pathology, The

Johns Hopkins University School of Medicine, to Mark D. Wilson, 31 Mar. 1987, Summary of Response to Bingham's *Passion and Prejudice,* item 7.

38. *Times* (London), 20 Dec. 1937; FDR to Barry Bingham, 22 Dec. 1937, PSF, GB:RWB, FDR Papers.

FDR particularly missed Bingham's influence during the election of 1940 because the president "had no close ties with the Associated Press as he did in 1936" when the Louisvillian kept a close watch over that group. Winfield, *FDR and the News Media,* 144.

39. *New York Times,* 20–24 Dec. 1937; *Times* (London), 12, 20, 21, 24 Dec. 1937; *Courier-Journal,* 19 Dec. 1937; *Manchester Daily Telegraph* and *Daily Telegraph and Morning Post,* 20 Dec. 1937.

40. *New York Times,* 21 Dec. 1937; *Louisville Times,* 18, 20 Dec. 1937; Barry Bingham to Marvin McIntyre, 26 Dec. 1937, OF 491, FDR Papers.

41. *New York Times,* 27 Sept. 1938; Barry Bingham to FDR, 24 Dec. 1937, FDR to Barry Bingham, 29 Dec. 1937, PPF 716, FDR Papers.

42. *Louisville Times,* 28 Dec. 1937; Summary of Response to Bingham's *Passion and Prejudice,* 24; Will of Robert Worth Bingham, Report of Audit, Estate of Robert W. Bingham, 24 July 1945, J. J. B. Hilliard and Son to Barry Bingham, 6 June 1945, Robert Bingham, Jr., to Barry Bingham, 12 Jan. [1938], Estate of Robert W. Bingham, Wilson W. Wyatt to Lisle Baker, Jr., 13 June 1941, Estate Tax Return, RWB-FC.

43. *Courier-Journal,* 9 July 1941, 17 May 1944, 8 May 1952, 9 Feb. 1966, 31 May 1987; *Louisville Times,* 29 Feb., 9 Mar. 1938, 14 July 1941, 16 Mar. 1957, 20, 21 Oct. 1960.

12. *From the Old South to the New South and Beyond*

1. Lesy, *Real Life,* 152–55.

2. RWB to Margaret Mitchell, 16 Feb. 1937, RWB to Haywood Parker, 1 Aug. 1937, RWB-LC.

3. Bingham Diaries, vol. 2, 30 Oct. 1934, RWB to FDR, 15 Oct. 1937, RWB-LC; Wyatt, oral-history interview, 26 July 1986; *Courier-Journal,* 29 Dec. 1937.

4. Bingham, *Descendants of James Bingham,* 71–83; *Courier-Journal,* 10 Jan. 1986, 16 Feb. 1987; *Courier-Journal Magazine,* 20 Apr. 1986; *Lexington Herald-Leader,* 19 Jan., 21 Dec. 1986, 21, 22, 31 Mar. 1991. In chapter 7 of *Across Fortune's Tracks: A Biography of William Rand Kenan* by Walter E. Campbell (Chapel Hill: University of North Carolina Press, 1996), the author firmly agrees that Bingham was innocent of all charges and that the Kenans acted out of greed.

5. *Courier-Journal Magazine,* 20 Apr. 1986; Bingham will, RWB-FC.

6. For an interesting description of the roles played by "liberal" southerners in the pre–*Topeka v. Board of Education* days, see John Egerton, *Speak Now against the Day: The Generation before the Civil Rights Movement in the South* (New York: Alfred A. Knopf, 1994), 251.

Bibliographical Essay

THE AUTHOR OWES A DEBT OF gratitude to the curators of primary-source repositories and the authors of numerous secondary works. In the following essay, primary sources will first be discussed in some detail. Then the most important published articles and monographs used in preparing this book will be briefly credited.

The Robert Worth Bingham Papers at The Filson Club in Louisville and the Manuscript Division, Library of Congress, Washington, D.C., proved to be indispensable in producing this book. Though there are disappointing gaps in The Filson Club holdings, particularly for the years 1910 through 1918, there is enough information to give an adequate view of the life of Bingham from the 1890s through World War I. When I first began using these papers, they were uncataloged in boxes. The microfilmed version of the Bingham collection presented difficulty in reading, as they were recorded on sixteen-millimeter film rather than the usual thirty-five-millimeter standard. Later James J. Holmberg, curator of manuscripts at The Filson Club, cataloged the entire Bingham collection into its current excellent state. The Henry Watterson Papers and other collections at The Filson Club also proved useful. I also viewed Bingham material located at the Mary and Barry Bingham, Sr., Fund, which cast light on the personalities of the family members and is now part of the larger collection at The Filson Club.

The Bingham Papers at the Library of Congress are a much more extensive collection and cover in profusion the years of the Louisvillian's diplomatic career, while containing a lesser amount for the 1920s. The author was caught between two cataloging efforts, causing some repetitious work. But persistence prevailed. The Manuscript Division is one of the most congenial of places for a researcher. Within minutes the staff will place virtually any important material in the researcher's hands. Other manuscript collections at the Library of Congress, the North Carolina and Southern Historical Collections, the Department of State records at the National Archives, and the Franklin D. Roosevelt Library filled in many of the gaps in Bingham's correspondence.

Insightful oral-history interviews with Barry Bingham, Sr., John Herchenroeder, A. B. Chandler, and Wilson Wyatt, Sr., provided eyewitness accounts of Robert Worth Bingham and his era. The Bingham interviews were surprisingly candid. Although not cited in the book, several other interviews with older Kentuckians gave the author an introduction to the rumormongering that dogged the Judge and his family through the years. Some of these conversations began with the statement: "Well, of course, you know that Bingham pushed his wife down the stairs." Very often the account then degenerated into a tirade against the liberal Bingham papers.

The microfilm files of the *Courier-Journal* and the *Louisville Times* proved to be invaluable. Other important newspapers cited extensively in the manuscript include the *New York Herald,* the *New York Times,* the *Lexington Herald,* the *Lexington Leader,* the *Louisville Evening Post,* and the *Louisville Herald.*

As mentioned in the Preface, the breakup of the Bingham dynasty and sale of the papers created a "cottage industry" of books about the family. Much of this has been of the Bingham-bashing variety. *The Binghams of Louisville: The Dark History behind One of America's Great Fortunes* (New York: Crown Publishers, 1987) by David Leon Chandler and Mary Voelz Chandler can be dismissed as an imaginative, jejune concoction by investigative reporters. See surgical reviews by Mary K. Bonsteel Tachau in the *Courier-Journal,* 10 January 1988, and Richard Lowitt, *The Filson Club History Quarterly* 63 (July 1989): 386–89, to dispel any doubts about the credibility of the Chandlers' effort. Samuel W. Thomas and James J. Holmberg contributed excellent rebuttals to the Chandlers' book in *The Filson Club History Quarterly* 63 (July 1989): 307–85. Marie Brenner's *House of Dreams: The Bingham Family of Louisville* (New York: Random House, 1988) is somewhat more professional. I was a bit put off by Louisville's being described as "a Jell-O and Velveeta town," and the pop-psychology interpretation of Mary and Barry Bingham's relationship. Nevertheless, it is a readable book and provides a good description of the breakup of the Bingham dynasty in the eighties. Sallie Bingham's *Passion and Prejudice: A Family Memoir* (New York: Alfred A. Knopf, 1989) is bitter, rumor filled, and self-centered. *The Patriarch: The Rise and Fall of the Bingham Dynasty* (New York: Summit Books, 1991) by Susan E. Tifft and Alex S. Jones suffers from the same mind-set as the Brenner book.

The ideas presented in numerous secondary works stimulated this work. For the post–Civil War years one must always begin with C. Vann Woodward,

Origins of the New South, 1887–1913 (Baton Rouge: Louisiana State University Press, 1951). It remains as stimulating as when orginally published. Although impressionist to a fault, W. J. Cash's *The Mind of the South* (New York: Alfred A. Knopf, 1941) must be included as an important intellectual study of the southern mind.

Three other books stimulated my own views of the impact of the reconstruction and New South years on the Bingham family. Allen W. Trelease's *White Terror: The Ku Klux Klan Conspiracy and Southern Reconstruction* (New York: Harper and Row, 1965), Paul M. Gaston's *The New South Creed: A Study in Southern Mythmaking* (New York: Alfred A. Knopf, 1970), and F. Garvin Davenport's *The Myth of Southern History: Historical Consciousness in Twentieth-Century Southern Literature* (Nashville: Vanderbilt University Press, 1967) provided the factual background and intellectual stimulation for the first part of this book. The numerous articles and pamphlets of Colonel Robert Bingham, most contained in collections at the University of North Carolina at Chapel Hill, explained most emphatically the cultural and familial milieu of the young Robert Worth Bingham.

For the era from the early twentieth century through World War II, George Brown Tindall's *The Emergence of the New South, 1913–1945* (Baton Rouge: Louisiana State University Press, 1967) is must reading, as well as his suggestive monograph, *The Ethnic Southerners* (Baton Rouge: Louisiana State University Press, 1976). Robert H. Wiebe's *Businessmen and Reform: A Study of the Progressive Movement* (Cambridge: Harvard University Press, 1962) gives an excellent overall interpretation of the intellectual framework of that movement in America, whereas Dewey W. Grantham's magisterial *Southern Progressivism: The Reconciliation of Progress and Tradition* (Knoxville: University of Tennessee Press, 1983) specifically explicates the southern form of progressivism. Norman H. Clark's often neglected book, *Deliver Us from Evil: An Interpretation of American Prohibition* (New York: W. W. Norton, 1976) provides an important interpretation of that movement.

Many authors who have written about the history of Kentucky have influenced this book. Foremost, of course, is Thomas D. Clark. His *Helm Bruce, Public Defender: Breaking Louisville's Gothic Political Ring, 1905* (Louisville: The Filson Club, 1973) provided important background material for chapters 2 and 3. George H. Yater in *Two Hundred Years at the Falls of the Ohio: A History of Louisville and Jefferson County* (Louisville: Heritage Corporation, 1979) has provided a starting point for any study relating to that region. A 1936 publication of *Who's Who in Kentucky* gave minimal biographical information about numerous people in this biography. Several books by James C. Klotter are now an indispensable part of any study of post–Civil War Kentucky history. One must begin with his *Kentucky: Decades of Discord, 1865–1900* (Frankfort: Kentucky Historical Society, 1977) coauthored with Hambleton Tapp, *William*

Goebel: The Politics of Wrath (Lexington: University Press of Kentucky, 1977), and *The Breckinridges of Kentucky: 1760–1981* (Lexington: University Press of Kentucky, 1986) in researching the environment in which Robert Worth Bingham functioned. The Kentucky Historical Society in Frankfort published Klotter's incisive *Kentucky: Portrait in Paradox, 1900–1950* in 1996.

Several recent books touching Kentucky themes influenced me as well. George C. Wright's *Life behind a Veil: Blacks in Louisville, Kentucky, 1865–1930* (Baton Rouge: Louisiana State University Press, 1985) describes the racial mores of Bingham's adopted city. John Ed Pearce, a longtime reporter, editorial writer, and columnist for the Bingham papers, published an excellent political study of the Commonwealth entitled *Divide and Dissent: Kentucky Politics, 1930–1963* (Lexington: University Press of Kentucky, 1987). George T. Blakey's *Hard Times and New Deal in Kentucky, 1929–1939* (Lexington: University Press of Kentucky, 1986) described well that terrible decade in Kentucky's history. George W. Robinson's "The Making of a Kentucky Senator: Alben W. Barkley and the Gubernatorial Primary of 1923," *The Filson Club History Quarterly* 40 (April 1966): 123–35, is an invaluable description of political turmoil in the twenties.

For the New Deal years a number of important works on American foreign policy were of special importance to the last four chapters of this book, including: Robert Dallek, *Franklin D. Roosevelt and American Foreign Policy, 1932–1945* (New York: Oxford University Press, 1979); Howard Jablon, *Crossroads of Decision: The State Department and Foreign Policy, 1933–1937* (Lexington: University Press of Kentucky, 1983); Richard N. Kottman, *Reciprocity and the North Atlantic Triangle, 1932–1938* (Ithaca: Cornell University Press, 1969); Arnold A. Offner, *American Appeasement: United States Foreign Policy and Germany, 1933–1938* (Cambridge: Belknap Press of Harvard University, 1969); Maurice Cowling, *The Impact of Hitler: British Politics and British Policy, 1933–1940* (London: Cambridge University Press, 1975); Charles Loch Mowat, *Britain between the Wars, 1918–1940* (Chicago: University of Chicago Press, 1955); and, David Reynolds, *The Creation of the Anglo-American Alliance, 1937–1941: A Study in Competitive Cooperation* (Chapel Hill: University of North Carolina Press, 1981).

Index

Robert Worth Bingham and the Southern Mystique
was designed and composed by Diana Gordy
in 10.5/13 New Baskerville
on a Power Macintosh 7100/80
at The Kent State University Press;
printed by sheet-fed offset lithography
on 50-pound Turin Book Natural stock
(an acid-free, totally chlorine-free paper),
notch bound over 88-point binder's boards
in ICG B-grade cloth,
and wrapped with dust jackets printed in two colors
on 100-pound enamel stock finished with matte film lamination
by Thomson-Shore Inc.;
and published by
The Kent State University Press
KENT, OHIO 44242